China's Socialist Revolution

China's Socialist Revolution

John and Elsie Collier

Monthly Review Press
New York and London

To Piers, Lee, and Sarah

Library of Congress Catalog in Publication Data

Collier, John.
   China's socialist revolution.
   Bibliography: p.
   1. China—Politics and government—1949–
I. Collier, Elsie, joint author. II. Title.
DS777.55.C6 1974   951.05   74–7782
ISBN 0-85345-336-5

First Printing

Monthly Review Press
62 West 14th Street, New York, N.Y. 10011
21 Theobalds Road, London WC1X 8SL, England

Manufactured in the United States of AMERICA

Contents

Some Introductory Notes

Below we have alphabetically listed a number of national figures who are mentioned in the text. Apart from these the names used throughout the book are not, in the main, the real names of those referred to.

Chiao Tzu-yang First Secretary, Kwangtung Provincial Party Committee. Denounced as 'top capitalist roader in Kwangtung and Canton' in 1967. Returned to a Party post after Ninth Party Congress

Chen Po-ta Member of Peng Chen 'Group of Five' from 1963. Chairman of Wen-ge from 1966. Editor in Chief of *Red Flag*. Denounced at Tenth Party Congress in 1973. Chairman Mao's secretary in Yenan in 1930s (see *Kang Sheng*)

Chen Yi Veteran PLA commander. Foreign Minister up to death in 1972. Major target of Peking Rebels in 1967. Defended by Chou En-lai

Chi Pen-yu Member of Wen-ge. Wrote first published attack on Liu Shao-chi in *Red Flag*, spring 1967

Chiang Ch'ing Mao Tse-tung's wife. Member of Wen-ge. Led reform of Peking Opera from 1963 (see *Kang Sheng*)

Chou En-lai Prime Minister since the establishment of the People's Republic

Chou Yang Lu Ting-yi's deputy in charge of literature and art. Denounced for 'black line in literature and art' in 1966

Huang Yung-sheng Commander of South China PLA forces. Chairman of Military Control Commission for Kwangtung and Canton from April 1967. Commander in Chief of PLA in spring 1968. Reported killed in air crash with Lin Piao, 1971

Kang Sheng Prominent leader of the Great Leap. Together with Chiang Ch'ing and Chen Po-ta formed the National Cultural Revolutionary Group (Wen-ge) which most often met Rebel delegations which travelled to Peking for guidance or assistance in 1967–68

Lin Jie Member of Wen-ge. Chief contact of Zhongda Rebels in early 1967. Wrote key editorial calling for criticism of capitalist roaders in PLA in summer 1967. Denounced late 1967 as ultra-leftist

Lin Piao Assumed leadership of PLA when Peng Te-huai criticised and relieved of major posts in September 1969. Effectively replaced Liu Shao-chi as deputy leader of the Party in August

7

1966. Designated successor to Chairman Mao. Killed in air crash September 1971. Denounced at Party Congress 1973

Liu Shao-chi Chairman of National People's Congress from 1968. Vice-Chairman of the Party. Designated successor to Chairman Mao. Referred to as (a) China's 'Kruschev' and (b) top Party person in authority taking the capitalist road

Lo Jiu-ch'ing Commander in Chief of PLA from 1959 to 1965. Opposed policy of People's war in 1965. Denounced for revisionist line in military affairs in Cultural Revolution

Peng Chen Mayor and First Party Secretary in Peking up to June 1966. First target in Cultural Revolution

Peng Te-huai Major critic of the Great Leap Forward movement in 1959. Replaced as leader of PLA by Lin Piao

Tao Chu First Secretary of Central South Bureau of the Party. Linked in July 1967 with Liu Shao-chi and Teng Hsiao-ping in the slogan of the Rebels: 'Down with Liu-Teng-Tao'. Replaced Lu Ting-yi as head of Party propaganda department in July 1966, thus assuming leadership of Cultural Revolution until end of 1966

Teng Hsiao-ping Secretary General of the Party. Referred to as 'the other top Party person in authority taking the capitalist road'. Closely associated with Liu Shao-chi from 1962. Reappeared in leadership of Party in summer 1973

Wang Guang-mei Liu Shao-chi's wife. Led pilot rectification campaign in Socialist Education Movement in 1963

Wang Li Member of Wen-ge. Wounded in Wuhan incident in July 1967. Denounced as ultra-leftist in 1967

Wu Han Vice-Mayor of Peking. In 1960 wrote play *Hai Jui Dismissed from Office* as veiled attack on Chairman Mao and in defence of Peng Te-huai

Yao Wen-yuan Launched Cultural Revolution by writing attack on play *Hai Jui Dismissed from Office,* prompted by Chairman Mao. Shanghai literary critic. Member of Wen-ge. Elevated to Political Bureau at Ninth Party Congress

We have also included a brief explanation of some terms used in the book which may be unfamiliar to the reader:

Unit: Productive, administrative, cultural working group.

Headquarters: Term applied to the amalgamations of groups to cover a whole unit, a whole town or city, or even larger area.

'Pulled out' or *'dragged out'*: The identification of reactionaries who are called upon to make self-criticism and brought before struggle meetings to answer charges made by those they had had authority over, or their colleagues.

Commandism: The tendency to issue orders rather than give leadership by explanation and personal example.

'Dazibao' (big-character poster): A wall newspaper similar to those used during the early struggles of the Chinese Communist Party.

'Lao-dung' (physical labour): Manual labour taken on by non-manual workers to get closer socially and politically to the workers and peasants.

Introduction

In 1955 I was a worker in the radio industry. Before the Second World War our industry had been plagued by severe seasonal unemployment, and we feared that this unemployment might arise again. I was asked by my trades union branch committee to prepare a survey of the growth of the Chinese economy, with the aim of encouraging the management of our factory to develop its exports to China.

At this time, I thought the major significance of the development of the socialist countries lay in their socialised economies, so I applied myself to studying China's industry and agriculture. In 1957, Mao Tse-tung's *On the Correct Handling of Contradictions Among the People* was published, which opened up the whole question of the development of social relations in a socialist country. This was followed in 1958 by the launching in China of the 'Great Leap Forward' campaign and the formation of the People's communes, which exemplified the processes which Mao Tse-tung had discussed in his article. In the spring of 1959, I spent six weeks on a delegation to China, which confirmed for me the historical importance of what was taking place there, particularly in relation to that which had taken place, along different lines, in the Soviet Union.

At the earliest opportunity I returned to China. This time it was to take up a post as English teacher at Sun Yat-sen University in Canton. I arrived at the end of April 1966, to be followed later in the year by my wife, Elsie, and our three grown-up children. The next month, the first poster was put up in Peking University making an all-out attack on the Principal Lu Ping. It turned out we were to leave China a month after the first worker and peasant teams entered Tsinghua University to help the students forward towards a new unity, so my stay covered the decisive years of the Cultural Revolution.

This book, though, is not only about the Cultural Revolution, an integral part of China's ongoing social revolution, it is also about its life today, and some of the people whose experiences make China what it is. I make no apology for the passages of social theorising appearing cheek-by-jowl with descriptions of ordinary events occurring in the factory, farm or college. Our

9

society has taken to the extreme the isolation of theory and practice, making it difficult to remember when reading a scientific textbook that it is nothing but the reflection of the living experience of men and women, or when reading a novel to be aware that the lives depicted in it could only be lived out in the context of such theories contained in textbooks. Because it is the conscious aim of revolutionaries in China to break down such isolation of one aspect of human life from another, it is particularly relevant in a book about the Chinese revolution to emphasise it, while at the same time trying to bridge the gap.

From April 1966 to January 1967, foreign workers in China were not able to take part in the Cultural Revolution and were not encouraged to do more than observe it. However, following the efforts of some Americans working in Peking, this restriction was lifted. Thus from February 1967 until mid-1968 foreign workers were, to varying degrees, enabled by their colleagues (with the support of the national leadership) to take an active role and study the movement from the inside (Appendix III describes the background to this decision). From June 1968, when a renewed period of intense struggle ensued, including some violence and death, we were again pushed to the sidelines until our departure from China in the August of that year.

I spent my first week in China visiting some units (see explanatory notes on page 8) in Peking that I had been to in 1959, and renewing my friendship with some English and American comrades who are resident there.

I started teaching in the Language department at the university three days after arriving in Canton, and stayed in the guest house on the campus until my family arrived in mid-August. Before all classes were suspended in early June, I was teaching the fourth and fifth years. I went on outings with the students and teachers, and also played games, swam and talked with them during their free time, which all but disappeared as the campaign intensified. From our arrival until we left we spent a good deal of time, most days, in the company of one or more of the young English teachers in our department, but we also made many personal friends among the workers and students.

In October 1966 we went to Peking for National Day, and spent a week visiting our friends. Shortly after this we did our first physical labour, or *lao-dong*, in the countryside, helping to dig an irrigation ditch in a poor hill village that was severely hit by the autumn drought.

In February 1967, we were enabled to work in a factory, which we had been pressing for for several months. It was to be assembling generators in an electric motor factory nearby the university (Appendix IV describes the factory and our work there). We left after three and a half months so that we could attend more meetings in the university which, by that time, we were attending (on average) twice a day.

In June we all went to the countryside with a group of students and teachers to harvest lichees and peanuts, and worked for two weeks at two villages belonging to the same commune.

The following month, a time of intense struggle, we left on a tour to visit historic revolutionary sites, factories, farms and colleges throughout the North. In Peking we found that a few of our English friends were in the thick of the struggle, in Tientsin there were barricades in some of the streets and lorries loaded with workers armed with pick handles, and in Sian we were prevented from visiting a college. Shanghai was comparatively quiet, except for fighting in one diesel factory. Our return to Canton was delayed by a few days because of the fighting, and when we got back we were persuaded to stay in a hotel for over a week before our friends thought it safe for us to return to the university.

After September, most of the frequent meetings at the university were aimed at forming an alliance between the various groups as a basis for setting up a new leading committee, but there were also disputes and disturbances from time to time, including some more violence. In late November, we again went with our colleagues and students to the countryside, this time to harvest rice for a week.

In December we resumed classes. We taught sporadically – mostly in the students' dormitories or outside in the open – until classes ceased again with the renewed period of struggle in June 1968. Meetings had continued until then, although most of the students went home for several weeks during the Spring Festival in February. In early June we were asked to join the other two remaining English teachers in a hotel in Canton. There we remained until, in mid-July, we began our last tour. This time to Hunan Province, and then on to Shanghai to visit units which were being taken as models for new forms of socialist organisation – notably the Shanghai Machine Tool plant.

The chapters and appendices fall into four groups: those dealing with the background to the Cultural Revolution from 1949 to 1965; those outlining the course of the movement during the period of our stay in Canton; a group of discussion chapters concerned with particular problems that arose in the Cultural Revolution related to the general nature of revolutionary struggles in a socialist country; and, finally, chapters depicting some aspects of life in the factory, the country villages and the colleges in which we worked.

This book is the result of my joint experience and joint work with Elsie. Because I wrote most of the text, and because on a few occasions Elsie was not with me, it is set down in the first person.

We would like, in addition, to acknowledge the help of several people: Richard Pfeffer, for the criticism of our draft and the suggestions which formed the basis of the final pattern of the text; Richard Handyside and Peter Sinclair, for their help with the final editing; and our friends and colleagues at Zhongda, without whose comradely help and patience in endless hours of discussion and argument this book would not have been possible.

John Collier

The Role of the Revolutionary Party

The development of feudalism in Europe was based on two factors; the advanced technology required in the use of iron, particularly in its application to weaponry and the plough, and the collision of the declining civilisation of Rome with the migrant barbarian warrior tribes from the East. Serfdom had already arisen within the splintering empire, and a new ruling class of lords, knights and priests was developing from amongst the Roman landlords, soldiers, priests and barbarian chiefs. Thus this class, from its inception, controlled economic, political and ideological power, however, much strife was necessary before society finally settled into the feudal, hierarchic social pattern based on armed force and landownership.

The European bourgeoisie grew up in the medieval city, a combination of feudalism and pre-existent 'Roman' trade and commerce. From the beginning it held enclaves of economic and political power. Its education and culture soon established its ascendancy, partly reviving the classic culture of Greece, partly merging with medieval clerical culture, and partly breaking new ground in science. Thus the bourgeoisie came to full political power on the basis of an already existing economic and cultural power.

The situation in the socialist revolution, when the working class wins political power, is quite different. The economic power of the working class lies in its power to paralyse production – to bring it to a halt; its political power resides in its taking to the streets in insurrection; and its ideological power exists in its collective solidarity, coupled with revolutionary theory developed by the revolutionary party. Thus the proletariat can only consolidate its political power, can only take over functioning economic power and can only transform culture and education (i.e. dominate ideological power) if it has its own political party which has come into existence and developed as the revolutionary vanguard of the working class in the process of prolonged class struggle. This is implicit in Marx's words, 'the proletariat can only finally liberate itself by liberating the whole of mankind'.

The membership of such a revolutionary party may predominantly be working class, and although its leading personnel may also derive from the same class, by the very nature of their function as both formulators of revolutionary theory and providers of day-to-day revolutionary leadership, they cannot be composed of people who are daily engaged, as workers, in production. Therefore they tend to be cut off from the very sphere of human activity which is the main source of working-class collectivism. This is true of capitalist society and is even more true during the early period of socialist society. Party cadres in socialist countries are involved in every sphere of social activity, and especially where decisions are being made. They are government leaders at all levels of government, and in close touch with other government personnel who are not members of the Party ; they are managers in industry, and in close daily contact with other non-communist managers ; they are educators who can be deeply influenced by leading non-Party teachers, writers and artists.

The Party in a socialist state can take measures to see that its leading members do not become corrupted by power and their close contact with counter-revolutionary social elements. All Party members can be expected to lead a simple life, without luxury or privilege. Leading cadres can be called upon to take part in manual work and other work at lower levels for part of their time. Offices can be kept close to production units and cadres' time spent there shortened. Social activity can be organised to ensure the greatest possible shared participation of workers, technical personnel and cadres in manual work, technical innovation and management. Finally, of greatest importance, there can be continual criticism and self-criticism, the momentum of revolutionary change being maintained so that new dedicated revolutionary cadres are constantly thrown up in the struggle from amongst the youth to take the place of those who have become too apathetic, too bureaucratic, too liberal, or just too old.

However, socialist society, during its early stages, is still a class society in which there remains a property consciousness and the existence of the capitalist relationship of one man having authority over another. Because of this the Party wields an oppressive power, and its leading personnel keep in contact with the old reactionary elements in the management, educational and cultural fields. The leadership of the Party therefore reflects the class struggle in socialist society, and has a constant tendency to integrate with all the elements of oppression in society to form a new oppressive minority dictatorship based on economic exploitation.

Ultimately it is only through the mass action of the least privileged sections of the workers and other groups rising up in class struggle that this tendency can be stopped. This may be expressed in another way ; periodically the degeneration of the Party, due primarily to its leading social role in a stabilised yet still class-divided society, must be counteracted from below by a movement of criticism, or social struggle and criticism, whose centre of action lies outside the Party.

Before workers' state power is established the centre of action lies in the relationship of the working class, and other oppressed classes, with the employers and the capitalist state. The Party can only lead the working class, it cannot control the class struggle. In China during the anti-Japanese war and the subsequent civil war, the Party could not dictate to the Chinese workers and peasants, but could only continue to exist for as long as it was nurtured by them.

Once there is a workers' state, the Party combines in itself both the centre of class oppression and the leadership of the advancing social revolution. But the dynamic of social revolution still arises from the political, economic and cultural oppression of the masses.

The role of the Party can be understood most clearly in terms of the 'mass line'. This concept is based on the view that history is made by the mass of the people as opposed to the view that it is made by a few gifted or particularly powerful individuals. It follows from this that social progress arises from the actual social conditions, both mental and physical, of the mass of the people and is achieved through their activity – their participation in production and class struggle. Out of this has developed the Marxist concept of social leadership. Social advance arises from the achievement of the needs and the fulfilment of the aspirations of the leading social class, therefore to give leadership it is necessary to acquire the standpoint and share the living experience of that class. Progress arises from the existing conditions, it cannot be created by arbitrary decisions about what is thought to be in some sense 'best' for the people, therefore it is necessary to study both the objective material conditions and the subjective state of mind of the various classes. Leadership consists further in relating these actual conditions to the summary of previous experience – which we call theory – summing it up in a way that is comprehensible to the masses, and taking back this 'essence' of their own thinking to the masses as the basis for action. Even then, only in so far as this 'essence' is accepted by the workers and peasants and thereby becomes once more their own, so that they act upon it in accordance with their own will, does social progress take place.

The major contradiction in socialist society is that it is a society progressing towards a classless society where there will be no authority of man over man – no State – yet socialist society itself is a class society which requires a strong State in its early stages to maintain the leadership of the working class against the still educationally and culturally more powerful elements of the old ruling classes. The solution of this contradiction expresses itself in the revolutionary Party.

What has been said here about the Party and revolution has been said very simply by Mao Tse-tung: 'In the last resort the whole of Marxism may be summed up in the statement; rebellion is justified.'

1 The Two Lines and the Two Roads

The focus of the Cultural Revolution – the central concept contained in most of the speeches and articles and the endless hours of meetings and group discussions throughout the three years of the movement – was contained in a directive prepared under the guidance of Mao Tse-tung and issued to the Party in January 1965. This directive concerned the nationwide rectification movement which was launched in 1963 and came to be known as the Socialist Education Movement. In the document Chairman Mao inserted this phrase: 'The main target in this movement is those in authority in the Party who have taken the capitalist road.'

This concept was developed in a directive issued by the Central Committee of the Party to leading Party committees throughout the country in May 1966, and further expounded in the definitive directive of the Cultural Revolution known as the 'Sixteen Points' passed by the Central Committee of the Chinese Communist Party in its meeting of August of the same year (for full text, see Appendix I). In a sense this book is an attempt to clarify the content of this concept, and its relationship to the events, now known as the Great Proletarian Cultural Revolution, that took place in China from 1965.

The basis of the formulation of this concept is this. The class struggle between capitalism and socialism characterises the whole era between the first establishment of workers' political power and the final achievement of a communist classless society, a society in which there will be no state, no oppression of man by man, no relationships based on the ownership of property. Mao Tse-tung came to recognise that this class struggle in the Soviet Union, eventually, during Kruschev's period of ascendancy in the Central Committee of the Party, resulted in a victory within the Soviet leadership of counter-revolution – of revisionism.

The victory of revisionism became expressed in the policies of the Soviet Government and the line of the Soviet Party. The Soviet Party gave up the revolutionary theory and practice of a Communist Party being a party of the working class and adopted the theory and practice of a Communist Party being a Party of the whole people. Likewise it gave up the theory and practice of the Soviet State being a workers' state based on the unity of the workers and peasants, and adopted the theory and practice of a state of the whole people. Revisionism in industry expressed itself in policies that increased the authority of the managers, increased the role of individual material incentives to the workers, and instituted a degree of managerial control of profit. All these measures were calculated to undermine socialist planning and retard or reverse the breaking down of the authoritarian division between managers and workers, and the professional élitist divisions between experts and ordinary workers. In agriculture new encouragement was given to private production and marketing, which already dominated the manufacture of some important products. The authority of state farm managers and collective farm chairmen developed to such a degree that, coupled with the encouragement of individual enterprise, there was in many cases the exploitation of collective and state farm workers to create individual wealth. In the sphere of education and culture, the Soviet Union is more and more adopting the individualistic culture of the capitalist countries. Similarly, the Red Army has adopted the same professionalism as its opposites in the West. Finally, in relation to the transformation of the Soviet State into a counter-revolutionary state, the Soviet Government has turned against world revolution, has adopted a policy of sacrificing the revolutionary struggles of the peoples of the world to placate and reach a *rapprochement* with the United States Government or as pawns to play in competition with United States power. The lead given by the Soviet Union, especially since Stalin's death, has been a large factor in many communist parties having ceased to be revolutionary and become, in essence, social democratic parties.

Undoubtedly there is a danger that China will become revisionist too, that it will turn back from socialism to capitalism. Mao Tse-tung pointed out this danger in 1964 in an article published in *Red Flag* under the title of 'On Kruschev's Phoney Communism and its Historical Lessons for the World.' Later, during the Cultural Revolution, it was explained that by 1962 the struggle between capitalism and socialism, which was inevitably reflected inside the Chinese Communist Party, had come to a head and resulted in the establishment of what amounted to two opposed headquarters (see explanatory notes on page 8) in the Central Committee of the Party – one led by Mao Tse-tung and the other by the chairman of the Government, Liu Shao-chi. These two headquarters supported two totally opposed sets of policies, the realisation of which would result in either a further development towards communism, or a turning back towards capitalism.

The crucial factor in the class struggle within a socialist society is the Communist Party. However many government officials, industrial managers, ex-landlords and rich peasants, scholars and professional experts there may be, whose ideology is largely capitalist, these elements cannot organise themselves into a unified political force sympathetic to capitalism so long as the Communist Party adheres firmly to socialist revolution and socialist construction or, in a word, remains dedicated to the collective interest. However, as we have already noted, the higher-level leaders of the Party are necessarily in daily contact with these bourgeois elements, particularly in state and industrial management and education. They tend to share their relatively high standard of living, and most importantly, also share their isolation from the workers and peasants. It is the transformation of the leadership of the Party, together with these bourgeois elements, into a new oppressive class that the Chinese Communist Party maintains took place in the Soviet Union, first under Kruschev and later under Breshnev. It was this that they argue was taking place in China from 1960 to 1965 with the initiative of Liu Shao-chi and Teng Hsiao-ping, acting through the executive hierarchy of the Party, and Lu Ting-yi and Chou Yang operating through the Ministry of Education and the propaganda department of the Party. And it was this which had reached such an advanced stage in Peking under the leadership of Peng Chen, that from 1960 to 1964, using the Peking press, those directly under him were able to mount a semi-clandestine propaganda campaign throughout China aimed at discrediting the revolutionary traditions of the Chinese Communist Party, the policies of the Party's Central Committee, and the leadership of its elected chairman – Mao Tse-tung.

Why was it the case that when workers' power had been established in China in conditions that resulted in the new state having very considerable support and acceptance throughout the population, and the Communist Party being able to establish its leadership very thoroughly in every aspect of social life, that nevertheless counter-revolution was able to become effective? The following attempts to give some of the reasons why this should be so

China having maintained what was in essence a stable form of society for over two thousand years, created an ideology that was to become deeply ingrained in the minds, habits and customs of the whole population. Some aspects of this ideology are helpful to socialism. The tradition of hard work, simple living and co-operative labour among the peasants, which was necessitated by irrigation agriculture in areas periodically inundated by flood, drought and locust swarm. No predominantly individualistic village society could have survived in such natural conditions. The tradition of one people and one country ; of secular government administered by a civil service composed of men of wide culture and personal integrity, in principle not related to property rights or specialist expertise ; and closely related to this, the lack of a strong legalist tradition. But, most important, the tradition that it is both inevitable and morally right that the people should rise up and overthrow a ruler who rules badly. However, all these aspects have both negative and positive sides in relation to socialism and social structure.

In China there remains a traditional awe of authority, and consequently a reluctance to get involved with it. The authority of the emperor down to his lowest mandarin official was absolute, while at the same time, any local administration was carried out by village elders, who were not themselves government officials. In periods of dynastic prosperity the village had a minimum of contact with the imperial administration. This means that it is still a constant struggle in China to keep most people involved in anything but their own immediate affairs, and anyone who has authority still tends to be avoided and feared. It also means that while the Party cadre remains close enough to the people he is leading to assume the aspect of the traditional village elder, he can call forth all the traditional Chinese capacity for co-operative effort and harmonious social intercourse. Once he has crossed the divide and assumed the aspect of the mandarin he is feared and shunned, and any task that he assigns is carried out only with reluctance as a drudgery. Thus the changed relationship between the Party and the masses which developed after 1959 and which, in the view of Mao Tse-tung, required a revolutionary struggle to re-establish working class power in the Party organisation, should not be seen purely as a degeneration of the revolutionary integrity of certain leading Party cadres. Rather, it must be seen as a qualitative transformation in class relationships, such that the Party organisation, from being the leading institution of the working class and poor peasants keeping the bourgeois, landlord and rich peasant elements isolated and in check, developed into an organisation for uniting these elements together, giving them leadership, and enabling them to re-assert their domination in society.

The traditional attitude to education and the intellectual also remains powerful. In old China, particularly in the heydays of the great dynasties when ideology was most deeply defined, education was the road to power and social status, and the scholar was the most respected man. Even the lowliest peasant lad might, if he showed sufficient promise, be subsidised by a rich relation or his community to receive an education, and once on the lowest rung of the education ladder there was no absolute bar to further advancement. Thus, although the vast majority of mandarins came from the ranks of the scholar gentry, the aspiration to become an official through education was diffused through the whole population, and remains a powerful ideological element in modern China. This tradition is in the process of transformation: education has been opened to women (thus helping to break down another Chinese tradition, the ascendancy of man); the tradition of gaining status solely through education and not its application in production has been undermined by the emphasis on the importance of applied science; and, through the dissemination of Marxism, the concept of the unity of theory and practice has been strongly asserted. However, when in 1960–62 there was a policy in China of giving the professors and experts more influence, freedom of action and privilege, because of the still powerful reverence for the intellectual, this process rapidly gained momentum and took place with the minimum of opposition. Thus, because of this, large numbers of new students from worker and peasant homes who entered middle school and university in the period of the Great Leap in 1958 and after, came very much under the social influence of the older professors and teachers. This influence was greatly reinforced by the still very powerful tradition of respect for age.

There is a further point that must be made. Many of China's

higher Party cadres, below the top leaders, were denied an advanced formal education when young due to being swept into the anti-Japanese war, and had only managed to scrape together such education as was possible during the course of years of overwork. Close contact with many people who had had the benefit of a full formal education when young and time to study and research when older, and who thus possessed a more sophisticated culture, tended to wean them away from their revolutionary ideology. Where this experience was coupled with long isolation from the workers and peasants, this tendency was reinforced. When you bear in mind that many of these cadres came from landlord, capitalist or professional families themselves, the effect of such experiences becomes all the more obvious. This problem of the cultural élite came to a focus in 1961–62. Up to 1957, the intellectual's traditional position and status in Chinese society was largely maintained. Certainly he was asked to adopt the new ideology of Marxism, but he was not required to make the change quickly and so long as he showed willingness to adapt, he retained his position of high status. Further, because of the rapid development of industry, education and the arts, his work was highly appreciated, and highly productive. With the Great Leap in 1958 there was a strong attack on status and privilege, both inside the Party and outside. During 1961–63, owing to the setbacks resulting from three years of natural disasters, the withdrawal of Soviet assistance and the mistakes committed in the setting up of the communes and the Great Leap campaign, an opposing set of policies was adopted which opened the way for the educational elite to fight back against the revolution.

The single strongest element in traditional Chinese ideology is the family. This is not the same as the European family, although, as in the bourgeois tradition, there is emphasis on the 'small family' of parents and children. Alongside the small family exists the Chinese 'big family' which ideally consists of grandparents, all their living sons and, in turn, their small families. The big and small families merge with the clan, a much larger unit and which to this day, in South China, usually includes a whole village or half a village of people with the same family name. In South China land reform cut through the village and thus cut through the clan, and thus much of the initiative for land reform had to come from the North. The successes of co-operative farming strengthened the new basis of village life, and with the formation of communes which united several villages together one of the central reasons for strife between villages and thus strife between clans (the fight over irrigation water rights) was largely brought to an end. However, in certain areas where conditions were particularly difficult in the hard years from 1959–61, the re-emergence of family and clan solidarity as opposed to reliance on Party leadership came about. With the encouragement of more individualistic farming and marketing in 1961 and 1962 there was a tendency for the old, rich peasants – the traditional village leadership – to regain influence in the villages.

Another serious threat to the revolution which specifically

related to the strong family tradition and traditional reverence for education, was the existence of schools particularly catering for the children of leading cadres. In the major cities many cadres lived in accommodation provided especially for them, presumably to facilitate easy communication. This was certainly the case in Peking in relation to government functionaries. Because of their location it resulted in certain schools having a very high proportion of the children of such people. These children tended to develop an attitude of arrogant social superiority. With the influence of their parents, coupled with the privileged educational opportunities they possessed, they were more likely to graduate into positions of authority and possess a further enhanced status. It is interesting to note, and this connects up with the launching of the Cultural Revolution in 1965–66, that this kind of school, though it existed in Peking and Canton – and no doubt other cities – did not exist in the same developed form in Shanghai, where Ko Ching-shi (who was to the fore in the revolutionary changes of the Great Leap Forward period) was the Mayor up to his death in early 1965. Although at times we encountered confusion, criticism and apathy concerning the Cultural Revolution among various young people, the most cynical attitude towards it was evinced by some middle-school students, precisely from such a school.

To the counter-revolutionary influence of China's traditional ideology must be added the reactionary influence of capitalist ideas and attitudes that came from Japan and the West. Industry and commerce already existed on a considerable scale in China at the time of the formation of the Empire, two centuries B.C., and although the merchants and manufacturers were always prevented from gaining political power, particularly by the organisation of imperial monopolies, nevertheless they have played an important role in China throughout the history of the Empire. Thus the ideas characteristic of a merchant community like that which came to flower in Europe with the Renaissance existed, if in an undeveloped form, in China, and with the full impact of the West in the nineteenth century were there to provide soil for the rapid development of capitalist ideology.

Counter-revolution in China was greatly strengthened by two 'imports' from the capitalist West; authoritarianism of management in industry, and 'economism' on the part of the workers. The former is reinforced by the traditional Chinese attitude to authority discussed above. Economism is the tendency among the working class to be concerned exclusively with material production and particularly individual material reward. It is probable that the critical struggle in the Cultural Revolution was that in December 1966 and January 1967 in Shanghai, later to be known as the 'January Storm', in which those taking the capitalist road appealed to the workers' economism, and the revolutionary rebels appealed to their fellow workers and students to expose and repudiate this appeal and to fight against their own selfishness. Perhaps the most meaningful and symbolic act of the whole movement was when thousands of Shanghai workers marched past the City Hall and threw down the money which they had received in the form of pay rises and travelling expenses as bribes to adhere to the leadership of their old managers and city officials.

There are less obvious ways in which capitalist ideology influences people's attitudes of mind in China. The liberal individualist tradition of Europe and America, although resisted because it was alien, was also welcomed in China from the late nineteenth century onwards, both as a weapon with which to destroy the degenerate and corrupt Manchu dynastic rule, and because it was closely associated in the Chinese mind with the strength the western powers had had to defeat China in war and dictate terms to the Chinese government in peace. Although Marxism gained in effect over bourgeois political thought in China throughout the twenties and thirties, nevertheless, from the turn of the century right up to the present, bourgeois ideas, literature, art and drama have exerted and still do exert a powerful influence. The essence of this influence is individualism.

Closely related to the ideology of individualism which pervades western culture is the concept of the 'expert' and the practice of professionalism. The European idea of the professional expert as the person who solves the problems, makes the plans and decisions, and instructs the technicians and workers as to what they should do and how they are to do it, is alien to Chinese tradition. In old China the two most important groups of people were the peasants and the mandarin administrators. The main social division recognised was that between the mandarin – the refined man who used his mind and governed – and the peasant – the rough man who worked with his hands. The mandarin had a 'liberal', not a specialised education. There was, however, only one education, and though its content varied from time to time to include such subjects as medicine, hydraulics or mathematics, it was always essentially a classical humanist education based on the writings of the sages. The peasant was a manual worker, but one who was respected for his skill in every aspect of farming. Against this, the structure of western society, built on a rigid foundation of private ownership, consists of a minority of specialists who do the thinking, who solve the problems and make the plans, another minority who issue orders and see that they are carried out (the managers), and a majority who do the work, (the manual workers and technicians). In the West, this system is carried over in modified forms into every aspect of our lives, and more and more every little problem of life is passed back to the expert or is solved by referring to a book written by an expert. In the Great Leap, the tradition of the Chinese revolution (which was a transformation of the tradition of old China) wherein each man must solve his own problems, was reasserted, but in 1961 the élitist expert came into his own again, a change that was to be combined with increased managerial authority, increased emphasis on individual material incentives (piece rates and bonus systems) and encouragement to individual agricultural production and marketing. One of the most consistent themes of the Cultural Revolution has been the onslaught on the concept of the 'expert', and the direct criticism of particular individuals who have cut themselves off from the masses to solve their problems behind laboratory or office doors, asserting their superior 'expert' status.

The last question in relation to the persistence of bourgeois ideology in China which must be mentioned is the most difficult to assess. This is the role of modern scientific education and theory. The contradiction may be expressed like this: it is asserted that modern scientific theory is not based on ideology, but on multiple observations of experimental and natural data; yet scientific truth is an aspect of the relationship between man and his environment which includes other men. However, 'western science' claims to have established truths (or near truths) which exclude man. What is incontestable is that most of scientific theory is built upon assumptions, not made explicit, of 'isolates' and 'identities', and that nearly all science teaching in China, as in other countries, is carried out in terms of a system of mechanistic logic. Most of China's engineers, if not her scientists in other fields, must surely have working minds in the main dominated by mechanistic patterns of thought. The only students who told us categorically that they could not understand the Cultural Revolution were physics students, who were very advanced in their work. Further, the scientific journals from the Soviet Union, America, Japan and other countries, which the Chinese students and scientists are reading avidly and on a vast scale, are infused with the ideology of individualism and the concept of the 'expert' – the élite who solve all the problems.

In summary then, the capitalist road is still open in China for the following reasons: the strength of certain aspects of her own heritage, particularly the tradition of authoritarianism and the status of the intellectual; the influence of bourgeois ideas, especially that of individualism and its expression in the concept of the 'expert'; the existence in China of the old exploiting classes – the capitalists, landlords and rich peasants – who still possess a disproportionate social influence owing to their generally higher level of education and culture, and the old privileged sections of people such as shopkeepers and professional people who are still deeply imbued with both traditional Chinese and bourgeois attitudes; the many institutions in China which are still organised in such a manner as to isolate the intellectuals from the workers and peasants, notably the universities; the backward material conditions, compared with the advanced capitalist countries and the Soviet Union, which constitute a continuous corrupting influence, especially on the higher-level cadres and students who inevitably come into most contact with foreign countries, and foreign writings; the backward material conditions in China in their internal aspect, especially the poverty of the Chinese village, which makes the breaking down of the divisions between workers and peasants, and the division between workers and peasants on the one hand and intellectuals and administrative cadres on the other such a slow and bitter struggle. Added to these are two indeterminates – the changing world context and China's weather. Among the factors determining the shift towards taking the capitalist road in the Chinese Communist Party in 1961–62, two of the most decisive were the decision of the Soviet Government to withdraw its experts and terminate its material assistance, and the three years of bad weather which created a critical food shortage and brought devastation to wide areas. The present emphasis put upon water control and national self-sufficiency in China derives from this bitter experience.

Marx said that when correct ideas grasp the minds of the masses they become a material force which advances history. Given all that has been described above, in the last resort it was the action of the masses of Chinese workers, peasants and soldiers activated by their ideas that was the decisive factor. If one is going to divide up history, the subject of this book may be said to begin with the demoralisation of large sections of the Chinese peasants in 1960–61, and to have reached its turning point with the revolutionary solidarity of the Shanghai workers in 1967.

So we return to Mao Tse-tung's phrase coined in January 1965, 'The main target in this movement are those in authority in the Party who have taken the capitalist road'. From the discussion we have carried out we may now characterise such Chinese leaders. They are those who lost faith in the workers and poor peasants, so that, faced with urgent problems, they resorted to individual material incentives and authoritarian discipline where revolutionary leadership called for efforts to rouse the workers' and peasants' initiative and enthusiasm. In industry they substituted managerial authority for leadership that is only achieved by sharing the living experience of the workers; and in agriculture they blamed the ordinary peasants and their directly elected leaders for all the shortcomings and failures, instead of focusing criticism on those higher up who wielded authority arbitrarily or corruptly To cure shortcomings they attacked the collective and encouraged individual initiative of a sort which boosted the influence of the old rich peasants, with their greater experience of marketing and individual farm management. In education they relied on the old professors and experts, increased their status and granted them privileges, and in turn they isolated education from productive labour. In the cultural sphere they gave up the struggle to produce a new culture that would express the lives and aspirations of the workers and peasants and inspire them in their struggle to advance socialism, and instead exalted the old culture of the Chinese court, and the culture of European individualism. In relation to world affairs they feared war to the extent that they were prepared to sacrifice the Chinese revolution and other revolutionary struggles in order to gain support from the Soviet Government and reach a *rapprochement* with United States imperialism. In their day-to-day work they sat in offices issuing orders, rather than getting out to solve problems together with all those involved.

It should not be supposed that everyone 'dragged out' (or 'pulled out', see explanatory notes on page 8) in the Cultural Revolution and characterised as 'a person in authority in the Party who had taken the capitalist road' had all these attitudes of mind, or that from 1961 all the organisational leadership of the Party that emanated from the Party Central Office, which was dominated by Liu Shao-chi and Teng Hsiao-ping, encouraged these attitudes. What is clear is that from about 1961 there crystallised two opposed factions within the Central Committee, and that the cultural revolutionary faction led by Mao Tse-tung, Lin Piao and Chou En-lai retained faith in the Chinese workers, poor peasants and the traditions of the Chinese revolution which are summed up in the writings of Mao Tse-tung, and adhered broadly to the collectivist line of the Great Leap Forward of 1958, whereas the faction led by Liu Shao-chi, Teng Hsiao-ping and Peng Chen, had lost faith in the initiative of the Chinese workers and peasants, had lost faith in the traditions of the Chinese revolution, rejected the path forward indicated by the Great Leap Forward and reverted to authoritarianism and individualism. It is important to note that between 1960 and 1964 a group of writers, including the vice-secretary of the Peking Party Committee, wrote plays and published a series of over one hundred and fifty articles which more or less explicitly expressed all these characteristics of those taking the capitalist road, and that they clearly wrote these articles as part of a concerted political and propaganda campaign which had as its aim the discrediting of Chairman Mao and the revolutionary policies of the Great Leap Forward.

2 The First Stage of Socialist Revolution, 1949-1956

In 1945 Chairman Mao wrote, 'Today two big mountains lie like a dead weight on the Chinese people. One is imperialism, the other is feudalism.' Feudalism meant the old ideas and institutions of the Empire, but most particularly the landlord system – the hold of the landlords on the land and over the poor peasants, and their support for reactionary government. By imperialism was meant every aspect of the penetration of China by military force, commercial and industrial interests, and the cultural influence of the capitalist powers, but primarily the power of imperialist countries to dictate to China's government. The combination of feudalism and imperialism was to be found in the bureaucratic capitalism of the most powerful financial families that surrounded Chiang Kai-shek – the 'Four Families', those comprador interests which on the one hand exploited China's workers and poor peasants, impeding the progress of Chinese industry, and on the other served the interests of the foreign imperialists, depending on them to support their continued power.

The victory of the People's Liberation Army and the setting up of the Chinese People's Republic in November 1949 removed the influence of imperialism in China, and the rule of Chiang Kai-shek and the Four Families. In areas of the North and the North East, the power of the landlords had also been broken, but over the major part of the country they still held sway in the villages, and in the newly liberated towns and cities, industry and commerce was still managed by capitalists.

The transformation of agriculture

The major political campaign from the defeat of Japan in 1945 to its final completion in South China in 1953, a period that covered the whole duration of the war of national liberation and that of the Korean War, was that of land reform.

From 1937 to 1945 the agrarian policy of the Chinese Communist Party had been designed to create the best conditions for unifying the Chinese people against the Japanese invaders. Land was only taken from landowners who collaborated with the

Japanese. To alleviate the poverty of the poor peasants a policy of rent and interest reduction was adopted.

With the defeat of the Japanese in 1945 land reform was instituted by the Party in those areas they controlled. Work teams were organised, composed of Party members, other peasant leaders, and people from the cities – particularly students, teachers and office workers. These teams after a period of instruction in the principles and clauses of the land reform directive went to the villages to participate in and guide the movement.

In accordance with the directive on land reform, the peasants were divided into categories – poor, lower middle, upper middle and rich. Poor peasants were those who had possessed no land and worked as labourers; very often they owned no property at all, having to live in the barns or outhouses of the landlord they worked for; they were frequently unemployed, and were the first to starve in years of scarcity. Lower-middle peasants were those who might own a little land, but in the main rented it, and at times had to work as labourers; perhaps part of the family worked on their own land while part worked for others; these families scarcely made a living, and paid anything up to a half or more of their harvest in rent; they too went to the wall in bad years, or when hit by family illness. (Poor and lower-middle peasants are often referred to simply as poor peasants.) The upper-middle peasants (often called middle peasants) mainly worked their own land and, except in very bad years, would normally have enough food and clothing for a stable life, but little more. Rich peasants worked their own land, but gained more than half their income from renting it or lending money. Interest rates were very high so that money lending was an acute form of exploitation: as those peasants who once got into debt seldom managed to escape short of parting with some or all of their land, borrowing was a short path to landlessness and the abject poverty of the labourer. The rich peasant was thus part landlord, but as he worked in the field he shared some of the day-to-day life of those less well off than himself. The landlords were those who gained all or nearly all their income from the work of others, both in the form of rent and interest. They lived a life apart in their superior houses, and dressed in scholars' robes, which were quite unsuited to manual labour. They sent their sons to school, and themselves were mainly literate in contrast to most of the peasants who were not; from their class was drawn the mandarin civil service. In the decades leading up to 1949, more and more landlords were absentees, living in the local town or, if large landowners, living in the provincial capitals or the great eastern cities.

The aim of the movement was that everyone should be given a class designation through unanimous agreement – an agreement that should include the person being designated. Thus there would be a general feeling that justice had been done according to the terms of the land reform.

With everyone in the village designated, the distribution of confiscated land, animals and equipment was carried out. The middle peasants retained their possessions. The rich peasants before 1949 – in the North, North West and North East – lost land over and above their share (as did the landlords), but after Liberation when land reform was carried out in the South, they were treated more leniently and left all land they could cultivate as a family, their houses, animals and equipment.

The land reform was tempestuous and uneven, many mistakes were made and there was strife and injustice, but overall the peasants stood up and their traditional oppressors, the landlords, were brought low. (See William Hinton's *Fanshen* for an excellent account of this process.) In 1948, in order to correct the abuse arising in the movement, the Party organised a rectification campaign in which the village cadres were interrogated and assessed by their fellow peasants, each one having to justify his actions and return any property wrongly appropriated.

The poor peasants benefited most from land reform, just as they had suffered most from the exploitation of the old society. Thus they were the firmest supporters of the revolutionary army – a large proportion of which was in fact made up of poor peasants – the Communist Party and the government. Further than this, the poor peasants were also those who benefited most from later socialist changes in the countryside. The middle peasants gained little from land reform, but also had little to thank the old society for, and gained from the new social and economic stability after 1949.

Further socialist measures were to the advantage of the middle peasants in that they gained from any general improvement of living standards. The landlords and rich peasants lost severely from land reform, and to the extent that they still constituted a privileged class in the countryside because of their higher standard of education and social contacts in the towns and cities, they suffered further blows to their position by each succeeding socialist transformation.

Where the poor peasants took the initiative in land reform, and together with the middle peasants isolated the landlords and rich peasants, and discussed at length the designation of families into one category or another, the result was a heightened self-confidence amongst them, and a valuable lesson learned in co-operation by relying on their own common action and uniting with the middle peasants. Closely related to this achievement was that of destroying the domination of the villages by the landlords, destroying their social morale and the fear of them in the minds of the poor peasants. Where the mass of the peasants was not roused into action and the initiative had to come mainly from the Party cadres and work team members, the actual distribution of land might be reasonable. But in so far as the poor peasants had not initiated or carried through the movement themselves, their self-confidence and co-operative spirit would not have been raised, and their traditional fear of authority would still remain.

The work team members lived with the poor peasants, shared their food and their household chores. In the course of many meetings and countless conversations they got to understand better the peasants feelings, their aspirations, and not least the arduousness of their work and the poverty characteristic of the mass of Chinese villages.

Thus land reform had an immediate material, concrete objective – to distribute land to the tiller; it had a progressive objective – to create a social and economic basis in the village for co-operative agriculture, the first step to a socialist countryside. It also had the objective of transforming people's social attitudes – raising the confidence of the previously downtrodden peasants and their feeling of collective strength, humbling the traditional arrogance of the landlord, and taking a step towards breaking down the traditional division between the city people and the country people, and the equally traditional separation between the intellectual who worked only with his mind and the peasant who worked only with his hands.

The completion of land reform signalled the completion of the stage of national bourgeois revolution. China thence forward entered the era of socialist revolution, and socialist construction. According to Chairman Mao's analysis in 1949, this era would be characterised by class struggle between the working class and the bourgeoisie. By this he meant that for the foreseeable future China would be faced with a series of major social problems, and each of these problems would in essence be capable of solution in two entirely different ways. One solution would mean a further consolidation of socialism and a step further towards communism; the other would mean a weakening of socialism and a step backwards towards capitalism. Both the adoption of a particular solution and carrying it out would entail social struggle. This struggle would take place within the minds of individual men and women – yes, and children – and between different groups of people, and would be an integral part of the transformation. Finally, the solution of each major problem would lead to a new situation with new characteristics, which in turn would throw up a new major social problem.

With land reform completed two futures lay open to Chinese agriculture. The first was to leave the individual family basis of production to develop freely; the second was to push on with collectivisation step by step. Because some families lacked manpower, for example the father was dead or in ill health, or there was a large number of young children, and some families had a shortage of land but some capital, for example many rich peasant families, there would be renewed buying and selling of land leading to a new polarisation of land holding. Owing to the vicissitudes of the climate, health or to differences in skill at farming, some families would prosper while others would again go under, furthering the process of polarisation. In 1953 Liu Shao-chi argued that allowing a rich peasant economy to develop for some years would result in increased agricultural production, and would allow time to develop industry to the point where farming could be mechanised, and that only mechanisation could create a suitable basis for collective farming. This line of argument resulted in a call for the 'Four Freedoms' – to rent land, to sell land, to hire labour, and to lend money. If this policy had been fully adopted the rich peasants would have come to dominate the villages. Further, the natural supporters of socialist advance, the poor peasants, would have been demoralised and disillusioned.

The alternative that was adopted on the basis of the leadership of Mao Tse-tung was to commence to develop forms of co-operative production immediately after land reform. In fact a good deal of polarisation did take place in the villages, indicating what would have happened if the alternative policy had been adopted.

Traditionally the Chinese peasants had from time to time formed mutual aid groups to assist each other at harvest time, at spring planting, or in the face of drought or flood. The first form of co-operation which was popularised throughout the country was this traditional form, but it was soon taken a stage further. Instead of just forming a group of a few families for a short period, groups were set up which worked together and loaned each other tools and animals on a permanent all-the-year-round basis. These 'mutual aid teams' led on quite naturally to the formation of small co-operative farms, where now the land of the whole group was consolidated and worked in common. These first (so-called 'lower-level') co-ops paid out part of their product in the form of rent paid in proportion to the land each family had put into the co-op, and rent for the use of the members' tools and animals, and the rest according to a system of work points.

The lower-level co-ops favoured the old rich peasants in that it was they who in general (particularly in the South) owned more land and capital for which they received rent. Secondly, many poor peasants felt that it was like the old society because they still had to work to pay rent to others. Another drawback to these small co-ops was that in most cases they were too small to utilise the land to the best advantage, whereas a larger unit could allocate different crops to fields with differing qualities of soil. Finally, as a great part of Chinese farming relies on irrigation, small units lead to endless quarrelling about water rights.

Thus again two tendencies arose: one was to attribute the problems that arose to the nature of co-operative farming, and to keep the co-ops as small as possible or even dissolve them – in some areas this was done on a large scale; the other tendency was to increase the size of the co-ops and change their constitution so that they would both favour the poor peasants and stimulate co-operative work. Again there was a cleavage of opinion in the Communist Party, and again Liu Shao-chi supported the conservative and more individualistic policy, whereas Mao Tse-tung convinced the Party that the peasants were ready for further collectivist change. (See *Socialist Upsurge in China's Countryside* Ed. Mao Tse-tung, Peking, 1957.) The advanced co-op farms were formed by the amalgamation of several small co-ops, or in some cases from among the individual peasants. In these co-ops rent on land was abolished, the capital of the members was bought out by the co-op thus abolishing rent on tools and animals, and ownership of the land was vested in the co-op.

The movement to form advanced co-ops swept the country, surpassing even the optimistic forecasts of Mao Tse-tung. Clearly the main reason for this was that it caught the imagination of the poor peasants – never again would they pay rent now that the land was collectively owned ; never again could the land be returned to the landlords now that individual title deeds were burnt ; never again would a family hit by ill health or other bad luck have to go begging while there was the collective to succour them in their times of trouble. But the landlord saw his chances of regaining his land disappear, and the rich peasant saw his privileged position as rent receiver vanish, so the movement for the formation of advanced co-ops was again an intense class struggle, and was only carried through successfully by the mobilisation and full participation of the poor peasants.

By 1956, the greater part of Chinese agriculture was collectivised, each village in the main formed a community of common economic interest, and most of the work of the co-op members was on land held in common.

The transformation of industry

If the basis and organisation of Chinese agriculture was transformed between 1949 and 1956, this was no less true in the case of industry.

With the setting up of the People's Republic, all industry previously owned by the Japanese and taken over by the Kuomintang Government became the property of the new Republic. This included all the heavy industry of the North East. Further, all industry owned by foreign companies and by Chinese who went with Chiang Kai-shek to Taiwan was nationalised without compensation. However, those capitalists who were independent of the Kuomintang monopolists retained their enterprises. Thus over half the industry of Shanghai, which by itself accounted for something of the order of half the industrial production of China south of the Great Wall, remained under private enterprise.

The policy adopted by the Communist Party and the government towards the national capitalists was based on the following assessment of their role. It was considered that during the anti-Japanese war the capitalists had suffered at the hands of the Japanese invaders, and in the main had supported the war effort and the national front. Further, it was considered that they had suffered from the domination of Chinese economic development by the imperialist powers and their Chinese supporters, and that in the period of the War of Liberation against Chiang Kai-shek from 1947 to 1949 they had in the main ceased their support of Chiang and shown a readiness to work in co-operation with the Communist Party to rehabilitate Chinese industry, and resist further interference from foreign powers. Finally, it was considered that given overall state control of the economy, in the years immediately after 1949 private industry could play a positive role in the reconstruction and advancement of the economy. However the Party also recognised that as well as having progressive features the capitalist class was by its nature opposed to working class power, and would take every opportunity to strengthen private enterprise and try and create conditions for the establishment of their political power.

On the basis of this assessment a dual policy was adopted:

on the one hand, to unite with the capitalists – recognising them as full citizens of the Republic, encouraging them to develop their production, and allowing them to enter into trading relations with nationalised industry; and on the other, to restrict them – increasing the power of the workers in private industry by organising trades unions and increasing the membership of the Party among the workers so that the workers could supervise the activity of their employers, control wages and working conditions, and control production by controlling the supply of raw materials and the trade in finished products. The policy of restriction also envisaged the gradual step-by-step transformation of private industry into state industry, and the transformation of the capitalists from share-holding independent managers into salaried employees in joint state-private industry, which would finally become state industry. At the same time the main growth was to be in the state industry.

A counterpart to the mass movement of land reform in the countryside was organised in industry and government administration. As the strength of the revolutionary movement had grown up in the countryside, the Party and the government had to take over running the cities and industry with little or no previous experience, thus in the main the old administrative and clerical workers had to be retained in their positions. Among these people were many counter-revolutionaries who had remained in China to oppose the new Republic, and countless others who had no scruples about making money by various corrupt practices. The campaign in government departments and state enterprises was aimed at bureaucracy, waste and corruption, and was entitled the 'Three Anti's'. The campaign in private industry was known as the 'Five Anti's', and was directed against bribery, smuggling and tax evasion, theft of state property, shoddy work and the use of inferior materials, and the misuse of government economic information for private gain. The third campaign aimed at uncovering counter-revolutionaries took place in all places of work and social activity.

Just as in the land reform, this movement in the towns had a threefold purpose: to achieve the material requirement of raising the efficiency of the Chinese economy; to raise the self-confidence and the participation in social affairs of the workers while at the same time reducing the sense of power and social morale of the capitalists; and to prepare for further steps of socialist advance. In so far as the movements relied on rousing the workers to denounce those in managerial positions who were transgressing the socialist principle of industry, that of serving the people and not individual gain, this both increased the sense of power of the workers and decreased that of the capitalists, and raised the collective consciousness of the workers. In the process of criticising the selfish and anti-socialist practices of the capitalists the workers also became more aware and critical of their own selfish individualistic tendencies.

In the 'Three Anti's' and and 'Five Anti's' movement those in authority, both capitalists owning enterprises and administrators in government enterprises and offices, were encouraged to make self-criticisms and to discuss these criticisms amongst themselves, so as to put their own houses in order, as well as accepting criticisms from the workers and office staffs. Those who came clean and where possible made restitution for losses they had caused to others or the state, were treated leniently, while severe punishment was meted out to a few of the worst offenders who persisted in trying to cover up their misdeeds.

In 1955 there were still 130,000 private industrial units employing two million people. This was excluding handicraftsmen working for themselves. But by this time the employers had become used to working closely with state agencies and their main activity was that of managers, as there was no stock market for them to buy and sell shares. In this situation a mass campaign was developed among the private owners which resulted in private industry and commerce merging with the state. The capitalists were issued with state bonds in place of their share capital, which would pay a fixed interest rate for a limited period. State nominees joined the boards of management, and those capitalists who had industrial posts were given salaries.

The policy of 'uniting with, while at the same time restricting' the capitalists thus had a three-fold purpose. Firstly, to ensure that immediately after 1949, at a time when knowledge of industrial management was very limited in China, all those with such knowledge would be employed to the full; secondly, to ensure that as quickly as possible Chinese industry would be developed in such a way that capitalist-type managers would no longer be required; and thirdly, so that the large number of capitalists in the major cities – who in many cases were trained scientists or engineers – would have the opportunity to remould their ideas and become supporters of socialist construction. However, Liu Shao-chi gave a different emphasis to this policy of the Party. In talks with industrialists in Tientsin soon after Liberation, and later in Shanghai, he encouraged them not only to increase the production of their existing plant but to build new factories, and told them that this would be in their interests because for a long period China would need capitalist industry, and even when this stage was past the present capitalists could become managers of even greater undertakings built by the state.

The development of education

The Communist Party in China administered areas of the country continuously from 1927. Thus it had to work out policies not only for production and civil administration, but also for education and cultural work.

In the course of the twenty-two years from 1927 to 1949 the Party's policy in relation to education had become based on three principles which all derive from Karl Marx. *Education should be conducted on the basis of a unity of theory and practice*: illiterate peasants should be encouraged to learn to read and write with material which related to their own lives, and in such a way that having achieved literacy they could immediately apply it to benefit both economically and culturally; soldiers who fought a battle should then discuss it so that they acquired an understanding of strategy and tactics; Party workers should study politics so that they could apply their knowledge to leading the people in solving their immediate problems, as well as understanding the general nature of revolution. *Education should be combined with production and other social activity*: those who were studying agriculture ought to combine it with growing crops, and they should do this in an all-round way, by actually taking part in all forms of agricultural work; those who were studying literature should write articles and fictional works for publication, and take part in meetings held to criticise published works – criticism which would relate the works to the lives of the workers and peasants. *Education should aim always to serve the workers and peasants.*

After 1949 education was rapidly extended in China. The highest recorded number of children in primary school before 1949 was 13 million, by 1956 the figure was nearing 60 million. Similar rates of increase had been achieved in the secondary schools and colleges. An important aspect of this expansion was the opening of new schools in the interior and remoter areas of the country, which had previously lagged far behind the large eastern cities and the capital.

Educational policy was distinctive in a number of respects. To conform to the needs of a rapidly developing industry great emphasis was placed on training scientists and engineers; school students took a general course which included both science and arts subjects, but most of the new places in higher education were for engineers and scientists. To raise the educational level of the workers and peasants, special efforts were made to help children from such families to get to senior secondary school and university, and adult literacy classes were organised. To ensure that the schools and colleges should conform to the needs of a socialist society, communist cadres were assigned posts as directors of educational institutions, and courses in Marxism were instituted. Also the old teachers and professors were expected to remould their ideas in the direction of Marxism, by study and discussion, and move their class standpoint towards that of the working class by adding periods of social criticism and self-criticism. The participation of the intellectuals in the land reform was considered a very important part of this process.

Reform in literature and art

In his talks on literature and art at the Forum in Yenan in 1942, Mao Tse-tung had elaborated the principle that in a socialist society, literature and art must be created for the workers and peasants and must be developed under political leadership. The content of artistic works should in future be predominantly the lives and struggles of the workers and peasants. The workers and peasants should be encouraged to produce artistic works, and professional artists and writers should live and work among the people so that their creative works came to express the standpoint of the workers and peasants.

A movement of thought reform was carried out in the spirit of the Yenan Forum in the early fifties, and again in 1955. The particular feature that characterised the movement in the latter

33

period was that it was focused on writers who were Party members, notably Hu Feng, who was denounced for attempting to build up a position of domination in the sphere of literature and for propagating the view that in this sphere it was the writers themselves who should be the arbiters, not the leadership of the Party. The criticism of Hu Feng was led by Chou Yang who held a leading position from the thirties up to the cultural revolution in the Party's propaganda department.

All forms of literature and art were encouraged. Book publication was greatly increased, which included much translation of foreign works, especially from the Russian, but also dramatic and literary works from all over the world. Peking and other forms of Chinese opera, which were enormously popular throughout the country, were particularly favoured, and efforts were made to build up new companies by finding all the old artists – many of whom were doing other work or were destitute – and getting them to train young people.

Music and drama were used a great deal in propagating the aims of the various social campaigns that were launched, especially for advancing the collectivist ideas behind land reform and agricultural collectivisation.

The mass campaign for adult literacy coupled the Party's educational policy with that in the field of art and literature. Groups of young people took plays and films to the countryside, both for the purpose of propaganda and for the purpose of carrying out work which would help the more privileged young people of the cities serve the peasants in the countryside. New theatrical companies and film studios were opened, and teams were organised to take theatrical performances and mobile film units to the countryside. Encouragement was given to workers and peasants to write, set up drama companies and develop all forms of cultural activity.

The People's Liberation Army

Up to Liberation the People's Liberation Army had been in the main a guerilla army based in the countryside, armed with small arms apart from the limited amount of artillery and heavy equipment captured from the Japanese or the US-armed Kuomintang. It was led by commanders who lived with their men in the field and were supported by allowances of food and clothing in kind.

In late 1950, MacArthur carried the Korean War to the Chinese border and large forces of Chinese volunteers entered the conflict. Fighting a foreign war gave many young Chinese a new experience of international solidarity. The 'Resist America, Aid Korea' campaign developed the concept of the PLA as an army of the whole people, and fighting the most up-to-date mechanised army in the world strengthened the need to review the guerilla traditions of the PLA in contrast to a modern army led by technically-minded professional soldiers.

In 1955 the organisation of the PLA was largely remodelled on the pattern of the Soviet Red Army and re-equipped with Soviet and Soviet-pattern arms. Officers' uniforms replaced uniforms which were the same as those of the ordinary soldiers. Decorations were instituted. Training establishments for specialists and staff were established. Officers were assigned salaries which were slightly above those of persons of equivalent rank in civilian posts. However, in one respect, the PLA retained its own tradition – companies of soldiers continued to give massive assistance to civil construction by building roads, bridges and dams, laying railway lines, and aiding areas hit by natural disasters such as flood, drought, earthquake or insect pests. By working closely with the national militia of workers and peasants the army was kept in contact with the people.

The structure of government

In 1954 after the 'Three Antis' movement against malpractices in government offices, the Republic established a new state constitution. This includes representative congresses at various levels, each of which elects representatives to the congress immediately above it, and a council to carry out its day-to-day work of government. At the lowest level are the village congresses and town district congresses which are directly elected by the whole people. Above these, and formed from delegates from the lower congress, are the district congresses, which in turn send delegates to form the county congresses. The county congress sends delegates to the provincial level, which in turn elect the national deputies for the National People's Congress. Several cities have the status of provinces, and the national minority autonomous areas elect their own delegates to the National Congress on the basis of a greater proportional representation because of their smaller populations.

The National Congress is the final state authority which elects the Chairman of the Republic, who in turn nominates the Prime Minister. The National Congress also elects the head of the judiciary and the head of the procurator's office. The Supreme People's Court and the Supreme Procurator's Office both come under the National Congress.

The constitution of the Republic recognises the working class as the leading class in Chinese society, and the alliance between the workers and poor peasants as the basis of the state. It also recognises that the purpose of the socialist state is to serve China's advance to communism, that is a society in which all oppressive institutions – the state, law courts, police, and military formations will be things of the past, as will the class divisions that gave rise to them.

The two alternatives

By 1957 China had been transformed into a stable socialist society with a thriving economy and an industrial base of raw material production and heavy engineering, although a poor peasantry still made up the great majority of the population, together with a working class which was hardly any better off. The future promised a gradual solution of the low material and cultural conditions of the country, but this did not necessarily

35

imply the further transformation of Chinese society towards communism. In every sphere of life considerable obstacles existed.

In industry, the structure was still characteristic of capitalist organisation, with each enterprise containing its own managerial, technical and trades union hierarchy. Based on managerial authority, the technical authority of the expert and a high degree of specialisation, much emphasis was put on individual material incentives and codified regulations and procedures. Membership of the Party was higher among the workers than other sections of the population, and the social ethos emphasised the status and leading role of the working class. Many workers were promoted to managerial and technical positions, particularly in the new industries being created in the interior. To a great extent, though, the managerial personnel were still drawn from the old capitalist class and professional strata, and the new engineers and technicians coming out of college were also predominantly from these social backgrounds. Bureaucracy was increasing, helping to perpetuate this traditional class pattern of worker, technician and manager. The very achievements of the system, the status and social security of the worker and the family, created complacency and acceptance of this structure, particularly as the growth of educational opportunities for the children of working class families, together with the growth of the economy, gave promise of social advancement. The relatively higher living standards in the town compared to the countryside reinforced this conservatism in industry.

In the villages the advanced co-ops were only semi-socialist. There were state farms where the employees received wages, as in industry, but these accounted for only a small part of the agricultural population. It was true that each year saw more young people from peasant families getting advanced education, but the conditions and form of this education were calculated to change the student from a rural peasant into an urban intellectual or bureaucrat, cutting himself off from contact with the life of his family, his village and the countryside in general.

If a fair degree of social equality between families in the village was now established, within the family and between the country and the town the situation was still one of inequality. The co-op was essentially a collective of families, with the man retaining his status as breadwinner and holder of the family purse by going out to work in the field, while the woman stayed at home to keep house and look after the children. (Women, though, did more farm work in minority areas, hill districts and all over South China, compared with their counterparts in the northern plains.) The village economy was backward compared to the towns, and with the growth of modern industry this was becoming more, not less, acute. Education, health services and other social amenities were far more advanced in the towns; and with the village economy largely restricted to a few main agricultural crops, culturally, it was in danger of falling further behind the towns and especially the large cities – a process only too apparent in most under-developed countries.

The separate administration of production and civil government meant that although the mass of the peasants were actively involved in production, civil government was largely carried out from the county towns so that peasant participation remained very limited.

Although greatly expanded, changed in emphasis, in the main brought under state control, and led by the Communist Party, education was very largely developing on the pattern and with the same content as education in capitalist countries. The reasons for this are not hard to seek. Firstly, the People's Republic had to build on the existing educational structure, in part administered by the Kuomintang and part by foreign foundations in the treaty ports and in some other towns prior to Liberation. The overwhelming majority of school staff, however sympathetic they might have been to the new Republic, were not socialist in their outlook, let alone revolutionary Marxists, and the only systems and methods they knew were those of old China, Japan or the capitalist West. The Chinese Government and Party, faced with this problem and the need to develop an advanced scientific education of which they had no experience, turned to the Societ Union for guidance. Soviet education was suited to a society which was more advanced technologically than China, but even this was largely modelled on that of the West. It is true, however, that Soviet education was in general more related to production and other social activity than in the West; more students came from the working class and the peasantry; girls had a greater degree of equality of opportunity, particularly in science, engineering and medicine; and Soviet education was strongly impregnated with certain socialist ideas and social attitudes. Yet, in spite of all this, Soviet education was still based on the acceptance of a professional and managerial structure of society much as it had developed in advanced capitalist countries. Its form and content, particularly in the universities, was in many respects similar to that in the West. Equally important, in the years in which China was following the Soviet lead, Soviet educators were looking more and more to the West, increasing educational and cultural contacts with capitalist countries, while class struggle was being denied as an aspect of socialist society.

Cultural activity – art and literature, the theatre and cinema, sport and other recreations – had developed in the same way. Much of socialist content had spread to the workers and peasants, influencing their thinking in a positive direction, yet the separation of the intellectuals from the labouring people still persisted. Old works of literature and drama that dealt with the lives of the former ruling classes continued to dominate cultural circles; new works which were unrelated to the lives of the workers and peasants were prominent. Competitive sport was taking on the specialised and socially isolated form of professional sport throughout the world; and of most significance, those engaged in cultural work were looking outwards to the Soviet Union and even the capitalist world for inspiration and cultural contact, rather than trying to find ways to break down the barriers between themselves and the mass of the Chinese people, enabling them to develop a new socialist culture.

The People's Liberation Army had been transformed to a

great extent into a professional, specialist, hierarchical military force, with the structure and trappings of the Red Army and capitalist armies throughout the world.

The state structure conformed to the needs of China's socialist society in that it established equal citizenship, encouraged universal participation in elections of national significance, and provided elements of representative government. But this structure isolated the State from production, particularly at the level of direct mass participation, and thus hindered further socialist development.

By 1956 the Chinese Communist Party had consolidated its position of authority and leadership throughout the country, and in every sphere of social activity. At its eighth National Congress in that year it adopted a new constitution similar in form to that of the Soviet Communist Party.

At every level communist leaders were out-numbered by non-communist experts drawn from the old privileged classes, who in the main possessed a more advanced education and a generally higher cultural level. The Party cadres were overworked in their everyday jobs, and at the same time were required to raise their educational and cultural standards. They were caught in the paradoxical situation that on the one hand they were required to be non-sectarian so that they could work efficiently with their non-communist colleagues, whilst on the other, they had to give political leadership and persuade those same colleagues to re-mould their ideas to fit in with the development of a new, social-ist society. Often they had to use their Party status to maintain authority, yet this very process was transforming them into a privileged and bureaucratic élite. Those who held aloof from their non-Party colleagues were criticised for commandism (see explanatory notes on page 8) and sectarianism, and those who merged with them for liberalism and professionalism. Thus the Chinese Communist Party, together with all the institutions of which were now under its guidance and leadership, had arrived at a crisis of direction.

China was faced with two alternatives: either it could adhere to the Soviet pattern, that is, concentrate the energies of the people and the leadership of the Party exclusively on increasing production, and spreading educational opportunity and culture to wider sections of the people, without substantially altering the structure of society; or it could commence to initiate further revolutionary transformations, recognising that if socialist develop-ment was to stop at the stage it had reached, social stagnation would rapidly be transformed into social polarisation and finally into counter-revolutionary reaction. The situation that I have just outlined shows that the crisis of direction existed in all social spheres. Thus the revolutionary changes would need to encompass every sphere of Chinese life.

There were clearly deep differences in the Party concerning the correct road forward, and these were closely related to con-flicting developments in Chinese society. In the countryside, some co-operative farms were moving towards larger units of admin-istration in the face of growing problems of co-ordination, where-as others were on the verge of breaking-up. In industry the cleavage centred on the question of one-man management authority as against the concept of collective leadership. In education and the arts there was conflict over whether to concentrate on a gradual build up of cultural standards by relying mainly on the older intellectuals, or whether to emphasise the need for a new revolutionary culture and pattern of education involving the mass participation of the workers and peasants. In the PLA the argument developed over the question of people's militia. If the militia was going to constitute an integral part of national defence, it followed that the army would need to retain its guerilla traditions of egalitarianism and democracy to allow the two to become an efficient fighting force. If the army were to develop along the path of professionalism, instituting authoritarian discipline and a hierarchic structure, then the militia could be no more than a training organisation serving the army as and when required.

Finally the Party chose revolutionary change, but the course taken and the early disputes indicated that the Central Committee, which launched the various movements, was at no time fully united in its decision.

It seems likely that the events that precipitated the crisis were the Hungarian uprising and the Suez débâcle. It had certainly become clear from the Hungarian situation that the whole question of the degeneration of the Party leadership in a socialist society and the Soviet leaders' role had been raised, and Suez opened up the possibility of re-uniting Taiwan with the mainland.

The policies of revolutionary transformation eventually adopted by the Chinese Party were clearly at variance with Soviet practice – so evident during the first Five-Year Plan. It is for this reason that the gradually developing schism between China and the Soviet Union must be understood as an integral part of the changes which took place in China after 1957. The decisive break came with the Soviet refusal to support China in her efforts to regain Taiwan from US domination, a decision which was consummated by Kruschev's withdrawal of all Soviet experts and aid in 1960.

39

3 The Great Leap Forward

By 1957 China's first Five-Year Plan for national construction was completed successfully. The country had created an industrial base which allowed for sustained economic growth. Industry had been socialised and agriculture was largely collectivised. But as we noted at the end of the previous chapter, in the city, industry was organised very much on the pattern of capitalist industry, and in the countryside the peasants' day-to-day lives were mainly confined to agricultural work. Education conformed to the old pattern – academic in content and isolated in organisational form from production and the lives of the workers and peasants. In administration bureaucracy had considerably increased. This situation was dealt with by carrying out a rectification campaign in the Party, followed by the implementation of a set of new revolutionary policies which came to be known as the 'Great Leap Forward', the 'People's communes' and the 'General Line – for building socialism by going all out to build more, faster, better, and more economically', or the 'Three Red Banners'.

The rectification campaign

The rectification campaign took place at a time when the facade of unity in Eastern Europe had begun to break up, starting with the initial upheaval of the Hungarian rising, the Soviet intervention and the crises in Poland and East Germany following the Kruschev revelations at the Soviet Twentieth Party Congress. Even before this, in 1955, Mao Tse-tung had proposed the line of, 'Letting a hundred flowers bloom and a hundred schools of thought contend', preceding the clear recognition by the Chinese Communist Party that it too was becoming bureaucratic and authoritarian.

In early 1957 Chairman Mao gave a report to the National People's Congress of Party and non-Party delegates, later to be published under the title, *On the Correct Handling of Contradictions Among the People*, which recognised the class contradictions in socialist society and asserted the need for dissident views to be allowed a hearing. A few weeks after the speech was

40

delivered the national Party press was thrown open for all forms of criticism, and meetings of criticism were organised in offices, colleges, schools and places of work all over the country. The most important aspect of this period of the rectification campaign is that the criticism was, to a large extent, levelled at the Party. The main demands voiced were for all forms of bourgeois democratic freedoms, such as the freedom of self-expression in writing, the freedom of independent newspapers, the freedom to broaden the sphere of activity of the minority political parties, and an end to the dominant role of the Communist Party in all spheres of social activity. The critics were overwhelmingly from the professional and educational sections of the population, with the workers playing a very limited role, and the peasants virtually left out. With the counter-criticism mounted by the Party more letters from workers and peasants were published and more meetings involving them took place.

The 'Hundred Flowers' campaign was of historical importance because it was the first major example of a Communist Party in a socialist state encouraging massive criticism from outside the Party. As such, it was also the precursor to the Cultural Revolution. But whereas the Cultural Revolution was a rectification of the Party from the Left – from the workers and peasants – the 'Hundred Flowers' campaign was rectification from the Right – from the bourgeoisie. It merely cleared the ground for the revolutionary movement represented by the inner-Party rectification, the Great Leap Forward, the commune movement and the development of the General Line.

The rectification campaign was at first primarily aimed at improving the style of work of leading cadres in the Party. It was run under the slogan of eliminating the 'Three bad styles' of work. These were bureaucracy, sectarianism and subjectivism. Bureaucracy was typified by officials sitting in offices giving out orders and putting on superior airs. This was contrasted with the communist style of work in which leading personnel recognised that they were ordinary workers who had particularly important work to do and, due to their greater experience and understanding, could set an example by hard work and simple living. Bureaucracy, if allowed to exist, cuts the leadership off from the masses with whom they are working. Sectarianism meant asserting authority and superiority because of Party position. The opposite of this was the capacity that the Party had developed during the pre-Liberation years for finding common ground with people of differing social position and political views where their major interest – say the defeat of the Japanese aggressors – was the same as that of the Party, and on that basis giving leadership. The struggle against sectarianism was particularly concerned with improving co-operation between Party cadres and non-Party intellectuals and administrators. Subjectivism was making decisions and taking action without making a full study of the facts, or of the objective situation (that is, not only the objective physical situation, but also the state of people's thinking). Thus being subjective meant cutting yourself off from reality.

In May 1957 came the call published in the Party press for everyone to criticise the 'Three bad styles' in the Party.

The Great Leap Forward

To counter the outburst of the 'Hundred Flowers' period the Party initiated an anti-rightist campaign. These two campaigns continued until the end of 1957 and to lesser extent into 1958. The anti-rightist campaign was again renewed in the latter part of 1959.

The Great Leap Forward campaign centred on decentralisation and a national drive for steel. This broadened to include a drive to extend heavy industry, support industrial expansion, and develop industry and mechanical pumping for irrigation and drainage in the countryside. In the winter of 1958 a large proportion of the population was concerned to some extent in steel production. Small iron-smelting furnaces dotted the countryside and backyard steel furnaces were operating – even in such unlikely places as the grounds of newspaper offices or government departments. When I visited China in May 1959 the nationwide steel-making campaign was over, and nearly all the factories I visited were producing (as well as their normal products) electric motors, generators and transformers to help water control in the countryside.

With the widespread formation of advanced co-operatives severe problems were created and new perspectives presented themselves. Problems of internal organisation and lack of trained personnel suggested arguments for retrenchment and cutting back, whereas problems of co-ordination with other co-ops, the possibilities of freeing women for production, the possibilities of the diversification of rural life by the development of industry and education in the countryside, and the possibility of breaking down the isolation of the peasants from civil government and the army suggested larger units quite differently organised. Both trends actually took place with local initiative. On the basis of a study of what was actually taking place among the developing co-operatives the Central Committee came down in support of amalgamation and transformation.

The People's communes

In 1958 the three quarters of a million co-operative farms of China became amalgamated into 26,000 much larger collectives – the People's communes. The co-ops, containing on the average 160 families, were predominantly small village communities, and on the formation of the communes retained their identity as brigades, a level where a good deal of the organisation of agricultural production was still carried out. The co-op work teams were also retained as work teams of the commune, and continued to be the level at which much detailed field cultivation was organised and led.

The commune, in general, covered the same area and population as the *Hsiang* or township, which was the traditional unit of civil administration. When the communes were formed the old *Hsiang* civil administration was merged with the administration of agriculture so that a unified leadership was created. As the resolution of the Central Committee meeting of the Communist Party of August 1958 put it, 'The size of the communes and the all-round development of agriculture, forestry, animal husbandry, subsidiary production and fisheries as well as of industry (the worker), agriculture (the peasant), exchange (the trader), culture and education (the student) and military affairs (the militia), demand an appropriate division of labour within the administration organism of the communes. A number of departments, each responsible for a particular kind of work, should be set up, following the principle of compactness and efficiency in organisation and of cadres taking part in production. The township government and communes should become one, with the township committee of the Party becoming the Party committee of the commune and the township People's Council becoming the administrative committee of the commune.'

The setting up of the communes and the reorganisation of rural life, which was part of the movement, served a number of purposes: it facilitated the planning on a larger scale both the utilisation of land and water and the use of manpower; by creating nurseries and communal dining-rooms it freed women for work in the fields; it created the organisational basis for developing industry in the countryside; the increased potential for local self-sufficiency strengthened national defence; and the diversification of village life created a new demand for education.

Income in the communes was divided between free issue, on the basis of family members or simply need (in the main this was limited to staple food), and wages, which varied according to work. The free issue was thought of as introducing the communist principle of 'to each according to his needs' and the wage part of income, which was emphasised after the first flush of enthusiasm had passed and the communes were being consolidated, was considered as adhering to the socialist principle of, 'to each according to his work'.

Associated with the creation of nurseries and dining-rooms was the establishment of 'respected homes for the old'. As these were provided for old people who had no family to look after them, which were only a small minority of the old people, it may seem strange that such importance was attached to them. However there is a ready explanation. Traditional life in China had been insecure because of the hazards of drought and flood, and poverty had increased due to the decline of the Empire and the growth of foreign exploitation. This was particularly true in the case of old people. Thus an important focus of adult life in China was providing for the security of one's old age. Traditionally the Chinese peasant was both strongly collectivist, and strongly family centred. One may think of it like this: when the waters started to rise, everyone had to co-operate to man the dikes; when the flood swept away the dikes it was each family for itself; after the waters subsided, co-operation was again dictated by the need to rebuild the dikes, clear the channels and rebuild the devastated village. Old age loomed before the peasant like a threatening flood. By emphasising the 'respected homes for the old', the appeal to the collective spirit of the peasant was reinforced, eliminating one of the factors lying at the root of his traditional selfish or family-centred attitude of mind.

When I visited China in the early summer of 1959 the commune movement was at its height. All over the country one could see exhibitions showing great plans for the future. Models and tables showing communities with both industry and agriculture, possessing all the facilities for culture and education befitting modern society. And these future perspectives had a very solid base, for in the preceding years great strides had been made in increasing agricultural yields and diversifying farm production. Small and medium sized local industry had been built up, social services with clinics and communications centres had been extended, and perhaps most successful of all, the great majority of village children for the first time were attending school, and their parents who had missed schooling were themselves learning to read and write.

The creation of industry in the communes was coupled with a policy of the peasants working in rotation in these local industrial establishments, so that together with the gradual mechanisation of farming the distinction between peasant and worker would be steadily diminished. The steel-making campaign of 1958 gave this policy an initial boost.

The General Line

In the towns and cities, where possible, workers and office staff were encouraged to take some part in producing their own food. Schools and colleges set up gardens and fields to help provide for themselves, and also workshops, where they organised repair and maintenance work for their own unit as well as production for the market. The army was also involved in this campaign, where it returned to its own tradition of self-sufficiency by producing food and many of its simple everyday needs.

A general policy was adopted throughout society for everyone to take part in manual labour, technical innovation and administration. This was connected to the policy requiring those in positions of authority to work at lower levels during part of the year, both to curb bureaucratic tendencies and to give them a fuller understanding of the spheres of activity where they operated. Factory managers and engineers worked in the shops doing ordinary production work and menial tasks, such as sweeping and cleaning. Commune cadres were expected to spend a certain amount of their time giving leadership at brigade or team level, and doing field work with the ordinary peasants. Army officers up to the generals served for one month each year as private soldiers. All students spent part of the summer vacation working in the communes, or in factories doing manual work. Factory workers were involved in organising the lay-out of work, in preparing blue-prints, discussing the supply of materials and so on. Groups of workers, technicians and administrative cadres were formed to solve particular problems.

In 1957 a million office staff were effectively transferred to production work, particularly in the countryside, and in 1958 a second contingent left their offices.

A system of leadership known as 'creating experimental plots' was popularised throughout the country. This began with a group of cadres on a commune taking over a piece of land and carrying out experiments to raise grain yields. Having achieved good results they then travelled round the district helping the peasants to adopt their experience. The idea was later tried out and widely adopted in industry and other spheres of activity. Where hold-ups were experienced a group of cadres would, say, take over the running of a workshop. Having solved the problems and got the shop working efficiently, they would then go to other similar shops and help the workers increase their efficiency. In these activities emphasis was put on freeing people's minds from the old ideas, culture, customs and habits – 'the four olds' – so that more and more people were able to create and adopt new ways of doing things. Much of this process of transformation was summed up in the slogan coined by the Changchun Motor Works: 'One, Two, Three'. One stood for, 'All old rules and regulations should be reviewed in the light of new experience'; Two stood for, 'Workers should take part in management, and managers should take part in productive labour'; Three stood for, 'Workers, technicians and administrative cadres should form one entity'.

Another aspect of the Great Leap was summed up in the phrase, 'Walking on two legs'. The idea here was that while it was necessary to develop the most modern and productive methods in production, due to the size, the diversity and the generally backward condition of China, and also due to her own particular historical experience, it was also necessary to utilise old methods and resources of knowledge. Foreign technology should be learnt, but traditional Chinese techniques should also be used, and new Chinese methods developed to surpass what had been achieved elsewhere. For example, 'western' medicine should be studied, but traditional Chinese medicine, such as acupuncture, should also be practised and studied. Plastics should be developed, but traditional bamboo and other handicraft production should also be extended and improved. Large-scale industry should be coupled with the development of small- and medium-scale industry where local raw materials, transport, and availability of labour made it economical. This combination of large and small was well illustrated by the national steel campaign, and also in the work of building dams and reservoirs for irrigation, flood control and power.

The policy for education adopted at this time may be summed up in the concept that everyone should eventually become 'a worker, a peasant, a soldier, with education and culture'. To this end many changes were introduced and, quantitatively, a great leap forward was achieved by the rapid increase in the number of schools, colleges and students. The main emphases were put on ensuring that a growing proportion of the students came from worker and peasant families, and that education was integrated with productive labour.

Communes started part-work, part-study middle schools. Spending half their time in agriculture and related occupations many of these schools became self-supporting – in food, at least – which made possible a very much faster expansion of secondary education in the countryside. In the towns, factories were encouraged to set up primary schools, middle schools and technical colleges. In Chengtu, capital city of Szechwan, I visited an instruments works which provided education from primary level to technical college. Incidentally, they were also duplicating their main production building, which was a modern factory built of ferro-concrete, using traditional timber, a direct illustration of 'walking on two legs'.

Primary school children started some productive activity at nine years old, for two hours a week ; this period was extended as they got older. The main purpose was to develop among children a socialist attitude of mind – a respect for manual labour and love of the working class ; acquiring productive skills and increasing production were considered of secondary importance.

The following is an extract from a report from Tsinghua, China's leading engineering college in Peking :

'. . . . Tsinghua's 11,000 students and several thousand teachers and workers have worked together to set up over sixty plants, workshops, engineering and designing enterprises. They have completed over 900 important projects in scientific research and trial production of new products. These include nodular cast iron rails and a model two thousand kilowatt multipurpose electric power plant, all of which are of considerable importance to China's economy. In addition to spells of general manual labour, the university students and teachers have also carried out 392 important designing and engineering jobs . . .'

During this period the enrolment at Zhongda, the university in Canton where we taught, more than doubled to several thousand. The students set up a brickworks on the campus, and the science faculties did much of their own construction work and built new equipment to expand their laboratories. The proportion of students coming from worker and peasant families rose to ninety per cent.

The policy of transformation affected every aspect of life. A report on Xeihe (Peking Union Medical College) in late 1958 compares very closely with what we heard at Huashan Hospital in Shanghai ten years later. Some of the main points of criticism which led to radical changes were that the senior staff concentrated on research which would bring them renown, and neglected diseases that were widespread among the workers and peasants ; that the senior staff spent little time actually attending patients ; strict rules and regulations prevented junior staff and nurses from carrying out the skilled medical work that they were capable of ; and the authorities failed to appreciate the value of traditional Chinese medical practice. The changes instituted, which included doctors taking part in routine work, such as cleaning the wards and feeding patients, were summed up in the report as follows, 'The leap forward was made when the focus of attention became centred fully on the patients, when classifi-

46

cations and ranks ceased to be dividing lines and all members of the staff began to work as a team.'

In late 1959 and 1960 the commune idea in a modified form was applied in the cities. It was begun in a small way by groups of city people – mainly housewives – who were up to that time not productively employed, starting up small productive units. In order to free women from household chores, various local amenities were set up to support these production units – nurseries, dining-rooms, district laundries, and eventually centres which dealt with a wide range of problems, like baby sitting, house cleaning and general repairs. From these beginnings some quite large undertakings developed, mostly making light consumer goods.

The organisational changes that we have already discussed were linked to campaigns to raise the political education of the people. This centred on the study of Marxism and the works of Mao Tse-tung. For example, in Shanghai, a core of 500 experienced party cadres was formed to lead Marxist studies throughout the city and district. There was a nationwide campaign for the workers and peasants to study philosophy using, in particular, the texts from Mao Tse-tung which were later to be featured in the Cultural Revolution, *On Practice, On Contradictions*, and *On the Correct Handling of Contradictions Among the People*. The movement started among workers in a Shanghai shipyard, but spread quickly throughout the country. In Peking University it was reported that nearly 400 study groups had been formed, comprising 80 per cent of faculty members. In Kwangtung a reading list of Mao's works was prepared for leading cadres, and in the army his writings on military questions were featured. Two particular aspects of this movement were to reappear in the Cultural Revolution ; firstly, the refutation of bourgeois ideas and theories, and secondly, the emphasis on relating study to the social activities that particular sections of people were engaged in. It was at this time that *Red Flag*, the theoretical journal of the Central Committee, was founded, and this was followed by a stream of new local theoretical Marxist journals.

The four movements – the rectification, the Great Leap, commune formation and the application of the General Line – formed an overall effort to transform Chinese society. They lessened the gap between town and country, between intellectual and manual worker, between worker and peasant, and the gap between those in authority and the mass of the people. This movement was followed by a period of reaction in which a great deal of ground was lost, but it set the course which was again to be taken up half a decade later. All the disputes and all the changes which comprised the Cultural Revolution had their origin in the Great Leap movement, if not before.

In the summer of 1959 exceptionally bad weather hit many Chinese provinces. Until 1962, the weather was to remain the worst the country had experienced for many years and, in particular, there was acute drought on the northern plain. During the same summer of 1959, the 1958 harvest was re-estimated, with the result that what had been thought to have been a harvest of 375 million tons of grain – almost doubling the very good 1957 harvest – was found to have been only in the order of 250 million tons. Other figures, including that for steel output for 1958, were also found to have been greatly over-estimated. In 1960 and 1961 the emphasis on steel and heavy industry was shifted to a policy of all-out aid to agriculture, and agricultural mechanisation.

In July 1960 Kruschev ordered the withdrawal of all Soviet experts working in China (some fifteen hundred), the termination of Soviet contracts for the supply of equipment for some of China's largest undertakings, and the destruction of existing blue-prints. This, with the natural calamities of drought, locust plague and flood, and the mistakes committed in the formation of the communes and in the Great Leap movement slowed down the revolutionary tempo. From late 1959 a reaction set in which reached its peak in 1961–62.

4 The Period of Reaction, 1960-62

The year 1960 constituted a watershed between the period of revolutionary advance and the following period of reaction. Over half of China's farmland was hit by drought and flood, and in July Kruschev ordered the withdrawal of Soviet experts. The emphasis of Chinese economic policy was shifted to one of massive assistance to agriculture. Several million people left the cities to take up work in the countryside. In late 1959 the policy concerning commune organisation was changed to one of decentralisation, making the brigade – usually the village or the old advanced-level co-op – the most important part of the structure (later, in 1961, the team was to replace it in importance).

Allowing for the bad weather conditions from 1959 to 1962, and the damaging results of the termination of Soviet assistance, very serious mistakes appear to have been made by the Chinese Communist Party leadership. It may be that had it not been for these adverse factors, what in the event appeared to be mistakes would now be looked back upon as either minor errors or not even mistakes at all. Clearly every major change in society has its positive and negative features, but the balance here remains uncertain.

It is not the function of this book to give a full analysis of the Great Leap, however it is necessary to consider some of these mistakes because they clearly constituted an important factor in determining the split in the communist leadership, which was to widen into a breach during the Cultural Revolution. One cause was the break in confidence in the Chinese revolutionary tradition – in the revolutionary changes of 1958, the leadership of Mao Tse-tung and the correctness of his theoretical works, in the Chinese workers and peasants as expressed in the mass line. In essence, the aim of the Cultural Revolution was to get China back on to the path of the Great Leap ; thus one dimension of the split of 1966 was between those who saw the Great Leap as the policy which had brought China to the point of collapse in 1961, and those who saw it as an historic step towards communism – marred, but not negated, by bad weather, Soviet perfidy and some serious errors.

Among the developments which led to the crisis in 1961, and

the breach in leadership, are the following. The withdrawal of vast numbers of male workers from fieldwork to work on steel, water conservancy and new industrial developments, both in the cities and on the communes, along with the fact that large numbers of women were working in the fields for the first time, both necessarily resulted in agricultural inefficiency. The acceptance of a high level of free food distribution on the basis of exaggerated production figures. This led to considerable wastage and, later, with the onset of food shortage, much bitterness among sections of the peasants. The high level of local inexpert initiative, resulted in large wastages of material and the construction of incorrectly sited industry, much of which could not be integrated into the national economy. Perhaps the worst mistake was that committed by the Party after the inner-Party struggle at the Lushan meeting of the Central Committee in September 1959 when the anti-rightist mood on the left prevented it from continuing the policy of regulation and restraint which had been commenced earlier that year. Even sensible criticism of excessive targets and adventurous projects were, in late 1959 and 1960, often labelled negative, or even rightist sabotage.

Of course, it must be noted that if there had been no labour crisis in 1959, the break with tradition in North China created by women working in the fields alongside the men, and receiving payment, might not have been made and this was clearly a revolutionary advance in women's emancipation. Again, however wasteful the free issue of food was for a time, and however bitter the feelings of some sections of peasants on this issue were, for many it stirred up a communist spirit which was to affect the whole country during the Cultural Revolution in 1967.

An example to become famous throughout China was that of Ta-chai, a production brigade of a commune in a very arid, infertile mountainous area of North China. On the basis of intense collective labour, despite severe setbacks, over a period of a decade of struggle with nature, and at times political struggle from above, they established high levels of output and stable living conditions. Since 1963 it has been a model of collective self-reliance.

To deal with the critical situation that had arisen in late 1961, the Central Committee adopted a number of policies which centred on all-out aid to agriculture, and were termed, 'Readjustment, Consolidation, Filling-out and Raising Standards'.

The Party responded characteristically. Leading cadres were sent to the countryside to share the hardships of the peasants and give leadership. However, there were a number of factors that must have made it very difficult, in many areas, to give leadership in the traditional way of setting an example and rousing the mass enthusiasm of the peasants. Because of the harvest failure in some areas, food had to be taken from other areas, which also, due to the nature of the bad weather for two years, had little surplus to spare. Food distribution had been free, rather than related to work done, and within each commune the more prosperous villages had to share with the less prosperous ones. With the onset of poor harvests, there must have developed a wide-

50

spread feeling of having been let down. Finally, after two years of hard struggle and the promise that three years of intense effort would achieve a higher and more stable standard of living, many peasants were faced with the need to work harder than ever just to produce enough food to keep going. Given this situation, hostility to Party authority must have become widespread, resulting in the local Party leadership degenerating into authoritarianism. On the other hand, many villages survived the bad weather because of the physical progress achieved in the Great Leap and the capacity of the commune to mobilise manpower for urgent tasks, such as transporting water from a distance to parched fields, or repairing flood-damaged dikes. Many other villages which suffered acutely from the bad weather were certainly saved by well-organised relief from other areas. In such situations, the increase in Party leadership at the village level, from cadres transferred from higher levels and the city, must have helped maintain morale and enabled the Party to keep to its traditional role and avoid authoritarianism.

The two lines and two factions in the Central Committee

It was at this critical time that it may be said that a split within the leadership of the Party and the State had begun to crystallise, and that two opposing factions were becoming established in the Central Committee.

A series of directives were issued by the appropriate government ministries affecting nearly every aspect of Chinese life, but which, in general, negated the policies of the Great Leap. They were not made public, but were made known in the particular spheres of work in which they were to become effective. (We were to get a broad view of the general impact during our visits to various units in Shanghai and Tientsin in 1967, and in the case of the directive for higher education, from our discussions at Zhongda.)

The directive for industry, which had seventy clauses, emphasised the authority and responsibility of management, and the technical authority of the professional and technical staff. It severely tightened labour discipline and put emphasis on rules and regulations, while at the same time increasing individual material incentives. (When we visited the No. 3 Steel Mill in Shanghai in the summer of 1967 the workers spoke about the directive with considerable bitterness.)

The fifty-point directive for schools laid emphasis on academic achievement, staff authority, and again on professional status. At one Shanghai middle school, students and teachers describing the trend from 1961, pointed out that it had led to teachers encouraging students to study hard with the promise of good jobs and high salaries; to the staff trying to obtain as large a proportion of academically-advanced primary school leavers as possible so as to raise the prestige of their school; and it had led to the students concentrating on their own studies, in some cases even to the extent of not wanting to share their knowledge, so as to acquire advantages over their classmates. The directive for higher education which contained sixty points had the effect of handing back the leadership of education to the old scholars.

Noted academics formed committees to plan educational courses, and were relieved of teaching duties to allow them to concentrate on research. They were also given personal privileges, such as special food rations, special seats on buses and the right to jump queues.

The directive for agriculture established the production team (in Kwangtung, this was composed of between thirty to sixty families) as the main unit for agricultural production in place of the brigade. It emphasised strict accountancy and workpoints assessment, and laid down the size of private family plots. During this period a further set of four policies, attributed to Teng Hsiao-ping, and which were strongly criticised in the Cultural Revolution, were tested throughout the country. They came to be known as the 'San zi yi bao' or the 'Three freedoms and one responsibility' – freedom to develop a free market; freedom to increase the size of private plots for individual family cultivation; freedom to develop small enterprises with sole responsibility for profit and loss; and the allotting of responsibility to individual families for the cultivation of particular fields belonging to the collective. No doubt many of the points in these directives were dictated by the critical situation facing the economy, and it was their adoption that assisted China's economic recovery. Also, it must be remembered that throughout this period the policy of all-out aid to agriculture continued and great progress was made in many branches of industry. Collective work at the commune level was maintained, especially in the continued development of water control, increased mechanisation and supply of artificial fertiliser, and this, to a large measure, laid the basis for the rapid recovery during 1962 and the following years. What is clear, however, is that in general the measures taken during this period had a retrograde effect in relation to advancing socialism. They strengthened the division between intellectual and manual work, and emphasised individual material incentives and authority rather than revolutionary leadership. In the countryside, particularly with the 'san zi yi bao', they stimulated private enterprise and helped weaken the collective spirit of the peasants.

Prior to and at the meeting of the Central Committee in mid-1959, Peng Te-huai, who was a member of the Polit-bureau and Minister of Defence, led an attack on the Great Leap and the communes. Peng had discussed these questions with Russian leaders and his criticisms were similar to those voiced by Kruschev. Peng was defeated at the Central Committee meeting, dismissed from his ministry and replaced by Lin Piao. However, he retained his position on the Polit-bureau. A number of other Party leaders associated with Peng were also dismissed from their government positions and Peng's criticism was denounced as being rightist. In 1960 Wu Han, a historian and Vice-Mayor of Peking, wrote a play called *Hai Jui Dismissed from Office* which described a Ming official who had stood up to the Emperor in defence of the oppressed peasants and had been dismissed from his position of governor of a province. The play was a veiled reference to the case of Peng Te-huai (who likened himself to Hai Jui) and implied that he had been wrongfully dismissed. There was also the implication that he had virtuously stood up for the peasants who were suffering from the mistakes of the commune movement.

From early 1959 to the middle of 1964 a group of writers, also associated with the city administration of Peking and the Peking papers, published a long series of hardly-concealed attacks on the policies of the Great Leap, the communes and the leadership of Mao Tse-tung, and in defence of such leaders as Peng Te-huai. Linked with these were demands that leadership should be handed back to the old professional experts, and assertions that the whole economy was in a mess and the leadership out of touch with reality. The writers encouraged journalists all over the country to take up their views and spread them.

In August 1962 a conference was held on 'Literature and the Countryside' in Darien, North-East China, run by Chou Yang, head of the Party propaganda department. In spite of the fact that it took place barely a month before the Tenth Plenum of the Party Central Committee (which was to reassert the essential correctness of the policies of the Great Leap), the main content of the speeches were attacks on it and on the communes. In 1964, Lu Ting-yi convened a conference on higher education in which he asserted the need to defend the 'sixty points' for higher education against growing criticism arising out of the campaign to reform education. This was clear evidence that these two leaders of the Party propaganda department, who also led the Ministry of Education, were in general agreement with the Peking leadership.

Following the publication of the fourth volume of Mao Tse-tung's works in 1960, many articles were written encouraging everyone to study and apply them to solving the problems facing them in their work. This movement declined in 1961, and in the summer of 1962, Liu Shao-chi's lectures, published in English under the title of *How to be a Good Communist*, were re-published, in an edited form, with a great fanfare. The importance attached to this may be seen from the fact that the lectures were printed in both *Red Flag* and *People's Daily*.

Liu's book emphasised the need for Party members to devote themselves to self-cultivation, as communists, by studying the works of Marx and Lenin, and said that they should subordinate themselves unconditionally to the Party, accepting decisions of higher organs even if they considered them wrong. It also emphasised the leadership of the working class and the Party in contradiction to the peasantry, which it claimed always suffered from petit-bourgeois egoism and individualism. The book explained that the Party exists to struggle for socialism and advancement towards communism, and that Party members could only develop in the course of social struggles, but the main emphasis was on the Party organisation itself and the need for allegience to the Party as such.

Thus Liu's book took a line distinct from that of Mao Tse-tung, for Mao always emphasised that study and self-cultivation, however much they might be a necessary part of the development of Party members, must always remain subordinate to practical struggle and leadership. Although he stressed the need for Party discipline he always made it clear that the Party's sole purpose was to serve the needs of the masses, that each Party member should always adhere to revolutionary principle, and that the workers were the leading class in the revolution. He had himself analysed the various backward tendencies of the peasants, but had always kept clearly in mind that the Chinese revolution depended on the alliance between the workers and the poor peasants and that the positive role played by the poor peasants in the Chinese revolution must always be recognised.

When discussing the significance of Liu's book with Party members at Zhongda, I said, 'Surely, if Party members read the book in conjunction with Marxist writings – as Liu recommends – and in particular the writings of Chairman Mao, the book would not be such a bad influence?' The answer I got was that after its re-publication in 1962, central importance was placed on studying Liu's book, and young people who wished to join the Party or the Communist Youth League read it again and again. Because Chairman Mao's works were only available as a large four-volume selected edition, they tended to be put off, so reading and discussion concentrated on Liu's book alone. Its re-publication at a time when the emphasis on studying Mao Tse-tung's works had died down, his policies of 1958 were being reversed and his leadership being sniped at in certain influential papers, can only be understood as part of a general effort to devalue Mao Tse-tung's leadership.

Given the critical situation, it was not surprising that great emphasis was placed on the discipline and leadership of the Party and on the importance of scientific knowledge, efficient accountancy, and the vital role the limited number of experts had to play following the termination of Soviet assistance. However, to properly assess the political significance of this period we must also look at the exceptions to the general trend of 1961–62, the most important of which were the developments in the PLA and the building of the Ta-Ching oil field, plus the model of self-reliance shown by Ta-chai.

Until 1959, when he was replaced as Minister of Defence by Lin Piao, Peng Te-huai had responsibility for the army whilst it was being reorganised on the pattern of the Soviet Red Army. In speeches, he had put forward the need to place increased emphasis on modern weapons and technical proficiency rather than political consciousness and a democratic style of work. In the Great Leap year of 1958, in line with the general policies of the Party, the system had been introduced of commanders serving in the ranks for one month each year. In May 1960, under Lin's leadership, 120,000 army cadres were sent down to basic units to 'promote the movement for cultivating the splendid 'Three-Eight' working style of the People's Liberation Army and to engage in political and ideological work in a big way. The 'Three-Eight' working style is summarised in three mottoes and eight characters. The three mottoes are: 'keep firmly to correct political direction; maintain an assiduous and simple working style; be flexible and mobile in strategy and tactics'. The eight characters mean be united, alert, earnest and lively. In October 1960, Lin Piao wrote a long article on the publication of the fourth volume of Mao's works, emphasising the need to 'put politics in command' and study Mao's works. At about this time he summed up his view of army leadership in the form of four basic principles, which came to be known as the 'Four Firsts':

'In the relationship between men and weapons, the emphasis must be put on man – his courage, spirit of sacrifice and political consciousness. In the relationship between political and other work, emphasis must be put on political work – when political work is done well the political consciousness, initiative and creativeness of men can be developed to the fullest. In the relationship between ideological and other aspects of political work, the ideological aspects must be emphasised – the Communist Party must carry on education among the masses in accordance with the needs of the masses themselves, and on the basis of living questions, not abstractions. In the relationship between ideas from books and living ideas, the emphasis must be put on the living ideas in people's minds – this is materialism. It has been thoroughly elaborated in Mao Tsetung's reports . . . books are necessary, but book learning must be related to reality.'

Both during the Great Leap, and the following period of difficulties, the People's Liberation Army was fully engaged in the struggles of production and distribution, so it might have been expected that the trends in the army would have reflected the trends in the civilian organisation of the Party, but from the above it can be seen that this was not the case. Even as early as 1961, Lin had had the book of Mao Tse-tung's quotations issued throughout the army.

In 1960 work was started on a new oilfield in the North-East. Up to this time, although there had been a considerable development in the Chinese oil industry, China was still heavily dependent on oil imports. The new oilfield, which by 1965 supplied all China's oil requirements, was called Ta-Ching. It was developed on the revolutionary principles of the Party's General Line, the Great Leap and the People's communes. Instead of building a single town to house the oil workers and their families and locate the offices and research centres connected with the work of the oil field, it was decided to combine the industrial work with an agricultural area large enough to feed the new population. Agriculture was to be developed by the families of the oil workers and staff and the total population to be housed in a number of housing areas, thus taking a step towards the elimination of the separation of industry and agriculture. From the start, emphasis was placed on maintaining a simple way of life, and the sharing of common living conditions by the workers, technicians and administrative staff.

In the organisation of work, leading personnel were encouraged to spend most of their time dealing with problems on the spot and spending as little time as possible in offices – which themselves were kept simple and located near the work sites they administered. Important problems were dealt with by forming groups made up of workers, technicians and administrative cadres. These groups operated democratically on the basis that all members of the group had equal status. Finally, the whole enterprise – industry and agriculture, education, civil administration and militia training – came under a unified administration on the same principle as that of the People's communes. (In reports about Ta-Ching in 1966, it was stated that a number of enterprises all over China had been developed along the same lines.)

The events of this period may be looked at in two ways. As has already been suggested, the Party's line from 1960 to 1962 can be seen as a retreat from the revolutionary policies of the Great Leap and the communes, the most important exceptions being the PLA and Ta-Ching. This view can be substantiated by the effort that was made to have Peng Te-huai re-established at the Central Committee meeting held in 1962, indicating a split in the leadership of the Party. However, it may be said that the Central Committee adopted the policies of retreat because they were dictated by the situation, and that they endorsed the revolutionary line of the PLA as the most effective way to maintain Party leadership and control, where a considerable proportion of the soldiers were from families in stricken areas. (It can also be argued that the pattern of development in Ta-Ching was followed, at least in part, because of the need for extreme economy in industrial expansion.) The fact that a split in the Party leadership was not felt acutely by wide sections of the Party membership until 1966 does indicate that this second view reflects a real aspect of the developing situation. Whether it was the divergent leadership that led to divergent policies, or that divergent policies reinforced divergent leadership can never be finally established. What is evidently true is that a process of polarisation set in from about 1957 in the leadership, only to be intensified still further by the economic crisis of 1961 and the changes of policy in 1958, 1961 and 1962.

In September 1962, the Central Committee held a meeting at which the correctness of the General Line, the Great Leap and the People's communes were re-asserted and, in general, policies were adopted and aimed at strengthening collectivism and combatting the individualistic, professional élitist and authoritarian tendencies which had developed in the preceding period. By this time the schism in the Party leadership had become so pronounced that from then until September 1965, when the Cultural Revolution was launched, can best be understood as a period of preliminary struggle between the two lines and two factions.

5 Preliminary Struggles, 1962-65

From 1962 the situation in agriculture improved. The three years of bad weather were at an end (since then, each succeeding harvest has been reported as surpassing the previous one). In industry, the period was one of consolidation rather than rapid expansion, but progress included some very important achievements, notably the development of atomic energy and the achievement of self-sufficiency in oil production. The policy of all-out support for agriculture resulted in a steady expansion of the production of artificial fertiliser, and power equipment for water control.

In September, the Central Committee met and Chairman Mao issued his call 'Never forget class struggle!' and raised the slogan 'Learn from Ta-chai', setting the tone for a number of policies designed to counteract the rightist trends which had developed from 1960. In industry and throughout the economy emphasis was again put on cadres taking part in physical labour and leaving their office desks to solve production problems where they arose. In agriculture, the policy of experimental plots where leading personnel developed new methods was maintained, and an allied policy was started of demonstration fields where new techniques could be tested on an expanded scale. All cadres were encouraged not only to run these ventures but also to take part in the toughest physical work.

Educational reform took two forms. Firstly, the content of school and college texts was reformed to relate more to socialism and contemporary problems, and a new emphasis was placed on students and teachers taking part in physical labour. Secondly, the policy of developing part-work, part-study schools both in the villages and country towns related to agriculture, and in the cities related to industrial production, which had been commenced in 1958, was given a new emphasis and clearly designated as the basic pattern for an advanced socialist education system.

A committee of five led by Peng Chen, Polit-bureau member and Mayor and First Secretary of Peking, was set up to lead a revolution in cultural life. Emphasis was again, as in the Great Leap period, put on creating works of literature, art, films and

57

plays which were for, and about the lives of the workers, peasants and soldiers. Chiang Ch'ing, Mao Tse-tung's wife – who was later to become the vice-leader of a reconstituted National Cultural Revolution Group – directed a movement of reform in Peking opera. This was looked upon as very important since Peking opera was, because of its renown and highly-stylised form, seen both as a stronghold of the old culture and stubbornly resistant to the acceptance of a new revolutionary content. The creation of such operas by the Peking Opera Company was later referred to as the first victory in the Cultural Revolution. These revolutionary operas came to dominate the Chinese stage during the struggle, and this has continued up to the present time.

Not only was it asserted that artistic work should be for the workers, about their lives, their work and their political struggles, but that these artistic works should lay emphasis on their heroic achievements as well. With this lead came a sharp criticism of a number of individuals in the cultural field for taking a rightist line. This culminated in late 1965 with the publication of an article criticising the play *Hai Jui Dismissed from Office* which can be taken as the first major shot in the Cultural Revolution.

In mid-1963 Lin Piao's 'Four Firsts' were officially established as part of the regulations of the People's Liberation Army, and subsequently these guide-lines were applied in industry in a national campaign for everyone to learn from the PLA its devotion to the cause of socialism and its democratic style of work.

That the movement initiated by the Tenth Plenum of the Central Committee of 1962 was intended to be a revolutionary movement to carry China forward to a more advanced level of socialism can be seen from the fact that the focus of the whole movement was to learn from the People's Liberation Army, the Ta-Ching oil field, and the Ta-chai production brigade. This meant a focus on precisely those spheres of activity where the three divisions of society – between town and country, between the peasants and the workers, and between mental and manual labour – were being struggled against most effectively and, further, these were the areas where China was demonstrating most clearly her capacity for self-sufficiency – seen as a necessary condition for her remaining on the road to communism.

The Socialist Education Movement

The most important decision of the September Central Committee meeting was to launch a mass movement called the Socialist Education Movement. The aim of this movement was to eliminate corrupt and bureaucratic practices which had developed particularly in some areas in the countryside, during the 'Three Hard Years'. It was also meant to counter all moves towards an individualistic economy – closely related to corruption and bureaucracy – and generally to raise the socialist consciousness of the whole people by bringing about mass participation in the struggle and relating Mao Tse-tung's works to it. The general lead for the movement was given in the slogan for everyone to take part in 'Class struggle, the struggle for production and scientific experiment', or the 'Three Revolutionary Banners'. It was first tried out in certain limited areas and then, on the basis of this experience, was developed throughout the countryside, which was the main focus of the movement, and in the cities. Four major directives were issued to guide it. The first issued in May 1963, contained ten points and became known as the 'First Ten Points'; the second was issued in September of the same year, also containing ten points, becoming known as the 'Latter Ten Points' (after some months this was redrafted, becoming virtually a new directive); and, finally, a directive of twenty-three points was issued in January 1965. The significance of these four directives lies in their divergence. The 'First Ten Points' implied a movement which, by rousing the class consciousness of the masses, would rectify the situation through a struggle to strengthen the collective spirit of the workers and peasants and fight against individualistic practices. However, the 'Latter Ten Points', and more particularly the redrafted version, encouraged a punitive policy focused on all illegal practices, and particularly the shortcomings of the lower-level cadres. The 'Twenty-three Points', on the one hand, was aimed at correcting the effects of the 'Latter Ten Points' and, on the other, re-asserted with increased emphasis the line of the 'First Ten Points'. It was in the 'Twenty-three Points' that the following phrase was first used: 'The main target of the movement is those in authority in the Party who have taken the capitalist road'.

After the issuing of the 'Latter Ten Points' a pilot scheme was launched in an agricultural production brigade called Taoyuan (Peach Garden) in Hopei Province. The scheme was led by Wang Guang-mei, Liu Shao-chi's wife. Both Liu and his wife condemned the whole Party branch at Taoyuan as anti-Party. Forty out of forty-seven cadres, past and present, of the brigade were denounced and more than one hundred and fifty ordinary peasants were made to make public self-criticisms. This experience was publicised throughout the country and led to the redrafting of the 'Latter Ten Points'. As an indication of the national importance of the Peach Garden trial, one of our teachers told us that Wang Guang-mei had held a meeting in Canton to brief cadres before they left for the countryside which took two days and was based on her own experience. Each meeting had lasted eight hours.

Thus, within the Socialist Education Movement there developed two opposed policies – the one aimed at raising the morale of the poor peasants and strengthening the collective spirit, the other tending to intimidate the mass of the peasants and strengthen those in authority at commune level and above.

Mao Tse-tung characterised the policy of the 'Latter Ten Points' as that of 'hitting at many to defend few' or 'waving the red flag to defeat the red flag'. It was Liu Shao-chi's adoption of the same tactic in June and July of 1966 which finally split the Central Committee. The importance Mao attached to this clash of policies in the Socialist Education Movement is seen by the fact that he drew particular attention to it when, in August 1966, he wrote his big character poster (*dazibao*, see explanatory notes

on page 8) headed 'Bombard the Headquarters!' which initiated the attack by the Red Guards on the top Party and government leaders who had attempted to suppress the Rebels up to
that time. From our discussions about the Socialist Education
Movement with people at the university who had taken part,
two things stood out clearly (this of course referred particularly
to developments in Kwangtung Province). One was that effective
criticism by the ordinary peasants seldom if ever got beyond the
level of production brigade cadres, and thus was essentially
criticism among the masses and their directly elected representatives and did not effectively touch those who held authority from above. Secondly, there was considerable variation from
one place to another in the way in which the movement had
developed, the main determining factor here being the date at
which it had commenced. Where the movement had been
launched just after the issue of the redrafted 'Latter Ten Points',
initiative was held by the work teams which went into the
countryside, and in effect 'many were hit to protect a few' and
most of these 'many' were ordinary peasants and team leaders.
Where the movement had not got under way until the work
teams had been briefed in the spirit of the 'Twenty-three Points',
the initiative had tended to accrue more to the poor peasants'
associations. To illustrate this point I quote briefly from one of
our teacher friends, Comrade Lo Tsin-min, and from Tung
Guo-hua from the university office:

> *Lo:* 'At first we criticised the cadres at team and brigade level;
> next we criticised individual peasants who had committed any,
> even very trivial offences; finally we criticised cadres higher
> up, at commune level, but this latter criticism was very super-
> ficial. Because they were liable to criticism for any trivial
> offence they might have committed, the peasants were reluctant
> to make serious criticisms of people higher up.'

> *Tung Guo-hua:* 'We were unable to get anywhere until we had
> become accepted by the peasants' association and by the poor
> and lower-middle peasants of the village. We had first to settle
> down in the village, working with the peasants in the field,
> helping them in the homes where we were staying, making
> friends with them. When we had done this, then they began
> to tell us about the situation in the village.'

As well as its significance in relation to the divergence of the
two political lines in the Party, the Socialist Education Movement was clearly of importance in conditioning the minds and
feelings of the people in the period leading up to the Cultural
Revolution. All our students, who had been at university for two
years or more, and the young teachers had spent from three
months to a year living and working as peasants, listening to
accounts of the sufferings of the poor peasants and the oppression
of the landlords before 1949, and engaging in the introduction of
new techniques in farming. I became aware of the extent to
which this had affected them in my classes in May 1966. My
most successful classes were those in which we discussed the
students' experiences in the countryside. They became so in-

60

volved in the subject that their normal shyness when speaking English mostly disappeared. The young teachers whom we knew best were themselves mostly from the countryside and they talked about the movement in a more matter-of-fact way, but two teachers, one whose father was a butcher in Shanghai and the other whose father was an emigrant tailor, had clearly been deeply moved by their experiences and contact with the poor peasants.

The Socialist Education Movement was also developed in industry. As part of the campaign to learn from the revolutionary example of the People's Liberation Army, PLA cadres were sent into industry. Also work teams were sent into some industrial units ; our university first secretary spent a period investigating in one Canton factory. We also heard from some workers in a sugar refinery that when workers had stood up to make criticisms in their factory, and other factories that they knew about, they had often been criticised for trying to make political capital for themselves. In some cases, they had even been victimised by being transferred to other factories ; thus many workers had been reluctant to make criticisms, especially those with family responsibilities.

From late 1959 when Peng Te-huai was replaced by Lin Piao as war minister, the general trend in the People's Liberation Army was back to its revolutionary traditions as expressed in Lin Piao's 'Four Firsts'. Nevertheless, here too the struggle between the two lines was continuous. Two aspects of the efforts to counteract the emphasis on political study and democratic discussion were attributed in the Cultural Revolution to Lo Jiu-ching, who was army Chief of Staff from 1959 to late 1965. He was charged with having developed army competitions to raise technical skill, in the course of which cutting down time devoted to political work, and with having condemned the action of certain army units for developing political rectification.

In 1965, with the war in Vietnam greatly intensified by the American bombing of the North, those who adhered to the idea of a professional army again put forward their case. However, the revolutionary line was firmly re-asserted, and clearly stated in Lin Piao's article 'Long Live the Victory of People's War', written at about the same time as Yao Wen-yuan was writing the opening attack on Wu Han's play *Hai Jui*. Major reforms were carried out in the army, including the abolition of official ranks, and rank uniforms and insignia, and a movement launched for a voluntary reduction in the pay of army commanders.

In the field of education it might be supposed that the advance towards socialist form and content was going according to plan. However, here too, there is reason to suppose that the situation was critical. With the adoption of the policy of developing part-work, part-study education the social and political effects would depend entirely on whether or not the old style, full-time education was reformed or not, and if reformed to what extent and how quickly it was carried out. If the old schools and colleges were to be left as they were then China would end up with the graduates from the full-time schools forming an élite, and those graduating from the part-work, part-study schools and colleges filling the manual and low-level clerical and technical jobs. Liu Shao-chi is said to have accepted this perspective. At Zhongda (Zhongshan Daxue) in May 1966, although the reform movement of 1965–66 had certainly resulted in considerable changes and the mass participation of the students in the Socialist Education Movement had obviously had a deep effect, there were no signs that anyone envisaged any transformation of the university sities to bring them into line with the part-work, part-study schools. Even the weekly afternoon of garden work was looked upon as recreation rather than a serious part of the struggle to bridge the gap between mental and manual work. But more importantly, the students and staff, while at university, had virtually no social contact with workers and peasants. Those who came from worker or peasant families might go for long periods, even years, without returning home, especially if they lived far from Canton.

The Socialist Education Movement overlapped the Cultural Revolution and virtually merged with it in the autumn of 1966. But it is reasonable to suppose that by the autumn of 1965, Mao Tse-tung had concluded that, in spite of the 'Twenty-three Points' directive, rectification inside the Party was being effectively blocked at a low level, and the only way to rectify the Party at higher levels was to take a new initiative specifically aimed at those in authority within the Central Committee. By choosing the Peking Party Committee as the first point of attack the struggle was taken to the highest level, but at the same time leaving every Party leader and committee, nationally, the option of which side to choose whilst the breadth of the target was temporarily limited. Again, Peng Chen, Secretary of the Peking Party Committee and Mayor of Peking, had been in charge of the campaign to revolutionise work in the cultural field of literature and art since 1964. Those who had most clearly put forward anti-revolutionary views in 1961–63 were directly under Peng's authority in Peking, and it was the Peking press that they had used to publish their attacks on Party policy and Chairman Mao, yet Peng had made no effort to expose or criticise them. Thus it is again reasonable to suppose that Chairman Mao had concluded that Peng Chen and a large section of the Peking Party Committee were firmly in the opposed camp. In relation to this question, it is interesting to compare the speeches concerning the Cultural Revolution of Peng Chen and Ko Ching-shi, the Mayor of Shanghai who died in 1965, which were published at about the same time in the summer of 1964. Peng Chen and Ko both state the need to transform literature and art to serve socialism and for the intellectuals to remould their world outlook, but whereas Peng gives the impression that this is, as it were, a routine and straightforward organisational task for the intellectuals to carry through by themselves, Ko states it in fervent terms of revolutionary struggle requiring mass participation.

6 Opening the Attack, September 1965-May 1966

It seems likely that the decisive factor leading to the struggle for power which took place during 1966 and 1967 was the division that arose in relation to the Socialist Education Movement. If this movement which intimately concerned the lives of the whole people was carried through without the workers and poor peasants fully participating then the chances of them being able to assert themselves against authority at any future date, short of civil war, would have been faint – this surely was one of the clearest lessons of the Soviet experience. However, in 1965 it was the external situation which brought the clash between the two lines to a head.

With the US escalation of the war in Vietnam, China's involvement became the over-riding issue and faced her with two broad alternatives. Either China had to align herself with the Soviet Union, which meant that the Chinese Party had to damp down the struggle against revisionism and remodel the PLA on the Soviet pattern of a professional army—as had happened in the fifties ; or she could stand by herself which, whilst the US possessed an overwhelming strength in armaments, would mean that she would have to rely on her superiority in manpower and morale, and maintain her policy of People's War. That the issue was contended is evidenced by the article written in April 1965, in commemoration of the victory over Nazi Germany, by Lo Jiu-ching, Commander in Chief of the People's Liberation Army. In this article he ends up by arguing that in the face of American aggression China and the Soviet Union must stand together. In August, Lin Piao wrote his article 'Long Live People's War!' which followed closely on the decision announced in June for the abolition of ranks in the PLA. However, there are also indications that Mao Tse-tung and Lin Piao had anticipated an all-out struggle for power even earlier. As we have already seen, in 1963 the campaign had been launched for the whole country to 'learn from the People's Liberation Army' its revolutionary work style, and that in connection with this campaign many PLA cadres had been sent into industry and communications units to enhance political leadership. In November 1963 Lin Piao had advanced five principles to guide the work of the

PLA. These, in conjunction with the campaign (apart from their military significance of extending the principles of People's War) were clearly, in retrospect, further organisational preparations for the Cultural Revolution. The five principles were: to creatively study and apply Mao Tse-tung's works; to persist in the 'Four Firsts' (putting man before weapons, and politics in command); for leading cadres to go to basic level units to give energetic and good style leadership; to boldly promote good commanders and fighters to key posts; and, to train hard, and master the finest techniques in close-range and night-fighting tactics. In January 1966, following the decisions of the Central Committee meeting, these principles were further emphasised at a three-week conference on 'political work in the Army' organised by its General Political Department. The close connection between the People's Liberation Army and the Cultural Revolution became clear when a high-level forum on 'Literature and Art in the Armed Forces', convened in Shanghai under the leadership of Chiang Ch'ing, brought out a summary of its work in February 1966. It stressed that the movement was a class struggle between the proletariat and the bourgeoisie for leadership on the cultural front.

The first blow is struck

In September 1965 a working conference of the Central Committee was held. Mao Tse-tung raised the question of the danger of revisionism arising within the Central Committee itself and called for criticism of Wu Han's play *Hai Jui Dismissed from Office*. By stating in so many words that 'Hai Jui is Peng Te-huai' and the 'dismissed from office' meant the dismissal from office of the rightists in 1959, Chairman Mao was indicating that genuine criticism of Wu Han meant political criticism. A month later Yao Wen-yuan, who had played a leading role in the criticism of rightism in literary circles in the preceding years, wrote an attack on the play in the *Shanghai Evening News*. The article was reprinted in *Liberation Army News* but not in *People's Daily*. From Peking came only a query as to the validity of publishing such an article without prior consultation. Only three weeks later did *Peking Daily* reprint the article as 'controversial' . . . the Cultural Revolution had begun.

As we have already noted, from 1960 through to 1964 a group of writers including Wu Han, the Vice-Mayor of Peking, entrenched in the administration of Peking, had published a stream of attacks on Chairman Mao, the Great Leap Forward, the communes, and on the Party's policy of self-reliance and independence from the Soviet Union and hostility to American imperialism. Yet Peng Chen, who was leader of the 'Group of Five' responsible for the Cultural Revolution campaign and First Secretary of the Peking Party Committee, had not raised any criticisms of these people who came under his leadership.

The attack being mounted in this way, it was ensured that either Peng Chen purged his own administration – which Chairman Mao alleged was so tightly knit 'that you couldn't even thrust a pin into it' – which would be a considerable victory against those in authority taking the capitalist road and clear the way for further revolutionising the cultural field, or Peng would stand his ground and thus bring the struggle out into the open more clearly. In the event the latter took place.

The 'February Outline'

Yao's article called forth a huge and conflicting correspondence in the press, then the matter died down in public. Following this, in February, Peng's Group of Five in charge of the Cultural Revolution brought out a report which was cleared for distribution throughout the Party by the office of the Central Committee. This report which was entitled *Outline Report on the Current Academic Discussion Made by the Group of Five in charge of the Cultural Revolution* determinedly diverted the discussion concerning the play *Hai Jui* and related subjects into academic channels. When I arrived at Zhongda at the end of April the students of the Chinese and History departments were making detailed historical investigations and holding long historical discussions, their normal classes having been suspended for this purpose. In Peking University it became known later the students were given literally thousands of historical references to follow up. As Wu Han and his colleagues had been in fact criticising contemporary policies and suggesting opposed ones, all this academic historical research and discussion was largely irrelevant.

To prepare people's minds for the further development of the struggle within the Party, two editorials were published in *Liberation Army News* in mid-April and early May. These were followed by Chairman Mao's 'May 7th' call for the revolutionisation of education. On May 10th, Yao Wen-yuan followed up his November attack on Wu Han's play with a much stronger attack on Teng To, Peking Vice Party Secretary, which not only underlined with detailed references the counter-revolutionary views developed by Teng and others from 1960 to 1964 but made out a fully substantiated case for there being a conspiracy between Teng To, Wu Han and others, and suggested, with clear implications towards Peng Chen, that they were supported by higher authority.

The *Army Daily's* editorials, 'Hold High the Great Red Banner of Mao Tse-tung's Thought', 'Actively Participate in the Great Socialist Cultural Revolution' and 'Never Forget Class Struggle', while being particularly addressed to fighters and commanders of the People's Liberation Army, were clearly also a general call for the whole people to 'actively participate'. At the same time, the editorials emphasised that this movement was a life and death struggle between two totally opposed roads – the capitalist road and the socialist road.

Chairman Mao's short statement concerning education was couched in his characteristically succinct terms:

'While their main task (the students) is to study, they should in addition to their studies learn other things, that is, industrial work, farming, and military affairs. They should also criticise the bourgeoisie. The period of schooling should be shortened, education should be revolutionised, and the domination of our schools by bourgeois intellectuals should by no means be allowed to continue.'

The general line was clear. The policy of part-work, part-study education was being reasserted as a general form for all education that was attuned to socialism. To call for shortening the period of education by indicating a practical step towards the achievement of the policy gave substantial assurance of action. The final sentence was clearly a call for intense struggle on the campus. However, immediately, the key sentence was 'They should also criticise the bourgeoisie', for the students throughout China were at this time being diverted into academic historical arguments. Here was a clear call to break through these restrictions. Chairman Mao did not leave this last point to chance; making contact with young teachers in Peking University he encouraged them to mount a direct attack on their Principal.

Yao Wen-yuan's detailed article on the 'Three Family Village' made clear a number of important political points. Particularly, that the defence of the dismissed rightists contained in the plays about Hai Jui was merely the beginning of a sustained rightist attack that was only reluctantly suspended in 1964 because of fear of exposure. That this attack not only criticised the Great Leap policies, but encompassed a whole array of criticisms which, taken together, added up to a rejection of the policies of the Party and the revolutionary advance of socialism. And most important that the conspiracy operated from the Peking Party Committee and the Peking press.

The 'May 16th Circular'

In May under the direct leadership of Chairman Mao, the Central Committee repudiated the 'February Outline' and criticised Peng Chen specifically in a circular to all Party organisations and down to county and equivalent level in other spheres. The 'May Circular', made public a year after its distribution, stated categorically the aims of the movement:

'The whole Party must follow Comrade Mao Tse-tung's instructions, hold high the great banner of the Proletarian Cultural Revolution, thoroughly expose the reactionary bourgeois stand of those so-called 'academic authorities' who oppose the Party and socialism, thoroughly criticise and repudiate the reactionary bourgeois ideas in the sphere of academic work, education, journalism, literature and art and publishing and seize the leadership in these cultural spheres. To achieve this, it is necessary at the same time to criticise and repudiate those representatives of the bourgeoisie who have sneaked into the Party, the Government, the army and all spheres of culture, to clear them out or transfer some of them to other positions. Above all, we must not entrust these people with the work of leading the Cultural Revolution. In fact many of them have done and are still doing such work, and this is extremely dangerous.'

The parallel between Peng Chen's handling of the campaign in the cultural sphere and Liu Shao-chi's handling of the Socialist Education Movement was brought out in section 9 of the Circular, although this parallel was not widely understood until a year later:

'At a time when the fierce struggle of the proletariat against the representatives of the bourgeoisie on the ideological front has only just begun, and in many spheres and places has not even started – or, if it has started, most Party committees concerned have a very poor understanding of the task of leadership in this great struggle and their leadership is far from conscientious and effective – the Outline stresses again and again that the struggle must be conducted "under direction", "with prudence", "with caution", and "with the approval of the leading bodies concerned". All this serves to place restrictions on the proletarian left, to impose taboos and commandments in order to tie their hands and to place all sorts of obstacles in the way of the Proletarian Cultural Revolution. In a word, the authors of the Outline are rushing to apply the brakes and launch a counter-attack in revenge.'

A week or so later the struggle was opened up in Peking University with a frontal attack on the university leadership for its attempt to stifle the movement among the students.

Because the movement burst into the open in June 1966 with the overthrow of the Peking Party Committee and the leadership of Peking University, and because the suspension of college and school classes for six months involved the dramatic mobilisation of the student Red Guards, the Cultural Revolution has been widely thought of abroad as beginning and ending with the students. In fact, the social changes which the Cultural Revolution was concerned with and the organisational forms created to facilitate these changes began with the Great Leap Forward and the People's communes in 1957–58, and concerned the workers, the peasants, the soldiers and the students in equal measure, and constituted a transformation of Chinese society in all spheres. The struggle which brought about the irreconcileable schism between the two political lines took place from 1963 to 1965 in the Socialist Education Movement and in the concurrent reforms in the PLA. Thus it is reasonable to view the events of June 1966 to the end of that year, in which the students played the most active role, and the events of 1967 up to September when the students still played a major part, as phases in the general struggle during which their role was central because there was a measure of stalemate on other fronts. It is also correct to see their role as that of a revolutionary vanguard, and this as both an actual reality of the Cultural Revolution, and in principle, an important factor in the continued advance to communism. Important because as social leaders of tomorrow, while at the same time inheritors of the past, if they do not become revolutionised through class struggle, the students of today will of necessity, as they rise to positions of leadership, support a stabilised pattern of society in the future, and thus create an obstacle to further advance.

7 'Zhongda'—Sun Yat-sen University, Canton

Education, educational institutions, students and teachers have been at the heart of the Chinese revolution in all its stages, and the universities in particular have focused and reflected the problems in Chinese society. As the traditional road to power and status in the civil-service-administered Chinese empire, education took on new dimensions of importance with the penetration of China by the foreign powers. The scientific technology and knowledge of the West seemed to offer China the only possible defence against foreign aggression and domination, and then it appeared that western forms of social organisation and culture could be used as an instrument for overturning the Ch'ing imperial rule. After the revolution of 1911 the problem of mass literacy arose both in relation to China's poverty and the isolation of the countryside from modernising efforts in the cities – the need for a widely read vernacular literature to unite the nation became pressing. Finally, with the Russian Revolution and the betrayal of Chinese interests by the allies in the Versailles Treaty, the universities became the focus of the struggle between capitalist ideas and revolutionary Marxist theory on the one hand and Confucianism and modern ideas on the other. Thus the Chinese universities, in their origin and in their present condition and situation in Chinese society are classical yet modern, scientific yet revolutionary, liberal yet Marxist, Chinese yet foreign. Indeed, many were originally foreign foundations – for example, Tsinghua College of Technology in Peking, so important in the initial Red Guard movement, and Lingnan College that was partly incorporated into Zhongda after 1949 – and today much of their study of science is still carried on in foreign languages and using foreign texts.

Chinese universities still have a very complex function in Chinese society, ensuring that they will remain, for the foreseeable future, at the centre of social struggle. At one and the same time, they are themselves centres of both privilege and revolutionary thought. Their graduating students have a wider view of the world but a weaker relationship to, and a shallower understanding of, the communities in which they will live and work. Therefore the students must be humble learners whilst being teacher and innovators, and certainly they must always be aware that they are at the heart of the revolution.

Zhongshan Daxue, or Sun Yat-sen University, is always referred to in China as Zhongda. Zhongshan means 'middle mountain'. Dr Sun acquired the name as symbolic of his central importance in China's struggle for national independence – the struggle to free herself of the degenerate Manchu dynasty – and the impositions of the imperialist powers. The contraction of 'daxue' into 'da' has a national significance because Peking University has always been known as 'Beida', and is never referred to as 'Beijing Daxue', and the first 'university' of the revolution, the Anti-Japanese Imperialism college founded in Yenan during the war against Japan, was known as 'Kangda'.

Zhongda is a national university, that is, it comes directly under the Ministry of Education, but it is also the primary university of South China, and the primary university of Kwangtung Province. It also has, as might be expected, a large number of students whose homes are in Canton. Thus Zhongda was a natural focus for the Cultural Revolution not only for the city of Canton, but also for the province, and for South China as a whole. This central position was also due to the fact that Canton contained the headquarters of the Central South Bureau of the Party and the Provincial Party Committee.

The original Zhongshan University was founded in 1925, the year of Dr Sun's death, at the time when the city was preparing for the Northern expedition, which ended in the victory of the Kuomintang and the beginning of the revolutionary civil war between Chiang Kai-shek and the communists in 1927. After Liberation the university was merged with other institutions of higher learning, including Lingnan University, the campus of which was taken over as the site of the new Zhongda. Lingnan was a United States missionary foundation of 1916.

Zhongshan consisted of faculties of physics, chemistry, mathematics, biology, history, geography, Chinese, philosophy and foreign languages. Perhaps three-quarters of the students were studying science, the physics faculty being the largest. All the science students studied Russian, English or both. Lingnan had had faculties of medicine and engineering, but these had been incorporated into other colleges.

After Liberation Zhongda, being a national university, was expected to achieve a high academic level by recruiting noted scholars onto its staff. One of the criticisms made against the ex-University Party Secretary, who held this position from soon after Liberation until 1965, was that he brought onto the staff a number of people with very black political records. A professor who was denounced at a university meeting was alleged to have been trained under the Nazis in secret police methods, and on returning to China and served in the Kuomintang secret police. Another had been a mayor who it was said, was notorious for hunting down guerilla fighters in the countryside and having them executed. In the 1957 anti-rightist movement a number of these professors were severely criticised and some designated as rightists.

Educational policies and Zhongda

In the Great Leap in 1958, following the anti-rightist campaign, the new educational policy was developed in Zhongda. Firstly, there was a very rapid increase in the number of students, and most of these were recruited from amongst children from worker and poor peasant families. Secondly, it was proposed that all students and young teachers should take part in physical labour. At Zhongda they started going to the countryside for several weeks in the summer, a brickworks was set up on the campus where they worked, and they did much of their own construction work. (We were told a number of times, in conversations about the years leading up to the Cultural Revolution, that emphasis on physical labour dropped markedly after 1960 until the Socialist Education Movement in 1964.) Under the national slogan of 'Red and expert' that is advanced in politics and professional work, more emphasis was also put on political studies in 1958.

In 1961 the education directive containing sixty points was issued to all universities and colleges at about the same time that similar directives were issued to other sections of the population – industry, agriculture, schools and research institutions. A friend at the university, Tung Guo-hua, summed up the effect that the university directive had at Zhongda, somewhat as follows: 'Authority for directing education was transferred to the academic authorities. Leading scholars were relieved of a lot of their teaching and routine work, and the function of the University Party Committee, in the main, came to be that of giving backing to leading committees of scholars'.

After 1960 most of the professors who had been designated as rightists and criticised in 1957 were rehabilitated. The acting First Secretary was later to admit in a self-criticism made in 1967 (see Chapter 12, The Cadre Question), that in 1960 he had gone to the homes of many of those professors and apologised to them in person for the way they had been criticised earlier. During the 'Three Hard Years' the old scholars received many privileges, including extra food rations and cards that entitled them to go to the front of queues and occupy reserved seats on buses. One of the criticisms levelled at Tao Chu, First Secretary of the Central South Bureau of the Central Committee, was that he unduly favoured the old scholars at Zhongda – often visiting them with presents and encouraging their privileged treatment. As a result of the new emphasis on academic achievement, the proportion of students recruited from non-worker or non-peasant families rose considerably in 1961 and 1962.

In the Language department during this period, it was said that there developed a strong tendency to admire and copy western customs. The more sophisticated students went in for ballroom dancing and wearing western clothes, which had been less marked with the Great Leap, and many avidly read novels about upper-class life in the West. These activities had become sufficiently noticeable for the students in other departments to refer to that department as 'The Western Kingdom'.

The English texts used up to 1964–65 were mainly the English

70

classics, from Shakespeare and Milton to the Brontës and Dickens, but also included contemporary authors, for example, Osborne and Amis.

After 1964 the situation changed fairly radically with the commencement of the Socialist Education Movement and the associated reform movement in education. All the older students and the younger teachers left the university for periods of up to a year to take part in the Socialist Education Movement. There was considerable criticism of the bourgeois ways and style of work of the staff of the university. The dean of the Language department was strongly criticised and removed from the University Party Committee, although being retained in his academic position of dean. The content of the language courses was criticised and changed, with contemporary material concerned with the Chinese revolution and revolutionary struggles in other parts of the world substituted for the 'classical' European texts. The direct method of language teaching was adopted and, again, a higher proportion of peasant and worker children were selected for university places. This reform movement was still going on when I arrived to start teaching a month before the suspension of classes. The weekend dances had been discontinued in 1964, and distinctive western style clothes, such as neckties, were conspicuous by their absence.

The students and young teachers went to the countryside as work-team members, as did some of the leading cadres. There they worked and lived with the peasants, helping to stimulate new ideas, while taking part in investigations to uncover corruption, mal-administration, private profit-making, and other practices which weaken the collective. One young teacher, Comrade Lin Chih-fu, described his experiences:

'I lived and ate with an old couple. I shared a room and a bed with the old man. I helped with the housework, cleaning, getting water from the well and wood for the fire. The old man used to talk to me of their sufferings before Liberation, and this moved me deeply. He was old enough to retire but as he was very knowledgeable about water control he volunteered for the job of keeping an eye on the water levels in the paddy fields. During the day we work-team members did a full share of the farm work, and in the evenings we wrote reports and took part in meetings. At meetings we encouraged the peasants to make criticisms of the cadres and the cadres to make self-criticisms. Very often the peasants were loathe to make criticisms, so we encouraged them to describe their hardships before Liberation, and what had been achieved since. Very often this moved the young cadres to tears, and afterwards, because they were so moved by these accounts, they would make sincere criticisms of their own selfish actions. At first, as I was city bred, I was not used to the hard work and my feet became very sore going barefoot over the rough, hard ground, but the fine example of the hard work and simple lives of the peasants helped me overcome my difficulties, and soon I got used to living and working in the countryside. One of our activities was to popularise new methods. There was a need to use liquid fertiliser (produced at a new plant near Canton) in the surrounding area because it is not so convenient to transport over long distances. At first the peasants were unwilling to use it, so we set an example. Seeing us apply it made them prepared to try.'

Another young teacher had this to say about the movement:

'Our professors in the Language department did not want us to spend a lot of time in the countryside away from our university work. They arranged it so that their students only went for three months while students from other departments went for a whole year. They also encouraged the students to take books with them so that they could carry on with their language studies.'

Lo Tsu-min, criticising himself for his lack of courage in making criticisms in the past, said,

'When I went to take part in the Socialist Education Movement, I knew the right thing to do was for us to live, work and eat with the poor peasants, yet when it was decided that we should eat separately – on the grounds that we were not used to the food the peasants ate and might become ill – although I knew this was wrong, I did not speak up against it.'

The campus

The campus itself, several square miles in area, lies on the south bank of the Pearl River. Across the river to the north lies what was the prosperous middle-class residential area of the city.

The river is over a quarter of a mile wide and the campus several miles from the nearest link with the northern shore, Hai Chu Bridge. Because of this, and because the south side was agricultural land until 1949, the original site of Lingnan must have been very isolated from the city. Even in 1966 the degree of isolation was still considerable, and intensified by the campus being surrounged by a high brick wall. All the walks and pathways were lined with trees, so with the bamboo groves and the many shrubs, the whole campus felt like a botanical garden.

The population was something in the order of seven thousand. Perhaps five thousand students, a thousand teaching and administrative staff and their families and a thousand workers and their families. As there were paddy fields, market gardens and various livestock, there were farmers, as well as building workers, craftsmen and service workers.

Physically, the campus was divided up between the workers' living areas, most of which were in the north-west district, and the academic body, with each faculty having its own blocks of student dormitories and dining halls. A further set of divisions existed between the living quarters of the students, the young teachers, the general run of older and married teachers, and the professors and senior administrative staff. The north-east district, where we were given a house, was mainly occupied by members of the University Party Committee and leading professors of the different faculties.

The material life of the students was very simple. They lived in dormitories, eight to a room. Half the room was filled with eight bunk beds, leaving just enough space in the middle for a table formed by eight 'school' desks pushed together and benches along each side. They took all their meals in student dining halls. Each student had a bowl and usually a spoon (rarely chopsticks) and after a one-course meal washed up his own things under a cold tap.

There were cold showers in the dormitories, and on certain nights the kitchens heated water for baths, which the students collected in buckets. They also washed their own clothes. Volley ball and netball were widely played, but there was also athletics, football and track sports. Badminton, swimming and table tennis were very popular free-time activities. All students and young staff have militia training – mostly rifle and hand grenade drill – and route marching with regulation kit.

The social activity of the campus included the free-time sports, playing musical instruments and singing, playing cards and several kinds of chess, watching films, amateur dramatics and going for picnic excursions to White Cloud Mountain which is a wooded hill with lakes just outside the city. Inconsequential relaxed conversation about family, food and health are perhaps the commonest way in which the people of Kwantung pass their leisure hours and make human contact. Kwangtung people are famous for their cooking and the enormous range of things that they eat, and since this is closely interwoven with a great body of health lore and both seem to vary somewhat from one part of the province to another, these subjects are inexhaustible. Very often, even during the most intense phases of the Cultural Revolution, when we had visitors to the house, and we were most anxious to go into the ins and outs of what was going on, our guests would be quite happy to chat on by the hour about acupuncture or what is good or not good to eat when you have a cold.

The students took a general course up to leaving school, but once at university specialised in one subject. Apart from that, everyone had political studies, sports and militia training.

Morning lectures were held from 7.30 until 11.30 and there was a study period of about two hours in the afternoon – followed by sports. After tea it was mostly self-study. The Language department had an administrative block that held a library, and there was also a general university library which contained a large number of books in English.

Most students stayed on the campus during the term, except those who lived in Canton and went home for the weekend. Two girls told us that they described their lives before the Cultural Revolution as a 'triangle': dormitory to classroom to library back to dormitory.

In general, it appeared that the students kept very much to the company of their own class and did not mix to the same extent with the rest of the students in their year. Their contact with the student body as a whole was not marked. They had very little social contact with the staff and the university workers, and it appeared that they had virtually none with the workers and peasants in the factories and fields that surrounded the campus. One of our young teacher friends who played a leading role among our language teachers in the Cultural Revolution, had been a student for four years before he had learnt Cantonese.

There is no doubt that a good deal of the verve and élan of the Cultural Revolution arose from the feeling of freedom generated by the simple act of breaking out of this limited circle of activity. Here one may mark a paradox. Chinese people tend to keep tightly within their own family, circle of friends or working group, yet when the occasion demands social intercourse outside this group there usually seems little difficulty in making personal contact. When we travelled north with a young teacher who came from a hill village in north-east Kwangtung, and had just graduated in 1966, he seemed quite at ease and almost immediately able to make friendly contact with people we met, whether in the villages of Hunan or the factories or schools of Shanghai. We, too, found it easy to make friendly social contact very quickly with peasants, workers or administrative people wherever we travelled in China.

The Communist Party at the university was organised in a manner similar to that of districts of the Communist Party in Britain. Each department had a Party branch, which was divided up into groups for political discussion and political education. Above the departmental branches was the Universtiy Party Committee – usually referred to as the 'Party Committee'. The university administration was separate from the Party in structure, with sufficient overlapping to provide for Party leadership. The two comrades who were responsible for foreign visitors and looked after our needs were both Party members. They worked in the President's Office. The president, as far as we knew, was not a Party member. He was an old man and had really retired from active administrative work. However he was a member of various provincial committees, and we understood that he still attended many meetings concerned with education. The First Secretary of the Party Committee, Li, was concurrently vice-president of the university. The members of the Party Committee were referred to in the university as leading cadres. We heard of about six of these but there may well have been more. Three leading cadres were of particular interest in connection with the Cultural Revolution and will appear prominantly in a later chapter. Liu had been First Secretary from the time that Zhongda was set up after Liberation. He was a left intellectual in the thirties. By 1960 he had developed a serious heart condition, and a new vice-secretary was appointed who virtually took over from him until a new first secretary was appointed in 1965. Vice-Secretary Yang had been a school teacher and educationalist who joined the Party about 1939 in Yenan. At the time classes were suspended he was away in the countryside taking part in the Socialist Education Movement, and he only returned to the campus in October 1966. The new First Secretary Li was a member of the Provincial Party Committee (in charge of education) when appointed to his post at Zhongda, and retained his membership of that body. President Li was the only one of the three we met, the other two we often saw around as they lived near us, but only heard speaking at meetings. We were taken to dinner at a neighbouring restaurant by President Li as part of our welcome to the university. I was invited out soon after I arrived, and again with the whole family when Elsie and the children joined me. Li also visited our house for an informal chat on one occasion. He was very much the executive – authoritative, urbane and relaxed. When I asked him about the Cultural Revolution in August, he said he thought it would carry on for sometime, and when things were a bit clearer he would give us a briefing. Liu remained a leading cadre in the university, and was still a vice-secretary, but because he was semi-retired with his weak heart, and Yang was away, Li became very much the man in charge during the first months of the Cultural Revolution, and being on the Provincial Party Committee gave him considerable authority. From observing Liu at the meetings at which he was criticised, listening to the criticisms, and observing the nature and manner of his defence, we judged him to be very much the Westernised liberal intellectual.

The people on the campus who were not connected with university education included building workers and farmers, kitchen staff and caterers ; tradesmen of all kinds, such as plumbers and electricians ; the security forces, who were a police and a militia responsible for militia training ; and general administration personnel, including drivers and postal staff. As has been said already, before the Cultural Revolution there seemed very little social intercourse between the students and teachers and the rest of the community, except in the offices. However, with the formation of rival groupings in 1967 which cut across occupational divisions, this isolation was to some extent broken down. There were of course exceptions, an example of which was the friendship between a driver and his wife, a cook, with a married couple who were both language lecturers. In this case, the friendship was partly an expression of the positive feeling felt by the teachers that the isolation of the academic staff from the workers and peasants was a bad thing which should be ended.

The reasons for this isolation and the extent to which it related to status was not easy to assess. Certainly the traditional tendency for each to keep in his or her own small social group was an important factor, typified by the students only mixing with others in their own class, even if there was another parallel class doing exactly the same course. Another factor was that most of the older teachers were of doubtful class background, whereas some sections of the workers were Party members who had served in the PLA. An important factor among the workers, which was highlighted in the Cultural Revolution, was that quite a large number of them were 'contract workers'. These people were taken on for a limited period and did not have security of occupation, nor the same trades union and welfare rights as other workers. As in other countries, segregation was also created by education and cultural status, diverse living standards and differing degrees of managerial, educational or technical authority.

The Language department

The Language department was composed of about six hundred students and about one hundred staff. The English section consisted of about four hundred students and something over thirty teaching staff. The remainder of the students studied French and German. There had been a Russian language section but this had been discontinued. However, a considerable number of the science students, something like a thousand, still studied Russian. There was also a General English department that taught English to science students.

Our classes ranged from about sixteen students to some with over twenty. The top three years had two classes each. In the second year there were three classes, and the first year had six. The number of girls in each class ranged from two to five. About half the students came from the families of poor and middle peasants, the remainder from professional and clerical families. A number were from overseas Chinese families, but most students came from Kwangtung Province. The lack of language students from workers' families was explained by their option for science courses. In the main, students ranged in age from nineteen to about twenty-two on the commencement of their studies, though many students from peasant families were 'over-age', reflecting the large increase in school places in the countryside created in the late fifties.

Each class had a monitor and a political instructor. A considerable proportion of the students were Communist Youth League members and there were also a few Party members; these were older people who had come from adult jobs.

The situation among the teaching staff was complex. The professors were more or less pushed aside during the Cultural Revolution. In so far as they took part, they did so as objects of criticism and struggle, or as sympathisers and advisers of one side or the other – their voices were hardly ever heard directly. Nevertheless, as repositories of much of the expert knowledge and training at the disposal of the People's Republic they were still very important. Of course, they also acted as a reservoir of anti-socialist thinking; indeed, no professor in our department was a Marxist. The two main factors in which they varied was the degree to which they were in sympathy with socialism, and the degree to which they were considered rightists. A third and more subtle factor was the extent to which their ideology was compounded of traditional Chinese ideas, bourgeois and Marxist ideas. Better than to try to categorise groups, a consideration of some individuals will illustrate what sort of problem they constituted, and will identify certain general aspects.

The dean of the Language faculty was a Shakespeare specialist. He dismissed his own writings as trivial. Being a Party member, I assumed he meant that he had not had a Marxist approach. During the Socialist Education Movement, he was strongly criticised and removed from the University Party Committee. I was told that he had little contact with the students and young teachers.

A certain professor of French was particularly unpopular with many students. He had an arrogant manner, believed that he was the healthiest person in the university, and boasted of his command of foreign languages and his travels abroad.

The clearest example of a pampered rightist was an old history professor who was blind. He was considered to be a brilliant scholar. There had been instructions from the Party Committee and, according to some reports, directly from Tao Chu, Secretary of the Central South Bureau of the Party, to give him all he required. Two nurses were detailed to look after him. The path leading to his house was made out of bounds to students so that he should not be inconvenienced in his movements. Several people told us that he constantly found fault with his nurses, never expressed any appreciation of what they did for him and frequently shouted obscene abuse at them. He demanded foreign foods, constantly read foreign journals and listened to the Voice of America, while at the same time abusing all that was Chinese. When those who had to deal with him criticised his behaviour they were told that he was a great scholar and must be cared for.

Two of our professors who had lived in America were popular among the students. They always seemed very friendly and good-natured. When we went to work in the countryside, they worked well and took the hardships of life in a poor hill village without any sign of complaint or attitude of superiority. They also showed little sign of being positively concerned about socialism, being prepared just to do what was expected of them and leave it at that. A third professor who had also lived in America stood out. In the few weeks before classes were suspended he had impressed me as one who was deeply concerned about his students and, in particular, concerned about the difficulties experienced by those from peasant families who had fallen behind. Throughout the time we were at the university he was constantly active, reading the posters, attending meetings, preparing material for the biannual trade fairs, going to work in the countryside and so on. When his son went off on a long march, heading for Hunan and Peking, he was obviously proud and intensely interested. When another son supported the opposing group he was glad to argue with him, but also to listen to his point of view.

The dean of the English department was severely criticised. She was a strongwilled and conscientious person. Having been brought up in the professional environment of Hong Kong, her attitude was that of the autocratic teacher.

The intermediate group in our English section, between the professors and the young teachers, consisted of perhaps half a dozen members of staff. They ranged in status between those who had been designated as rightists, and one who was a Party member from a poor peasant family. One older man had been on Chiang Kai-shek's staff in a technical capacity. He was shy and retiring, but always worked very hard when we did physical labour. Several of these teachers had lived in Hong Kong and came from middle-class families.

The assistant professors and those teachers with families lived in terraced two-storey houses divided into flats. If unmarried, they lived in one-storey buildings – single people usually two to a room.

I saw a good deal of one of the young assistant professors before classes were suspended. He was engaged on preparing new teaching material, so was not doing any actual teaching. He was a Party member and clearly looked upon in the department as an able Marxist. He acted as my interpreter and often took meals with me; on several occasions we went on expeditions together. He had travelled abroad to India and Indonesia acting as an interpreter and had a keen interest in world affairs. We had innumerable discussions, including arguments about Chinese policy towards Pakistan, Indonesia and Vietnam, and also the Chinese attitude to the Soviet Union and the nuclear test ban. He talked very much in the sort of terms used by western Communist Party intellectuals. He defended the policy of the Chinese Party and government in reasoned terms, and enjoyed discussion. His wife, who taught at an engineering college, had been away in the countryside for over six months with her class, taking part in the Socialist Education Movement. I asked him what his attitude was to her being away for such a long time and he said, 'A major reason for going to the countryside is to advance your own political consciousness. For this it is better that husbands and wives do not go together.'

The lives of the young teachers were not far removed from the students. One of these had graduated early in the spring of 1966 and still lived in his old student dormitory. Another, a girl who had only been teaching for a few terms, did likewise. About half a dozen young teachers lived two in a room in a house next to the student's dormitory, sharing a kitchen and shower room. Also in the house was one older teacher who was married, his wife working in a middle school in town. Even in the Cultural Revolution the young teachers tended to keep to themselves. Most of the dozen young English teachers became our personal friends and for longer or shorter periods of duty, our interpreters and helpers.

Lo Tsu-min arrived back at Zhongda in January 1967 after two years at Birmingham University studying English. He had originally gone to take a course in Shakespeare, but this had been changed as a result of the education reform to modern English. He came from a poor hill village, where his wife is still a working peasant. During vacations he returns to the village to help with harvesting. He is a Party member, very earnest and very conscientious. In April 1967 he made an interesting self-criticism. Two of the main points of this self-criticism were firstly that he had feared war, and secondly that he had lacked the courage to make criticism.

Comrade Lin Chih-fu's experience in the countryside working with the peasants has already been described earlier in this chapter. Lin always spoke with great feeling about this experience of his, and usually ended up by saying, 'We here in the university are lucky, we should never forget the hard life of the peasants.' He earns about £2.10 ($6) a week, and of this salary he sent a quarter to his sister who was a student in Peking.

78

All the young teachers impressed us as being conscientious in their work and concerned about the development of their society. They, like the students, seemed to lead a happy social life in which games and swimming were an important part. In the Cultural Revolution they were broadly speaking as active as the students although, in the main, less sure of themselves and less prepared to show initiative and give a lead. Several of our young English teachers threw themselves fully into the struggle in 1967, whereas several others remained throughout rather on the edge of the movement.

The students

I think in the spring of 1966 the prevailing feeling among the students was that of well-being. They felt that their lives were worthwhile, they were not living in luxury but in comfort. They worked and played hard and the great majority enjoyed themselves. The reforms being carried out in their way of life and in their courses were sensible and realistic. They could look forward to a secure and constructive future of great interest and opportunity. But as well as this general feeling of well-being there were feelings of oppression.

To understand the first stages of the Cultural Revolution it is necessary to recognise the nature of the oppression felt by the students. In the main it was of two kinds.

The more academic students, those most successful in their courses, felt oppressed by Party bureaucracy. Either because they were from families who were politically suspect or because they devoted so much time to their special subject that they neglected political studies, they felt uncertain when criticising the class monitors or political instructors. Yet because of the political line being pursued by the Party Committee, the political leadership was heavy-handed, the content of political studies uninspiring, and in some cases the class leaders oppressive.

The students who found the whole set up most alien and were least successful in their studies were mainly from poor peasant families, and they felt oppressed academically and socially. In their political studies, at least, the workers and peasants would be given a place, and they would not feel the negation of socialism felt in the academic situation where everything would seem to favour those from the old exploiting families.

Our Zhongda students who came from the countryside would mostly have attended a local primary school. Even at this stage it is probable that many of their parents would aspire for them to rise above being peasants. However, at this stage, they would still spend much of their time in the fields and in the social atmosphere of the village. At thirteen, or older if they had started their education late, they would have graduated to a boarding school in the local town. There they would receive a general education in which emphasis was put on political studies and the general economic and cultural progress of China since Liberation. They would have had, in the main, to look after themselves and take part in manual labour. In the holidays they would return to the village and take part in the farm work, especially the hard work of the summer harvest. However, by the time they graduated to senior middle school – normally at sixteen – they would consider themselves, and be considered by their own people to be intellectuals. Already their thoughts and way of life would be considerably removed from that of their own age group in the village, who had ceased their education at thirteen or fifteen and were now engaged entirely in farm work. On leaving the senior middle school for the university, the young villager would no doubt be in an inner state of considerable tension. He would be leaving his own locality and moving to the city; it would mean parting with class-mates who had failed to make the same high grade and who would now be returning to the village or taking up minor posts in a local town; he would have already achieved a status that perhaps no one in his family had achieved in many generations, and the future offered him boundless opportunity.

Coming to Zhongda in 1961 or 1962 what did the young peasant high school graduate find – what solution was offered to the contradictions in his mind; his desire to be true to his peasant background, his desire to serve his country, his ambition to progress as an intellectual and thus a man of influence, his conflicting feelings about physical labour, his desire to be a good communist? The need to fulfil his parents' ambition for him?

At that time China was just coming out of a period of great difficulty – the 'Three Hard Years'. Three years of natural calamities and consequent food shortage and shortage of agricultural raw materials; years of industrial disruption; and years which followed the optimism, even euphoria, of the Great Leap Forward and the formation of the People's communes in 1958. As has been described, during those hard years the professors in the university had been shielded from the general hardships by special privileges. Academic entry qualifications had been raised which increased the proportion of students recruited from the families of the old, privileged sections of society. The English department encouraged the students to devote all their energies to studying English literature at the expense of politics. Participation in physical labour was continued but with reduced emphasis. Students who did poorly in their exams were transferred to other departments, and generally made to feel inferior, or even sent away from the university. There was a tendency among the more sophisticated students to adopt western customs and dress. The major emphasis in political instruction was put on allegiance to the Party, derived in the main from Liu Shao-chi's *How to be a Good Communist*. Thus it is clear that both the social life and the content of their studies had been, in important respects, alien to these students from peasant families.

Those students who came from professional and administrative families must have found Zhongda very similar to what they had been accustomed to. Those from country towns, however, would be unfamiliar with the intense specialisation, the sophistication of the professors, or even the acquired sophistication of the older students and young staff. Caught between the rural ways of their comrades from the villages, and the more urbane manners and interests of those from the big cities, it might be expected that many would be anxious to acquire sophistication. However, those who had developed a strong socialist consciousness, perhaps coming from families where the parents kept in close contact with the lives and work of the countryside, on meeting this sudden cleavage with what they had assumed was natural to socialist society, would have reacted strongly in sympathy with their village comrades against the bourgeois ways of the university.

No doubt there were students who felt both kinds of oppression, who recognised that the whole set-up departed from the socialist road, and to a greater or lesser extent understood that in a socialist society, bureaucracy and professionalism, authoritarianism and bourgeois liberalism, were twin aspects of counter-revolution. In general, though, there developed a cleavage in the student body between those who felt politically oppressed, and those who felt academically oppressed.

8 Initial Rebellion, Suppression and Mobilisation, June—November 1966

On May 25th, 1966, seven members of the Peking University (Beida) department of philosophy posted up a fierce attack on Lu Ping, president of the university and first secretary of its Party committee. They charged Lu with attempting to guide the Cultural Revolution into purely academic channels and limiting the activity of the students and staff to holding small group meetings and to writing articles for internal circulation only. The poster asked: 'By guiding the masses not to hold big meetings, not to put up "big character posters" and by creating all kinds of taboos, aren't you suppressing the masses' revolution, not allowing them to make revolution and opposing their revolution? We will never permit you to do this!' The poster ended with this call: 'All revolutionary intellectuals, now is the time to go into battle: let us unite holding high the great red banner of Mao Tse-tung's thought. Unite round the Party Central Committee and Chairman Mao and break down all the various controls and plots of the revisionists; resolutely, thoroughly, totally and completely wipe out all ghosts and monsters and all Kruschev type counter-revolutionary revisionists, and carry the socialist revolution through to the end! Defend the Party Committee! Defend Mao Tse-tung's thought! Defend the dictatorship of the proletariat!'

This poster was broadcast on Peking Radio on June 1st and acclaimed by *People's Daily* on June 2nd. On the 4th an editorial announced that a work team had been sent into the university by the Central Committee, that Lu Ping and his vice-secretary had been dismissed from their posts, and that two party leaders from the North China Bureau of the Party had been appointed to reorganise the Peking Party Committee.

Following the Peking broadcast of the poster, mass activity commenced at Zhongda. On June 3rd, Vice-President Li announced the suspension of all classes and called a meeting for the whole university in the Small Auditorium, at which he called upon the students to make criticism of the university staff, and, in particular, announced, 'It is permissible to criticise anyone from myself downwards'. In the days that followed posters were written criticising nearly every teacher, and particularly the old professors. Demonstrations, mass meetings and meetings of small groups, were held continuously, many of which were in support of the students' actions in Peking and the decision to reorganise the Peking Committee. About half a mile of hoardings were erected and soon covered, sometimes two or three layers deep with posters. Loudspeakers were set up in the open spaces and, as well as broadcasting local speeches, carried speeches and broadcasts from Peking.

On the morning of June 3rd, President Li presided over a Party Committee meeting to prepare for a meeting that was to be held that evening, the purpose of which was to brief departmental party committees and political instructors. That evening they issued instructions that a particular watch must be kept for criticism of the Party Committee, and materials should be collected concerning students who made criticisms aimed at the Party, socialism or Chairman Mao.

At about the same time, a group of students in the German department put up a poster suggesting that the situation at Zhongda was the same as that at Peking University. The implication of this was that the Party Committee at Zhongda had followed a policy that was anti-socialist. The group was criticised on the authority of the Party Committee, more or less confined to their dormitory to study Mao Tse-tung's writings and called upon to make self-criticism on the grounds that their insinuations about the Party Committee were tantamount to an attack on the whole Party and socialism.

On the morning of the 14th, as I was walking towards the main gate to go to our department library and then out shopping, two small buses drove in. As they came towards me some hundreds of students standing on either side of the central walk cheered and clapped excitedly. When I enquired who the visitors were I was told that they were a working party, sent to the university by the Provincial Party Committee to lead the movement. Later I was informed that they were mainly teachers and administrative workers from other educational units. The work team took over the supervision of the running of the university and organised the formation of a University Cultural Revolution Committee and departmental Cultural Revolution Committees. Members of the team joined the classes and other small groups for the study of Mao Tse-tung's works and for making criticism and self-criticism.

Shortly after the team had arrived there were several days of particularly intense arguments and quarrels which I observed taking place in small gatherings by the poster hoardings. Comrade Lin Chih-fu explained to me that he had been worried because the Party leadership in the university had seemed to be losing its grip in the face of criticism, but that now there had been a new lead from Peking to the effect that the Party cadres should humbly accept criticism, but at the same time stand firm and give leadership to the movement. He said that this new lead had greatly reassured him.

On the 24th, a second work team arrived to replace the first. This action was presumably in response to the directive from Peking to strengthen the leadership of the movement. A year later, at a struggle meeting with President Li, we learned that he had had fourteen political instructors dismissed at about this time—in mid-June—to placate the rebel students and divert them from criticising the Party Committee. One of these instructors said he had heard of his dismissal on arriving back at Zhongda after a year spent in the countryside taking part in the Socialist Education Movement, and so it could not have had any proper foundation. One of Li's vice-secretaries also alleged that Li had procured his dismissal, and had said to him, 'Do not worry, I will see that you are restored to your position once the students have calmed down'.

During the following six weeks poster-writing, meetings and broadcasting continued intensively. After the arrival of the first team even the sports activity had been cancelled and the swimming pools closed, a situation that existed for several weeks, so that the students were devoting the whole day to their activities. However, those in authority had largely been able to head criticism off themselves and redirect it against the academic staff, particularly some professors whose behaviour had already attracted the students' criticism. One arts professor was notorious for heaping scorn on his less advanced students, and for being unpunctual in his attendance at classes. On one occasion he had waved the essay of one of his students before the class to show all the parts corrected in red ink, and shouted at the writer of the essay, 'There's your "red", now show me the "expert"'. On another occasion, when he had been criticised for repeatedly being late for his lectures, he had said, 'What can you expect, I've got an alarm clock that was made in China?' Another professor was criticised for waving a cheque in front of his class which he had received for a book he had published in Hong Kong, and saying, 'There, that is what you may get if you work hard enough!'

The following exchange I had with Comrade Sung, a leading Party intellectual in the Language department, was an indication of the line emanating from the Party Secretariat at this time. Comrade Sung said that everyone was studying Mao Tse-tung's works, particularly certain articles, and that general guidance for the movement was coming down from Peking. I said to him, 'I suppose the main question in this movement is that of revisionism?' To my surprise he said, 'No, I don't think so. This movement concerns the sphere of culture and education'. This answer may partly be attributed to his reluctance at that time to reveal to a foreigner the full significance of the movement, but in view of articles that were published in the press for foreign readers – emphasising that it was essentially a political struggle – I think Sung's answer is a fair indication of the lead that was being given in the university by President Li and the work team. Later in meetings, Li admitted to having in effect adhered to Peng Chen's 'February Outline' directive, and having failed to act on the 'May Circular' or in other words, having tried to limit the movement to the academic sphere.

After the defeat of Peng Chen, and the reconstruction of the Peking Party Committee, the next most important political development was the replacement of Lu Ting-yi as director of the

Party's propaganda department by Tao Chu, and the 'pulling out' of Chou Yang, Lu's deputy. Because at this stage the main focus of the movement was in the field of culture and education, and it was being asserted that to a marked degree capitalist and traditional ideas still dominated this sphere, it was not surprising that the two men mainly responsible for Party leadership in culture and education should come under attack. Also, as has already been indicated, there is evidence that by the sixties both Lu and Chou were committed to the rejection of the revolutionary policies of the Great Leap and the communes. However, their being 'pulled out' in July of 1966, at a time when the initiative in the struggle was in the hands of the Party Secretariat directed by Liu Shao-chi and Teng Hsiao-ping, suggests that, with the clearing out of the propaganda department, their position was strengthened.

In all socialist societies there is a deep-rooted contradiction within the intelligentsia. On the one hand, the writers, artists, teachers, doctors and other professional people are anxious to serve the people, and at the same time they provide the main force which can raise the educational and cultural level of the mass of the workers and peasants. On the other hand, it is precisely amongst them that the ideology of individualism is most deeply ingrained, and the structure of cultural and professional élitism is most tenaciously defended. Therefore, it is in the cultural sphere that the class struggle in any socialist society presents the most difficult problems.

Following the new wave of rebellious activity that commenced with the meeting of the Central Committee in late July and August, the diversion of the movement into purely academic channels was prevented, but the class struggle in the field of education and culture remained an integral part of its development. The main thrust of the Cultural Revolution, in relation to education and culture, was against individualism and professionalism. Thus, it was the defence of these tendencies on the part of Lu and Chou in the sixties that came under the heaviest attack, together with their alignment with Peng Chen's Peking leadership, rather than their authoritarianism. The charge of political authoritarianism, or 'commandism', that was levelled at Peng Chen, when further developed centred on Liu Shao-chi.

The raising of criticism of the University Party Committee at Zhongda, and the activities of the work teams against the rebel students and young workers, was a reflection on what was happening simultaneously in Peking, as was the onslaught on the socialist integrity of large numbers of university cadres in order to ward off criticism from those at top level. The clearest picture of what was happening in Peking came in reports from Tsinghua Engineering College, where Wang Guang-mei, Liu Shao-chi's wife, led the work team.

Early in June all the cadres at Tsinghua were set aside and the work team took over control. Several candidate members of the Party were given positions of leading responsibility in the university, and several of the old University Party Committee were allowed to absent themselves from the campus. Notable among these being Chiang, the First Party Secretary, who was reported to have taken refuge in the Ministry of Education. It was later alleged that over two thirds of the cadres at all levels were condemned as either members of 'the sinister gang' led by Lu Ting-yi and Chou Yang, or as camp followers. The cadres having been thus intimidated in June, they were then encouraged to denounce Kuai Ta-fu, the student leader of the rebellion. It was suggested that by so doing they would help to prove their own good faith. In one department, the whole leading Party Committee was branded as members of 'the sinister gang'. The cadres were called upon to confess their previous support for it and to denounce the rebels' earlier activity as an uprising against the Party and socialism. When the work team left Tsinghua, they left the Provisional Cultural Revolutionary Committee and the Provisional Headquarters Committee of Red Guards under the control of their own nominees, while the criticised cadres were still restricted to their living quarters and assigned physical labour to help them reform.

The 'Sixteen Points'

On the 23rd July, Chairman Mao had returned to Peking. He had been away from the capital, mainly in Shanghai, since late 1965. Shortly after his arrival, he convened the Eleventh Plenum of the Central Committee of the Chinese Communist Party. In the middle of the period of the conference, on August 5th, he wrote a large character poster which was immediately made public throughout the capital and, soon after, the country. The poster was headed, 'Bombard the Headquarters!' and was squarely aimed at the chairman of the government and vice-chairman of the Party, Liu Shao-chi – although this did not become clear until some weeks later. At the end of the Central Committee meeting a directive, to become known as the 'Sixteen Points', was issued which was to provide a general guide for carrying out the movement for the next two years. This directive is certainly one of the historically most important documents of the Chinese revolution.

The aims of the 'Sixteen Points' were summed up in three words: 'Dou-pi-gai' ; translated into English they mean, 'struggle, criticism, transformation'. They were stated in the first of the 'Sixteen Points' as follows (see Appendix I for the text, and 'Notes on Some Major Documents of the Cultural Revolution' at the back of this book for a fuller discussion):

'At present our objective is to struggle against and overthrow those people in authority who are taking the capitalist road, to criticise and repudiate the reactionary bourgeois academic "authorities" and the ideology of the burgeoisie and all other exploiting classes, and to transform education, literature and art and all other parts of the superstructure not in correspondence with the socialist economic base, so as to facilitate the consolidation and development of the socialist system.'

In his poster, Chairman Mao made three points: One, that the initial rebellion of the students and young workers in June was sound and that its suppression in June and July by the work teams was counter-revolutionary; two, that to find out who was responsible for this counter-revolutionary action it was necessary to look back to the rightest trend in 1962; and, three, for further enlightenment as to who was the 'top Party person taking the capitalist road' – the main enemy – it was necessary to study the two conflicting policies in the Socialist Education Movement in 1964.

The Red Guards

Before Mao's return to Peking, many middle-school students had already organised themselves into groups for carrying forward the movement. This was to be done by studying Mao Tse-tung's works and modelling themselves on the revolutionary traditions of the PLA. They limited their membership to children of workers, poor peasants, revolutionary cadres and revolutionary martyrs. As well as adopting the working style of 'hard work and simple living' of the PLA they also, where possible, copied its uniform of khaki drab, peaked cap, gym shoes, and Sam Brown belts. Red armbands proclaimed their identity. This was the start of the Hong Wei Bing – the Red Guards.

The normal ages for Chinese school pupils were seven to thirteen for primary school; thirteen to sixteen for junior secondary; and, sixteen to nineteen for senior secondary. However, because education had been expanded very rapidly and because it was policy not to exclude older people from starting, many pupils were over-age. Thus the leading middle-school Red Guards were mainly around sixteen years old in the lower schools and eighteen in the higher, but there would be significant numbers both above and below these ages. When the movement spread to the primary schools, leading pupils were aged from thirteen upwards. The middle-school Red Guards played a central role in the movement of criticising the 'Four Olds' from August to November 1966, and it was they who, in the main, carried out the methodical street by street searches of houses of all those suspected of concealing money, weapons and documents for counter-revolutionary purposes, and the confiscation of possessions – books, works of art, etc. – which were considered corrupting. After November the initiative passed more and more to university and college students.

The Red Guards were welcomed by Mao and the Eleventh Plenum, and the movement developed rapidly. On August 18th, a million Red Guards, who by this time included students from the colleges as well as the schools, assembled in Tien An-men Square to acclaim the leadership of Chairman Mao and the 'Sixteen Points' of the Central Committee. Similar rallies were held repeatedly until the end of the year, by which time great numbers of students (both Red Guards and others) from all over the country, had travelled to Peking to take part. As well as students, many young teachers and workers had also joined in.

From this time, three members of the National Cultural Revolutionary Group (Wen-ge), set up to replace Peng Chen's group in May, took a particularly prominent part in directing the movement and constantly appeared beside Mao, Lin Piao and Premier

Chou En lai at public demonstrations. These were Chiang Ch'ing, Mao's wife ; Chen Po-ta, who had worked closely with Mao since Yenan in the thirties ; and Kang Sheng, who was closely associated with the policies of the Great Leap in 1958. Chen Po-ta had been a member of the Peng Chen Group of Five, and the 'May circular' specifically charges Peng Chen with having brought out his 'February Outline' directive without Chen Po-ta's knowledge. Chiang Ch'ing had played a leading role in the movement to produce new dramatic works dealing with the political struggles of the workers, peasants and soldiers which had become important in 1963 as part of Socialist Education Movement. In November 1966 she was appointed cultural adviser for the PLA. In the early stages of the Cultural Revolution she had been very active at Tsinghua Engineering College in supporting the rebel students and it was at the school attached to the college that Red Guards first appeared. Throughout the movement, Chiang Ch'ing had been personally associated with the Red Guards – defending them against their critics and giving them encouragement. The first account we heard indicating that she was playing a leading political role concerned contract workers. It was alleged at the beginning of the Cultural Revolution that they had been denied certain rights and benefits enjoyed by other workers. Chiang Ch'ing attended a mass meeting in Peking at which she denounced the secretary of the National Trades Union Committee for being responsible for the exploitation and oppression of the contract workers. Later, when Zhongda delegates from the different groups went to Peking, they usually reported back as having attended meetings presided over by Premier Chou and these three members of Wen-ge.

After the first mass gathering in Peking in August, student Red Guards started to appear on our campus, at first only amongst the younger students, but soon spreading to the older students, the young teachers and the workers. Two young cooks who looked after a dining-room where we took our meals for a couple of months, became Red Guards, and both went up to Peking. Several of our language teachers also became Red Guards, including Kang Hai-ching, who later became the leader of the language teachers' Rebel group, and Ni, who represented the Conservative when the two sides negotiated in 1967 and 1968. By the time the second mass rally of Red Guards took place in Peking on the 31st August, the first contingent of our students and young teachers had reached the capital.

The history of the early stages of the Socialist Education Movement was now repeating itself, albeit in a modified and more developed form. The repudiation of Peng Chen can be likened to that of Peng Te-huai in 1959, and again in 1962. The re-establishment and development of the revolutionary movement in education associated with the repudiation of Peng Chen, Lu Ting-yi and Chou Yang was the counterpart of the earlier movement in the PLA. The reaction of Liu Shao-chi and the Secretariat, under General Secretary Teng Hsiao-ping, was in line with their response to the launching of the Socialist Education Movement in 1963 ; firstly, they hastened to assert an authoritarian control from above and protect leading cadres from criticism, and secondly, they adopted the policy of 'hitting at many (at lower levels) to defend the few (higher up)'. In 1964 they had encouraged criticism of large numbers of lower-level cadres, particularly for legal malpractices, and by widespread criticism of ordinary peasants had discouraged the mass of the peasants from developing the political struggle against those in authority who were diverging from the revolutionary path. Similarly, from June to August 1966, the student rebels had been discouraged and suppressed, while at the same time the movement of criticism was diverted in a one-sided way against the old scholars and low-level cadres. In both cases, the criticism of lower-level cadres gave the impression of a Party rectification campaign. To complete the parallel aspects, just as in 1965 Mao Tse-tung and the left leadership in the Central Committee had come out with the 'Twenty-three Points' and the call to 'Boldly arouse the masses' and to direct the main attack against those in authority in the Party who were taking the capitalist road so, in August 1966, the Central Committee issued the 'Sixteen Points' decision concerning the Cultural Revolution, and repeated these two rallying cries. Here the parallel ends, for with Chairman Mao's poster, 'Bombard the Headquarters!' and the clause in the 'Sixteen Points' encouraging Red Guard organisation, the struggle to revolutionise the Party became decisive.

The major aspect of the movement from August to November 1966 was that of rousing the students and, in the process, neutralising the bureaucratic control of those in the Party who opposed it. This was done under the slogan of, 'Destroy the "Four Olds" to make way for the new'. As well as students from all over the country travelling to Peking, and students from Peking spreading the message of rebellion, the students visited many other cities and stopped off to work with and rouse workers and peasants on their travels. The young people freed their minds, extended their social experience, raised their political understanding, and greatly built up their self-confidence. Perhaps most important, they deepened their class-consciousness.

Many of their overt actions, which so impressed foreign journalists, such as changing street names, denouncing sophisticated behaviour and dress styles, damaging old emblems or monuments, raiding hostile embassies and marching people about capped with dunces hats, were mainly of a symbolic significance. But even the most trivial of these actions contributed to the students' self-confidence and developed their initiative, and when outrageous things were done the argument and criticism that followed was part of the process of gaining political discrimination. For example, there was a demand voiced at Zhongda to take down the statue of Sun Yat-sen because some people said he was bourgeois. This gave rise to a heated discussion about the nature of Sun's historic role and the relationship of the bourgeois revolution he had led to the socialist revolution. However, much of what the students did was directly constructive and related to developing socialism. Many of the methodical raids on the houses of ex-landlords, ex-capitalists and others, revealed stores of arms and money, and perhaps of more importance as social instruction for the young people, title deeds to land and other records hidden away against a possible restoration of Kuomintang rule.

It was significant that most of this activity was carried out by middle-school students who were at the most impressionable age, rather than the older college students. Many students were making investigations into the past activities of leading officials, discussing and arguing about the information that they brought to light, and publishing it in Red Guard broadsheets. Students working on farms, in factories, in small groups or individually, on their own initiative as they travelled across the country, gained a new experience compared with their previous experience of such work organised by established authority, and carried out locally.

An important aspect of all this activity was the erosion of the concept of the all-powerfulness and sanctity of authority, so deeply established in Chinese history. The slogan of the day was, 'It is justified to rebel!' Equally important, this slogan was closely related to, 'Serve the people!' and the inspiration of the PLA tradition of being modest, dedicated to the common good and living a simple life of hard struggle.

The three most studied texts of Mao Tse-tung at this time, and throughout the Cultural Revolution, were *In memory of Norman Bethune*, which extols international revolutionary solidarity and individual self-sacrifice and dedication ; *The Foolish Old Man who removed the Mountain*, praising selfless, untiring effort in the face of adversity ; and Mao's short tribute to an ordinary soldier who was killed whilst tending a charcoal burner, while *serving the people*. In the Autumn of 1966 these texts came alive to the students in the songs and sketches of their propaganda teams, in their demonstrations in support of the Vietnamese people, and above all in their working travels through China. (These texts are included in full in Appendix II.)

In mid-July I received a telegram from Elsie and the children to say that their departure had been help up on account of the Cultural Revolution, and was being put off for a year. We soon sorted this problem out, but Elsie appears to have been the last foreign worker to have come to China from a capitalist country during the movement. By this time, the academic staff of our Language department who were most responsible for the direction of education – three in number – had been pushed aside. The departmental Party secretary was still working under the first secretary of the university, President Li.

After the publication of the 'Sixteen Points' there was a new surge of activity. On August 13th, I noted in my diary that many visiting groups from other colleges and schools were to be seen around the campus, and two days later we were invaded by a huge crowd of middle-school boys and girls who spread all over the campus, reading our posters, holding discussions in small groups, standing in the walks by the screens full of posters or sitting on the grass.

On the 15th, a large-scale demonstration of our people formed up and marched to the headquarters of the Central South Bureau of the Party, both to welcome the 'Sixteen Points' and to denounce the work teams. After spending the whole night demonstrating outside the Bureau offices, the marchers arrived back worn out after their ten-mile walk there and back. A few days later the provincial Party secretary, Chiao Tzu-yang, came to address a mass meeting on the campus. We went over to join the meeting which was held in the Cinema Field, but at this stage no one thought of us taking part in the movement, so we were not told the content of Chiao's speech. The meeting was well attended and listened to attentively, but there was little sign of enthusiasm.

After the first mass meeting of Red Guards in Peking, a major concern of our people was to get to Peking. Several preliminary decisions about how many should go followed each other in quick succession. At first it was one in ten college students and one in a hundred school students. But towards the end of August, Premier Chou suggested that all students should travel to Peking, group after group, and that travel on the trains should be free. There was tremendous jubilation at this announcement. Our first group reached the capital in time for the second mass meeting on August 31st. On their return in September, some of the most militant of the rebellious students formed themselves into an organisation which they called the 'August 31st Fighting Group', and soon became well known as just 'August 31st'. This group, which varied in membership from one to two hundred, was to play a prominent part in events until our departure in 1968. On September 10th, I wrote in my diary, 'Campus almost deserted with most students away in Peking'.

During the autumn, the campaign against the 'Four Olds' took place in Canton, as in all the cities of China, but not being as politically important as Peking, nor so much a centre of capitalist industry before 1949 as Tientsin and Shanghai, the campaign was not so intense as in those cities. Another reason was, no doubt, that the whole movement in Canton tended to lag behind that in Peking and Shanghai, which were respectively the focal points of the political and industrial struggles. However, the middle-school students did complete the street by street search of the houses of suspected class enemies.

To safeguard foreigners and overseas Chinese from being troubled, we were all issued with red ribbons to wear. We wore ours once or twice, then put them away in a drawer. No noticeable damage was done on our campus at this stage, except a large marble lion was tumbled from his plinth. After discussion, both Sun Yat-sen's statue and the library and exhibition building set up in his honour were left untouched. Some schoolboys set about digging up a plaque set in the ground, but our students told them to leave it alone and that they would deal with the 'old things' in the university.

The Rebel 'Zongbu' and the Conservative 'Bingtuan'

At mass meetings, much of the discussion took place in small groups – the students being in no mood to listen quietly to speakers they disagreed with – and from these group arguments and discussions, organised groups formed of people with similar views. From the beginning, the Red Guard groups started to polarise into two opposed sides, mainly on the basis of their assessment of the events of the summer. Those who had rebelled against the Party Committee and those who now sympathised with the rebels formed one side (which I will henceforth refer to as the Rebels) ; and those who had rallied to the support of the Party Committee in June and had been sympathetic to the work team and most critical of the Rebels formed the other side (which I call the Conservatives). All groups considered themselves revolutionary rebels.

Early in October, nearly all the students and teachers who remained in the university, including ourselves, went to the countryside to help combat the drought, which was very severe that autumn. The Pearl River delta itself was alright because it had been well supplied with irrigation and drainage pumping stations since 1957, but the nearby hill districts were hard hit. We did not observe any hostility between the different groups on this excursion, although already in September the Red Guards of the university had organised themselves into two big group-ings, which they called 'headquarters', the Rebel 'Zongbu' and the Conservative 'Bingtuan'.

On our return from the countryside, criticism of the University Cultural Revolution Committee became very strong, and the criticism of President Li, which was under way in September, intensified. The Committee was denounced for having failed to take a strong lead, for having been set up without proper elec-tions, and having mainly concerned itself with routine organisa-tional work (such as issuing ration cards to those who were going away on long marches, and arranging accommodation for visiting students who had been arriving in increasing numbers since the first Peking students came in late August). Our friend, Fan Fu-sheng, who had only returned from two years in England in July, had been made chairman of the Language department Cultural Revolution Committee. He confirmed these accusations against the Committee and certainly, himself, had been taken up with much routine work. Finally, the Red Guards of Zongbu sealed the Committee headquarters and painted a black cross over the doorway.

Meanwhile, a national campaign had been brewing up round the question of dossiers that had been collected on the June rebel students. The Central Committee issued a statement that such dossiers ought never to have been prepared, and that where they existed they should be destroyed or handed over to those concerned. With this blessing from the Central Committee, the Rebels went into action – their criticism clearly focused on leading members of top level Party committees in their various units.

9 The Seizures of Power, November 1966 – January 1967

On November 3rd, the largest mass rally to date was held in the capital – over two million students, teachers and young workers and peasants attended. Lin Piao made a speech in which he emphasised the importance of 'extensive democracy'. He said, 'By this extensive democracy, the Party is fearlessly permitting the broad masses to use the media for the free airing of views, big character posters, great debates and extensive exchange of revolutionary experience to criticise and supervise the Party and government leading institutions and leaders at all levels.' Later in the month, posters started to appear criticising many of the top Party leaders, including Liu Shao-chi, Teng Hsiao-ping and Tao Chu. Liu Shao-chi made a self-criticism in which he admitted having suppressed the rebels after June 1st by sending the work teams into the schools and colleges.

On our campus, there were days of peaceful if heated argument about the dossiers, which came to be known as 'black material', the Rebels demanding that it be returned and those in authority, in particular President Li, asserting that they had no such material. Then the Rebels started to debate whether or not they should take direct action by forcibly raiding the Party offices.

One night, we heard a commotion so went along to see what was happening. On arrival, we found a crowd of students gathered around President Li, who was standing on the steps leading to the Party offices. They were clearly having an argument, and there was a good deal of shouting. Li was arguing back firmly. This happened two nights running. Lin Chih-fu was very worried because he could not make up his mind whether it was right or not to take direct action. He put the arguments like this: The dossiers should certainly be returned or destroyed because if such material was kept, it would inhibit people from freely making criticism of others in positions of authority. Further, the Rebel Red Guards had repeatedly asked for the material to no effect, thus they appeared to have no alternative. However, against this was the possibility that in the course of raiding the offices for black material, confidential documents might be interfered with.

The 'Red Flag Commune'

On the 10th of November, the Rebel Red Guards of Zongbu, including members of 'August 31st', and some workers belonging to Rebel groups raided the Party offices. One of the university drivers who was on duty at the office at the time, and was very critical of the Rebels, told us later that the students had been 'violent and irresponsible', in that they broke into offices and drawers where there were confidential files and were careless about what was taken away. However, there was no evidence of anyone getting hurt. The Conservative Red Guards of Bingtuan opposed the raid for the same reason as Cde Lin had hesitated to support such action, and later added the accusation that some people with dubious records had joined in the raid to find and destroy dossiers on their own past, which pre-dated, and were not connected with, the Cultural Revolution. Two weeks after the raid, the groups that had taken part in or supported it came together and formed a new headquarters, which took the name 'Red Flag Commune'. The new organisation was not limited by family background. There was a large overlapping membership between the Red Flag and Zongbu, but they did not actually merge. Until the time we left China, 'August 31st' and the Red Flag remained closely related organisations, but they too kept their separate identities, with 'August 31st' usually acting more radically. A further raid on the Party offices was carried out at the end of November. The Rebel side throughout Canton and the province, became known as the 'Red Flag' side, and two other 'Red Flag Communes' were set up in the South China Engineering College and the Medical College.

The significance of the raids on the Party offices went much further than the importance of the issue concerning dossiers. These raids amounted to a direct physical attack on the Party organisation. Individual Party leaders had been criticised and even denounced before, and in rectification campaigns the workers and peasants had been encouraged to criticise and even struggle against large numbers of Party cadres in struggles against bureaucracy and other malpractices, but these movements had been led by Party cadres and the Party organisation. In this case an extra-Party organisation was making the attack. This was the thin end of the wedge that opened the flood gates of struggle, preparing the students and young workers for the seizures of political power in the following months.

At Zhongda, the dossier raids completed the schism between the Rebels and the Conservatives, although this was to some extent obscured in the following weeks by the Rebels carrying all before them, and Bingtuan losing the initiative and temporarily disintegrating, with many of their members leaving the campus. Later, we heard reports from other units indicating that dossier raids had played the same part in the development of their struggles.

Before leaving these events it is important to say something more about the distinction between the Red Flag and Zongbu. It has already been explained that the Red Guards were limited to those who came from worker, peasant or revolutionary family background. In general, the most self-confident young people were those whose parents were leading Party cadres. Many sons and daughters of workers and poor peasants who felt they owed so much to the Party, deeply respected the revolutionary cadres and carried this respect over to the children of old revolutionaries. But in the early part of the movement many of the parents of these young people had been criticised and humiliated. Thus there was a considerable tendency for cadres' children to become Conservative and to draw after them numbers of other Red Guards. A factor that added to this, which has already been mentioned, was that particularly in some cities, including Peking and Canton, there were schools at which a large proportion of the children came from leading cadres' families, and where an élitist atmosphere had developed.

By limiting the recruitment of Red Guards in the way that it was, the possibility of the students coming under the leadership of those from the more cultured and educated homes of the ex-landlords, capitalists and professional people was prevented, and the character of the Cultural Revolution as a class struggle was emphasised. However, in the autumn of 1966, this class aspect of the Red Guard movement was being utilised by the Conservatives to their advantage. Just as some of those students who had most fervently rallied to the support of Party committees in June because their parents were being criticised, were children of leading cadres, so also were many of the June Rebels who had felt most oppressed by bureaucracy and authoritarianism, from the families of ex-landlords, rich peasants, ex-capitalists or professional people. Under the slogan, 'A hero's son is a real man, a reactionary's son is no damn good!' the students were being set at each others throats and many of the Rebels discredited.

The New Year editorial of *People's Daily* attacked this line, likening the slogan to the old imperial saying, 'A dragon begets a dragon, a phoenix begets a phoenix, and those begotten by rats are only good for digging holes'. The formation of headquarters which were wider than that of the Red Guard groups, which at the same time did not deny the role of the Red Guards as such, was the organisational means of countering this rightist strategy. From this time the Red Guards still had a special prestige, but in the main they operated through the wider form of organisation that allowed every one to play an active part. Such was the Red Flag Commune. In March 1967, a Conservative headquarters was also formed in Zhongda, which was closely allied to the Conservative Red Guards of Bingtuan, but it also maintained a separate existence.

In August and September, the student Red Guards had been advised not to get involved with the workers and peasants. The Socialist Education Movement was still carrying on and Premier Chou pointed out that the workers and peasants were well able to manage their own affairs. One of the basic aspects of the social transformation which lay at the heart of the Cultural Revolution was that of breaking down the divisions between the workers, peasants and intellectuals and, as Mao Tse-tung had always asserted, at a certain stage the revolutionary action of students must become integrated with the struggles of the workers and peasants or it would come to grief. Thus, this was clearly only a temporary policy.

Late in October a group of engineering students set out on a six hundred mile march from Darien to Peking, stopping on the way to work alongside and exchange experiences with the workers and peasants. This action was commended in the *People's Daily* and ushered in the period of the 'long marches'. In November the students and young teachers started going into the factories to make revolution, while working with the workers. We discussed this with our friend, Gao Su-wan, who was interpreting for us at this time, and she said that some students would go into the factories or work on farms individually, and some in groups, and that she thought they would stay for about a month.

At this time the Rebel workers were in the minority in Canton, as in most other cities, so that it was easier for the Conservative students. Until late January 1967, the factories were still largely dominated by the old management and Party committees. The Conservative students thus saw their task to be that of joining the workers in their work, taking part in their meetings and discussions and helping them write posters and put on propaganda performances. The Rebel students, however, meeting strong opposition and fresh from their struggles over the dossiers, saw their main function as that of stirring up rebellion, and it seemed pretty clear in retrospect that in many cases they created antagonism between themselves and the majority of the workers.

In the university, with the Cultural Revolution Committees more or less crushed, the Rebels brought President Li and other members of the University Party Committee before a struggle meeting. The Conservatives were in a state of demoralisation: many of them had left the university for home or to work in factories or communes. The Rebel Red Flag Commune was in a position to take power.

'Struggle, criticise, transform'

The joint New Year editorial of *People's Daily* and *Red Flag* published on January 1st, 1967, was entitled, 'Carry the Great Proletarian Cultural Revolution through to the end'. It outlined the course of the struggle up to the end of 1966 and stated the aim for the coming year: 'It will be a year of decisive victory in carrying out the struggle to overthrow those in authority taking the capitalist road, the criticism and repudiation of the reactionary bourgeois academic "authorities" and the ideology of the bourgeoisie and all other exploiting classes, and the transformation of education, literature and art and all other parts of the superstructure (of society) that do not conform to the socialist economic base'. This aim had already been stated in the first point of the 'Sixteen Points' decision of the Central Committee in August. The Tenth Plenum itself had constituted the initial victory. The mobilisation of the Red Guards and their deployment throughout the country, coupled with the initial exposure of Liu Shao-chi, Teng Hsiao-ping and Tao Chu, took the struggle a stage further. Now with the opposition counter-attacking by organising Conservative forces among the people, the Central Committee was calling for an all-out struggle for power.

The editorial went on to detail four tasks: firstly to 'Grasp revolution and promote production. The Great Proletarian Cultural Revolution should be carried out on a large scale in the factories and rural areas, so as to stimulate the revolutionisation of the people's thinking and promote the development of industrial and agricultural production'; secondly, '. . . revolutionary students, teachers and intellectuals should go to the factories and rural areas in a planned and organised way, to integrate themselves with the workers and peasants . . .'; thirdly, 'fully develop extensive democracy under the dictatorship of the proletariat. This extensive democracy means arousing hundreds of millions of people under the command of Mao Tse-tung's thought to launch a general atack on the enemies of socialism and, at the same time, criticise and supervise leading organs and leading cadres at all levels . . .'; and fourthly, 'continue to carry out mass criticism and repudiation of the bourgeois reactionary line . . .'

One implication of this lead was that, although the students still had an important part to play, the main struggle had now shifted to the workers and poor peasants, and particularly the workers. Further, as this was a socialist revolution, the struggle in industry was the decisive struggle.

Already by the end of 1966 Left leadership had established itself in four provinces; in Heilungkiang in the north-east, in Kweichow in the south-west; and in the two strategically situated provinces commanding either side of the great northern plain, Shansi and Shantung. This meant that the Revolution had, as it were, substantial rural bases, and with the secure if not complete allegiance of the main forces of People's Liberation Army the Central Committee dominated the situation physically. This was what Chairman Mao meant by this being a revolution under the dictatorship of the proletariat. However, unless the working class was fully aroused into participation and won for the revolutionary line there could be no socialist victory.

Shanghai is far the biggest and most important centre of industry in China, and has the oldest established and most experienced working class. The Cultural Revolution had been launched from there, and thus it was of decisive importance. However, the Shanghai Party Committee had oppressed the Rebels and had organised Conservative worker's detachments to oppose the Cultural Revolution, although Mayor Ko Ching-shi had been a firm supporter of the revolutionary line up to his death in 1965.

The opposition adopted three main tactics in relation to the workers in Shanghai, which were copied to a lesser extent in Canton, as well as other cities. At first they took the Central Committee directive of August to promote production and grasp revolution – and divided it into its two parts. In the autumn they denounced the Rebels for sabotaging production, which at the time could appear reasonably in line with the Central Committee directive for the student Red Guards to keep clear of industry. Later, when the call went out for the Red Guards to rouse the workers, they encouraged the workers to leave Shanghai to take their complaints to Peking and visit other cities to exchange experience.

Thus, at first, revolution was obstructed in the name of safe-guarding production, whilst later, production was crippled in the name of revolution. Part of the encouragement for workers to leave Shanghai was in the form of money paid out as travelling and living expenses. This was linked to a general policy of buying the allegiance of the workers and other sections of people, mainly by granting pay rises. In some cases wages were raised retrospectively or paid in advance – we visited several places in Shanghai where this had taken place, including a school where the teachers had been paid some months in advance. Workers who had gone to the countryside in 1960–1961 when there was an all-out effort to assist agriculture, were told they could get their old city jobs back. These workers were organised into anti-Rebel forces. Finally, in the New Year, Conservative groups on the docks and railways, and in the power stations, were directed to bring transport to a stop and shut off power supplies.

The Rebels denounced the doling out of money as both a policy of squandering state funds and 'economism', that is put-ting individual material incentives before service to the people, and they maintained that the policy of the Central Committee for freezing incomes until the end of the movement should be adhered to. In response to the withdrawals from production and closing down of power and transport services, the Rebel head-quarters called upon its members to stay by their production posts, and make revolution in their spare time.

Red Guards from Peking were an important factor in initially rousing the Red Guards in Shanghai, and the PLA carried out a lot of propaganda work, but the main struggle was among the workers. The decisive moment came a few days after the Rebels had gained possession of Shanghai's two main papers and printed a message to all Shanghai people calling for united action to carry the Cultural Revolution through to the end. On January 9th, they printed a ten-point 'Urgent Notice' from the Shanghai Workers' Revolutionary Rebel General Headquarters and thirty-one other revolutionary mass organisations, denouncing the Shanghai Party Comittee for adopting the policies discussed above, and calling upon the people to counter them. A significant aspect of the notice was that it issued instructions involving legal proceedings – for example, those who did not vacate the build-ings they had taken over would be dealt with by law – and thus the Rebels took upon themselves the authority of local govern-ment. The last point gives the 'notice' the form of a demand to the Municipal Committee. However, the rest of the points clearly indicate a rejection of the Committee's authority.

On the 11th January, the revolutionary headquarters in Peking sent a message giving maximum support to the Shanghai Rebels and the 'urgent notice', in the name of the Central Committee, the State Council, the Military Affairs Commission of the Party, and the National Cultural Revolution Group (Wen-ge). The most important directives from the Centre were always issued on the authority of these four bodies.

The message from Peking confirmed the Rebel's victory in Shanghai, and was also a clear call for similar seizures of power throughout the country.

With the news of the struggle in Peking, Shanghai and the four provinces, and the directives for action coming from Peking, struggle also flared up in Canton. The limited amount of physical violence is evidenced by my January 24th diary entry; 'Trip up river to visit sugar-refinery. No noticeable fighting in Canton. Thousands of Shanghai and other workers in the city. No signs of pillorying for months.' This was when the struggle was at its height.

With the disintegration of Bingtuan at Zhongda, its members increasingly left the campus to go to work on farms or in factories, or to go home. The Red Flag Commune dominated the university.

Visiting students, mainly from Wuhan and Peking, joined the Rebel students of Canton and together with the Rebel organisations of the workers and peasants from the suburbs, prepared to seize power from the Provincial and Municipal Party Committees.

'Hong-zong' and 'Di-cong'

Early in January, two workers' headquarters opposed to the Rebels were formed, which came to be known as 'Hong-zong' (Red General HQ) and 'Di-cong' (Ground Command). These two organisations, which grew to include a majority of the workers of Canton, maintained a close unity and came to share a common headquarters building. However, Di-cong – mainly recruited in state-run units – always appeared to be rather more militant than Hong-zong, which was mainly recruited in locally administered units, and was in particular more hostile to our Red Flag Commune.

One of the first large-scale clashes between the two sides concerned a mass meeting planned for the Sports Stadium, where all the largest citywide meetings were held. The meeting held on January the 18th was for the purpose of denouncing Tao Chu, First Secretary of the Central South Bureau of the Party and in July 1966 promoted to lead the Party propaganda department, who just prior to this time had been 'pulled out' in Peking. The Rebels opposed the meeting on the grounds that it was intended to sabotage production by being held in working hours. They said that the workers were being told that they could stay off work to attend without loss of pay. They also alleged that the organisers, by putting up posters saying that Tao Chu would be brought to the meeting and Chiang Ch'ing would be there to make an address, were misleading people, as neither of these assertions was true. The Conservatives denied these allegations and claimed that the Rebels were only opposing the meeting on factional grounds because they were hostile to Hong-zong and Di-cong. Considerable contingents of Rebels, including one from our Red Flag, went to the stadium, and at the start of the meeting rushed the platform and tried to disrupt the proceedings. The meeting was preceded by a poster battle in which these accusations and counter-accusations were made. Accounts by students and workers who were there indicated that there was not much physical violence and the meeting was able to proceed, but it left a lot of bitterness among the Conservative workers, who felt outraged at what they considered to be the arrogance of the students.

'Sheng-ge-lien'

The Rebel groups and headquarters of workers, peasants, students, ex-servicemen, security men and others, formed into a loose federation which became known as 'Sheng-ge-lien' (the three characters standing for Provincial Revolutionary Union) and launched a movement to seize power in the city and throughout the province.

In the latter part of January and February, Sheng-ge-lien occupied the offices of the *South China Daily* and other papers, sent groups into the local radio stations and occupied some offices of the municipal and provincial government and Party – seizing their seals of office. Power was seized in some factories, and also in some other places of work and educational institutions. There were also active demonstrations at the headquarters of the Kwangtung Command of the PLA. Non-combative units of the army were involved because both Rebel and Conservative groups had been formed in them.

At the end of January, one of the Rebel workers' headquarters withdrew from Sheng-ge-lien, and there was disagreement between the Red Flag of the South China Engineering College and our Red Flag concerning the mass organisations of the security men. With the inexperience of the Rebel leaders and the withdrawal from public activity of most leading cadres who were not actively opposing the Rebels, there was great confusion. This confusion may be illustrated by the following accounts of some particular events.

Red Guards including students from Peking and Wuhan occupied the headquarters of the security forces on the 22nd January. A couple of days later, students of the South China Engineering College intervened and returned power to the two mass organisations of the security men. They argued that it was wrong for revolutionary rebels from outside to intervene and that the security men should be left to sort out their own problems. There was further intervention from outside and for a time one faction of the security men held a dominant position. Many of our people from Zhongda went to the security headquarters to take part in the arguments, as did people from all over the city. When we passed along the street where the headquarters was, large numbers of people were filling the entrance and overflowing onto the nearby pavement and street, arguing in groups. This issue was never sorted out, and right into 1968 there was contention among different Rebel headquarters concerning the security forces and which, if any, of their organisations should be recognised as genuine revolutionary groups.

100

This next account is straight from Elsie's diary:

'*February 14th, 1967*. More than 100 branches of the Red Flag Workers' Headquarters announced their withdrawal from Sheng-ge-lien. Forty-five branches disagreed with the withdrawal, and in the evening of the same day, went to their headquarters' office and created chaos there. They removed loudspeakers, cycles and other property. A hundred students from 'August 31st' supported them and on arrival found PLA men there keeping the peace. At first, the students could not get in, but eventually they did. One student was taken captive by the Conservative workers, as were two Rebel workers. The following day more than 2000 workers paraded the Rebel prisoners round the city with cards around their necks. Finally they marched out to our university threatening to break up the office of a workers' group on the campus. In the evening a large meeting was held outside this office, and loudspeakers mounted on lorries carried the speeches, slogan shouting and singing. There was no violence. (It was reported) demonstrating workers said, "If you want to make trouble with us, this is what will happen". The three captives were taken back to Canton but released the following day'.

Lee, my daughter, and I, who were out for a walk in the fields in the afternoon, came across the march on the main road out to Zhongda and accompanied it part of the way back before cutting across the fields again. After supper we went across to the meeting, but it was over except for groups of people chatting by the loudspeaker lorries. We looked for someone who spoke English, but the only person we knew there was one of our cooks who did not know English. She was chatting with some of the workers. By her side was her eight-year-old daughter, and it was for all the world like a group of casual evening strollers.

The PLA had orders not to use force. At the end of January and again in early February, Rebel groups demonstrated and sat down outside the military headquarters demanding student dossiers. Some groups entered the headquarters' grounds and disconnected loudspeakers and then used them for their own broadcasting. PLA men took photographs of the students' operations, but did not interfere. Some of our English teachers went to the PLA headquarters and after making investigations put up posters in the campus criticising the Rebel actions. The Rebels put up posters strongly criticising Huang Yung-sheng, the head of the South China PLA Command.

Sometime towards the end of February and the beginning of March, Sheng-ge-lien disintegrated, and in mid-March, the PLA took over supervision of the administration of the province and municipality.

What had Sheng-ge-lien achieved, and what was the cause of its final failure? The events of January and February had roused masses of workers, peasants and other sections of people into action, and it had caused them to 'concern themselves about state affairs'. The pattern of power, the bureaucratic structures in the press, in the security forces and in the provincial government and Party had been disrupted. The failures of Sheng-ge-lien were clearly brought out by contrast, following a report of the seizure of power in the extreme northerly province of Heilungkiang, an analysis which was published in the *People's Daily* on February 10th.

In Heilungkiang, the Rebels united with a section of the Provincial Party Committee, thus increasing the possibility of the new leadership being able to re-establish order out of the chaos of struggle, and equally important paving the way for uniting with 'more than ninety-five per cent of the old cadres' which Chairman Mao had asserted was a necessary basis for success in the movement. The Rebels also established their control of the press and security forces well before tackling the Provincial Committee and government. This enabled them to establish their own revolutionary order and prepare public opinion for their seizure of political power. The Rebels attacked certain organisations which were directly opposing them, and through this and their propaganda work among the vacillating Conservative groups, managed to disintegrate the rightists and win over intermediate sections of workers and others. Finally, the Rebel leadership united with leaders of the PLA, thus avoiding the friction between the Rebel leadership and the Army command that had been a feature of the developments in Canton and other places.

Why had the Kwangtung command acted as it did? Why, instead of taking over supervision of the administration of the province and the city, had it not supported Sheng-ge-lien in its effort to seize power? There will be more said about this further on, so here it will suffice to mention just two factors. Kwangtung includes Hong Kong and Macao, and is virtually a front line province in relation to Vietnam, and so the military command was especially security conscious and concerned about maintaining transport and communications. Therefore, Commander Huang had assessed the Rebels very severely in relation to the attacks on the PLA, on the chaos created among the security forces and the loss of confidential documents in the 'dossier raids'. Secondly, Sheng-ge-lien's failure to win over a majority of the workers and, in fact, antagonising most of them, coupled with its failure to win over a significant number of leading cadres, limited the extent of the shift of political power.

The policy of the Central Committee and the Military Affairs Commission was that the PLA should hold the ring, but stand apart politically. With the experience of the 'January Revolution', as this period came to be called, this policy was altered to that of calling upon the PLA to give political support to the left, while helping to propagate Mao Tse-tung's thought in all units.

10 Revolutionary Pattern and Counter-current, February—April 1967

January and early February was a period in which, following the example of Shanghai, there were intense struggles throughout the cities of China. Revolutionary organs of power had only been set up in the four provinces of Shansi, Shantung, Heilungkiang and Kweichow and in the city of Shanghai. The Municipal Revolutionary Committee of Peking was not established until mid-April. From the experience of these struggles the weaknesses and strong points of the Rebels were analysed by the revolutionary leadership. A pattern for action was worked out, including the setting up of revolutionary administrations, which on the one hand conformed to the 'Sixteen Points' and on the other, combatted the new forms of opposition and disruption.

The positive aspect of the Shanghai January Revolution was that the working class had been roused, and the struggle had been fought out mainly in terms of the basic issue of individual material interests versus collective interests. The victory was best illustrated when thousands of Shanghai workers paraded outside the 'Town Hall' and threw down onto the road money which had been given to them to divert them from production and political struggle. The negative aspects of the seizure of power were that, in the struggle, the majority of those in authority had been swept aside and insufficient effort had been made to win leading cadres over to support the Revolution ; the workers and students were divided up into hundreds of groups, which were involved in numerous factional disputes, and were also dividing into two hostile groupings of Rebels and Conservatives.

A campaign for studying Mao Tse-tung's thought and the Cultural Revolution had been initiated in the PLA at the beginning of January. Towards the end of the month – no doubt related to the Shanghai experience – the policy was adopted of the PLA joining in the struggle to propagate Mao Tse-tung's thought among other sections of the people, with the emphasis on 'serve the people' – promoting the public interest and fighting self-interest – and giving support to the left rather than just holding the ring. In the report of the seizure of power in Shansi Province published in *People's Daily*, it was made clear that the PLA had taken much of the initiative, and had given leadership to the Rebel workers, peasants and students in seizing power, and this was commended. As well as the new political tasks allocated to the PLA, they were also instructed to go into industry and transport to help maintain industrial production and distribution, and go into the countryside, on a vast scale, to assist with the spring ploughing and transplanting.

One experience, in Shantung Province, which was particularly noted and commended was that following the seizure of power in the major port of Tsingtao. The Rebel groups had initiated a rectification movement within their own ranks to combat various forms of individualistic and sectarian action, and had set out to form alliances of groups, at various levels and on the basis of places of work, in order to combat sectarianism. The type of self-criticism made may be illustrated from a poster written in February by a group of Shanghai sports students. The poster listed the following shortcomings: *The purely military viewpoint* – where some leaders of the group thought the only thing of importance was to overthrow certain revisionist people in authority, and thus neglected their own political studies and political work among other people; *Putting collected material in first place* – a tendency to emphasise the importance of collecting evidence against some leading cadres, and then using this as a basis for holding big meetings at which those who held the dossiers held the limelight and dominated the proceedings, while the mass of the members became more or less idle spectators; *Counter-revolutionary economism* – the poster said, 'Some of our comrades have changed a bit . . . they chase after motorcycles, telephones and cycles, and they are careless with paper belonging to the State, saying a little waste does not matter. They yearn after high standards of living and material benefits . . . If this trend is allowed to continue our revolutionary spirit is bound to weaken . . . We must . . . insist on (the) "practice of economy in carrying out revolution" '; *Closed-doorism* – a tendency for Rebel groups to refuse to unite with those who had previously opposed them, regardless of their present attitude.

The triple alliance or the 'three-in-one' combination

The most important positive experience came from the seizure of power in the province of Heilungkiang (which was contrasted to the pattern of developments in Canton in the last chapter). In Harbin, the old provincial first secretary, Pan Fu-Sheng, had joined the Rebels and taken on a leading role, and there had been a close liaison with the provincial military command. In this case, the seizure of power from those in the Municipal and Provincial Committee who opposed the Revolution was carried out by a triple alliance of mass organisations, revolutionary leading cadres and the PLA. This triple alliance, which became known as the 'three-in-one' combination, was recommended by the Centre as the general form most suited to the setting up of revolutionary organs of power at all levels, with the modification that at lower levels, in the main, the place of the PLA was to be taken by representatives of the People's militia of the particular unit concerned.

Before the Cultural Revolution, the general pattern of direction, leadership and administration in China was largely a continuation of the old bourgeois patterns, modified by the pervasive influence of the Party. At the lower levels, Party influence operated through rank and file Party members, Party cells and branches and directives coming from above. Commune organisation took a step away from this pattern in that it integrated administration of government, production and other social activities, including military affairs, in the form of running the militia. At production team and production brigade level there was direct participation of working peasants in administration and technical innovation. Also at the Ta-Ching oil field and other industrial units the 'three-in-one' system had been developed, whereby *ad hoc* groups were formed of workers, technicians and cadres to solve particular problems or carry through new tasks, helping to break down the divisions between physical labour, mental labour and administration.

The experience in forming a revolutionary committee in Heilungkiang provided a pattern for organisationally bringing together the three necessary dynamic parts of socialist society. Liberation Army participation reduced the isolation of the physical power of the workers' state from production; facilitated army militia integration; and provided an example for other sections of the people to learn the simple style and dedication that traditionally characterised the PLA. The cadres provided administrative and technological experience, and the experience of long years of revolutionary struggle. The major aspect of their participation in the new committee was that it was not just any leading cadres, but those who had come through the struggles and mass criticism of the Cultural Revolution. Also, with the participation of the PLA and revolutionary representatives of the masses in the new committee, there would be less likelihood of cadres becoming authoritarian or liberal. The inclusion of representatives of the revolutionary masses on the committee indicated a new level of collective consciousness and the possibility, therefore, of a more open style of leadership. It also indicated a new educational and cultural level among the people, sufficiently high for 'shop floor' representation to be realistic. But most important, it militated strongly against a renewed isolation of the leading cadres from the masses, and kept governmental, economic and military decisions close to the thinking of the people.

To summarise the importance of the new 'three-in-one' revolutionary committee, it may be said to further the revolutionary forms of the commune and the 'three-in-one' *ad hoc* committee, and combine these with the experience in the Cultural Revolution of the joint participation of the PLA, the Party leadership and the militant leadership of the mass organisations. A critical question in relation to the future working of such 'three-in-one' committees, at all levels, will be the success of the rectification of the Communist Party itself, whose leadership will be expressed through the new committees.

The negative experience of sweeping aside a majority of old leading cadres was combatted with a series of articles in *Red*

Flag and *People's Daily* concerned with 'treating cadres properly so as to unite with the great majority'. The problem of cadres was particularly acute in Peking, as it was in Shanghai. In the capital, the revolutionary struggles of January and February had mostly taken the form of Rebel attacks on the national ministries, in which the several hundred ministers and vice-ministers of the central government had nearly all come under heavy criticism from one section of students or another, and in some cases the work of the ministry brought to a standstill.

To both deal with the problems that had arisen in Peking specifically, and to set an example for the whole country, the establishment of a revolutionary committee in Peking was preceded by a series of measures adopted to avoid the negative features experienced by other committees. Conferences were held of PLA representatives from all services, workers in industry, transport and communications; and peasant representatives from the countryside round the capital. Two mass meetings of students were held in connection with the setting up of a united Red Guard congress of student groups of universities and colleges, and then of primary and secondary schools. Three main points were stressed at these gatherings: first, that the time had come for people to carry on struggle, criticism and transformation in their own units; second, that workers must integrate making revolution with improving production; and finally, that further seizures of power should be preceeded by the revolutionary organisations and groups forming 'great alliances', achieving unity with a majority of the old cadres and working in harmony with the PLA.

The counter-current

Beginning in February, and coming to a head in late March, a counter-current arose. Three factors in particular gave rise to this counter-current: the inevitable dislocation and confusion arising from the struggles of January, the related mistake of the Rebels in attacking leading cadres indiscriminately, and the comparative inexperience of the PLA in the Cultural Revolution, faced with the job of having to play a leading role in re-establishing and maintaining sufficient order so production and distribution, national defence and assistance to Vietnam could be kept up. The success of the revolutionary struggles in Peking, Shanghai and the four provinces no doubt made the opposition see the writing on the wall, but the limit to the success of the seizure of power movement gave it confidence that the tables might be turned.

The policies adopted by the revolutionary leadership to re-establish and maintain economic and military stability, and to bring more coherence and discipline into the Rebel forces dictated the form taken by the counter-current. This was to pick on the self-criticisms of the Rebels and the criticism of them by the leadership, and extend this into an all-out campaign of denunciation. At the same time, the Conservative organisations formed new, allegedly revolutionary committees which, in fact, were largely dominated by opponents of the movement.

As already noted, Canton is seen as a vital strategic centre in China – it is the principle city of the whole of China south of the Yangtse basin, it lies near Hong Kong and Macao and it is important in relation to communication with Vietnam. When the PLA at the end of February moved to take over supervision of the administration of the province, they were particularly security conscious in their assessment of the situation and the nature of the various groups. In judging whether groups or head-quarters were truly revolutionary, misled or reactionary, the PLA Command took as the main criteria the seizure of con-fidential documents in the course of the raids on Party and government offices, the attacks on the security offices and inter-ference with security work, the interference with press and radio, and most particularly, the interference with the work of the PLA itself. Not surprisingly their assessment came down heavily on the Rebel organisations, especially the most radical Rebel groups, and more or less in favour of the Conservative organisations. Arising from this, certain Rebel organisations were disbanded on instructions from the newly set up Military Control Com-mission, the Rebels were strongly criticised, if not specifically, then by implication, and the Conservatives gained the initiative.

The confused situation at the end of February and beginning of March is well illustrated by this extract from my diary:

March 2nd, 1967. Our thousand-strong Red Flag Commune is in control of the university. It belongs to a larger grouping that has been supervising the provincial administration for several weeks. About a week ago they raided the area PLA headquarters expecting to find some incriminating documents. They also tampered with a PLA loudspeaker van at the HQ. There is very strong opposition to the Rebel Provincial Com-mittee (Sheng-ge-lien), especially among sections of the workers (our factory that we are working in is pretty solidly against it). This attack on the PLA has strengthened the opposition. The Rebels have admitted making serious mistakes, and our Red Flag leadership are carrying out self-criticism. A new university opposition (Conservative) grouping was formed at a meeting last night. Already it claims some eight hundred supporters, and is considering taking over the university.

The night before last, Elsie and I took a walk to the main gate and found a large student gathering prepared to march into Canton. Going out to the main road we found thousands of workers and peasants already marching towards Canton, about eight abreast, with flags flying and loudspeaker vans blaring. We assumed at first that it was an anti-Rebel group-ing going to demonstrate against the new Rebel committee, but in fact it was the Rebels themselves, with our Red Flag Com-mune to the fore. So there is plenty of life in the Rebels yet! On the whole we are supporters of the Rebels, partly because they appear the most militant, partly because many people we admire are members, and many people we feel are luke-warm towards socialism are agin them, but perhaps mainly because we feel it is their actions that have really got things moving in Canton, and probably throughout the province.'

On March 10th, the Red Flag organised a march around the campus, ending at the Auditorium with a meeting to celebrate their first raid on the Party offices for 'black material' four months earlier. By this time, though, they were already retreating – and a week later it became a full retreat.

After the PLA took over their supervisory role in Canton, several public notices were put up throughout the city. One announced the setting up of the new administration and the action it was going to take:

1. Committees would be formed at all levels and in all units to carry on the Cultural Revolution and promote production. Reactionary organisations would be disbanded and those who had committed serious crimes, such as arson and killing would be arrested.
2. Everyone should give support to the spring sowing. Those who had been designated as rightists in previous years and sent to the countryside, but had returned during the Cultural Revolution, should now return to the countryside and their jobs. Students who had gone to work in the countryside after leaving school before the Cultural Revolution, and had gone on 'long marches' in 1966 and then returned to (their parents') homes in the city, should now return to the countryside to their work.
3. Students, workers and poor and lower-middle peasants should carry the Cultural Revolution through to the end, should expose reactionaries, and distinguish between those who had taken the capitalist road and the overwhelming majority of the leading cadres who were true to socialism.
4. Primary-school children were to return to school.

Another notice announced the arrest of seven people, and gave details of what they had been charged with. They had been travelling back and forth from Hong Kong and Macao as agents of organisations in those places.

A third notice announced the disbanding of an organisation called the 'Red Group of old Soldiers of the PLA'. This group was alleged to have taken a leading part in the raid on the PLA headquarters. They were forbidden to re-form under a new name, and called upon to study their mistakes, to study Mao Tse-tung's thought and return to the revolutionary line.

A final notice dealt with civil disorder. It called for the return of all vehicles that had been commandeered by mass organisations, for everyone to assist the security forces to keep order, and for individuals who had taken other peoples' cycles and property to make self-criticism.

Throughout the province a number of groups and mass organisations were disbanded on the instructions of the Military Control Commission, on the grounds that they were counter-revolutionary. Among these was an organisation of workers and clerical staff of the university, composed mainly of contract workers. It came under suspicion for two reasons. It was said that most of its members had bad class backgrounds, that is, that they were from landlord, capitalist or commercial families, and it was also alleged that in raids on the university Party offices for 'black material', members of the organisation had destroyed their own personal files dating back to before the movement. A few members were arrested for having smuggled secret documents to Hong Kong.

The PLA had taken over the supervision of the railways throughout the country, and in Canton it was clear that the railways constituted a focal point of the Army's efforts to maintain production, distribution and the requirements of national defence. Therefore, it came as no surprise when the first announcement of the setting up of a new revolutionary committee came from a sector of the Canton railways.

However, the Rebel organisations and, in particular, our Red Flag and those groups mostly closely related to it, alleged that the new committee had been set up as a front for the old leadership to suppress the Rebel workers. The Conservatives welcomed the setting up of the committee as 'the spring thunder' (thunder that heralds the spring rains that would nurture the rice seedlings) and were greatly encouraged, particularly as it had the support of the PLA. 'August 31st' put up a poster attacking the new committee. The text was in the form of ten questions:

1. How did it come about that the new committee on the railway had been set up at the height of the reactionary counter-current?
2. The revolutionary masses ask, 'Why have we heard the spring thunder, but not seen any rain come down? (i.e. why was the formation of the new committee not followed by the formation of other committees?)
3. Why does the 'Rebellious Committee' praise so highly the railway committee, when it is only the first 'spring thunder' in Canton?
4. Why are the majority of revolutionary workers reluctant to join the committee?
5. Why has this committee become a tool of suppression, why does it carry out 'white terror'?
6. Why in a cable to Chairman Mao did they dare to reassert the prestige of the Conservatives?
7. Why during the 'January Storm' were the true rebels slandered and called the tools of Chiao Tzu-yang, the provincial Party secretary, and called royalists?
8. After the committee was set up, was the lid taken off class struggle, or was it not put back on?
9. Why did the first 'spring thunder' use the methods of distortion and rumour-mongering in Canton to deceive the masses?
10. Why are the members of the Railway Committee so afraid of the masses? They daren't tell people who go there about the members of the committee.

The dispute over the situation on the railways was to continue throughout the summer, when it featured strongly in a later period of more acute struggle.

The plight of the Rebels in Canton during March reflected what was happening all over the country, as I mentioned earlier.

That the situation was similar in most urban areas of Kwangtung, we had evidence of in the following weeks from students returning from Swatao, in the north-east of the province and Chanchiang. Also we had a visit from two sugar-refinery workers, from about fifty miles west of the city, who told us that the Rebel group in their factory had virtually been crushed in March. They had come to Zhongda to get information and advice from our Red Flag. One of the workers expressed the view that the struggle in Kwangtung was complicated by two particular factors. Firstly, there was the traditional enmity between North and South China, which was felt acutely in Canton and, secondly, there was Canton's centuries-old commercialism. They also told us that after 1961 there had been a marked increase in authoritarianism (commandism) in the factories. When young workers made criticisms of the administrations they were sometimes denounced for attempting to make political capital for themselves and, on occasion, transferred to other departments or factories. They went on to say that one reason why most of the Rebel workers were so young was that many older workers, who had families, were still afraid of victimisation.

The 'Revolutionary Rebellious Committee'

On March 1st, the Conservative groups and individuals, who by this time had rallied their forces in the process of criticising Sheng-ge-lien, with the moral support of the PLA unit on the campus formed a new university headquarters, the Revolutionary Rebellious Committee. They held a mass meeting in the Cinema Field to inaugurate its formation, with the participation of the newly-arrived PLA group stationed in the university. A PLA man spoke encouraging the new organisation to adhere to the line of the revolutionary leadership and carry the Cultural Revolution through to the end, and at the end of the meeting the PLA presented the 'Committee' with a banner. Throughout March and early April, the Revolutionary Rebellious Committee went from strength to strength, and was clearly intent on finishing off the Red Flag completely. They also denounced 'August 31st' as a reactionary organisation which should be officially disbanded. Nearly all the young language teachers who had belonged to the Red Flag resigned, and several of these and most of the others joined the Rebellious Committee.

The PLA administration of Canton and Kwangtung Province was set up on March 15th. Three days later the Red Flag organised its rectification committee, and on the 20th the Rebellious Committee held a mass meeting in the Cinema Field to denounce the Red Flag, and 'August 31st'. The main speakers were factory workers. It was alleged that the Rebel students had gone into the factories, joined with minority groups of workers and had seized or attempted to seize power. Further, they had behaved arrogantly, wrote long complicated posters using many characters that the workers did not know, failed to consult with the majority groups of the workers and made no attempt either to learn from them or to assist production. It was also said that they had in many cases put their own members onto factory committees.

It was clear to us that the behaviour of the students in the factories had varied greatly, and an important factor in this was the proportion of the workers who had rebelled. In the cement factory, where there was a group of six PLA men who had gone in during January and stuck by the Rebels and the proportion of the workers who had rebelled had been high, the situation had been quite different to that described by the workers at the Rebellious Committee meeting. The following account of the actions of a Rebel student group at a printing works in Canton gives the other side of the picture:

'. . . We stayed (at the printing works) from 4th January until the 5th March. . . . The Central Committee had called on us to work and learn from the workers. Chairman Mao tells us that students must integrate themselves with the workers or they will not be able to make revolution. The workers are the leading class in socialist society . . . We wanted to live with the workers so we took our bedrolls with us. The manager did not want us to stay at the factory because we were members of the Red Flag, and said there was no room. The workers said that this was nonsense, and arranged for us to stay in a room at the factory. They fixed a door on the room, a light, and even built us a table to write on.

The first month we worked full-time and listened to discussions and read the posters to find out the situation. After this we worked half days, and with the encouragement of the workers, started to put up posters and take part in discussion ourselves. . . .'

The PLA group on the campus held two interviews with students to explain their attitude to the Red Flag and 'August 31st'. One was a delegation from the Rebellious Committee, the other was a delegation of Conservative students from the Medical College. The results of the interviews were put up as posters in the campus, and read to us. The gist was that the Red Flag was guilty of making a number of serious mistakes, but only a small group of leaders was mainly repsonsible for this, so the members should be re-educated to understand their errors. 'August 31st' was likened to some organisations that had been disbanded but the students, being young people, had to be dealt with differently from adults. A five-day ultimatum which had been given to certain leaders of 'August 31st' to return particular documents removed from the Party offices had expired without the return of the documents, but the matter was now considered to be under control.

During March the Red Flag seemed under attack from all directions, and many of its members resigned. To a major extent it was Zongbu, the Rebel Red Guard headquarters that held the line, first by refusing to denounce the Red Flag and the actions of Sheng-ge-lien and, secondly, by keeping in existence a mass organisation of the Rebel students that was not itself directly under attack. That the mass of the membership of the Red Flag was critical of its own leadership was clearly reflected in the setting up of the rectification committee. I dropped in on a mass meeting in the Auditorium at which one of the Red Flag leaders was being criticised by other members. He was coming under very heavy fire, but was also answering back forcefully and firmly. The main criticism was related to the attack on the PLA headquarters, people shouted at him, 'Don't be stubborn—admit your mistakes'.

At the beginning of April, Huang Pao-ti visited us with our young teacher friend, Lo Tsu-min. They brought with them the Chinese text of the new directive from the leadership in Peking which gave new encouragement to the Rebel organisations throughout the country. The following is a summary of the directive as Lo Tsu-min translated it to us:

1. Military units should not denounce organisations or groups as counter-revolutionary without reporting and getting authorisation from the Central Committee.
2. No one must be arrested without thorough investigation. If organisations have disturbed military units, this is not a very serious matter, and people should not be arrested for this reason alone. People who have been arrested in this way must be released forthwith . . . Where such actions have occurred, military units should do political work among the people . . .
3. If the leader of an organisation is arrested for counter-revolutionary activity the rest of the members should not be stigmatised.
4. Organisations must not be dissolved without the reasons being publicly explained. Organisations and leaders should not be denounced in posters. If they have made serious mistakes this should be dealt with by criticism and self-criticism. Pillorying people is not allowed – it is no crime to speak out. It is not permissable to suppress the masses in the name of suppressing counter-revolution.
5. Military units and leading cadres must resolutely support all mass left organisations, and must not support one against another where there are two or more.

Following shortly after this directive the PLA group in the university announced that it recognised our Red Flag, 'August 31st' and Zongbu as truly revolutionary organisations, as did the Provincial Military Commission.

The old Party structure dominated by the Secretariat had been destroyed. In the process two opposed factions had come into being. Both sides criticised oppressive and élitist aspects of the old situation, and in this respect they complemented each other ; but, whereas the Conservatives, in the main, saw their interests being served by salvaging much of the old position, the Rebels tended to see their future in terms of a complete sweeping away of the old leadership. The contradiction between this basis for alliance, and equally strong basis for a struggle to the death, was to dominate the movement for the next year, and see the consolidation of an ultra-left faction within the Rebel side and within Wen-ge.

11 Struggle Meetings

In 1926, in his travels round the Hunan countryside, Mao Tse-tung noticed that the peasant associations, in their struggle against the landlords, would pick out those who had been most despotic and extortionate and, putting dunces' hats on their heads, would drive them through the villages. Peasants who had suffered at their hands would shout abuse and recriminations at them as they passed. Mao commented that this treatment was often more effective in destroying the prestige of the landlords, than imprisonment or fines.

The struggle meetings of the land reform and subsequent movements have their origin in this peasant custom. To understand the significance of struggle meetings in the Cultural Revolution, it is also important to see them in relation to China's legal system, the Marxist concept of social contradiction and social struggle, and the growing recognition in China that revolution not only consists in struggle against the class enemy, but also in identifying and struggling against the reactionary ideas in one's own mind, whoever one maybe – worker, peasant, intellectual or veteran revolutionary leader.

In China, since Liberation, the State has recognised the legal concepts of crime and punishment – prison sentences and execution. Execution is rare and is not a recognised punishment for any specific crime, being mainly limited to extreme cases of anti-social behaviour involving loss of life. In the land reform movement, landlords who had committed extreme acts of brutality against the poor peasants were sometimes executed, and since then there have been reported cases of men being executed for acts of extreme negligence leading to loss of life. Early in the Cultural Revolution a man was executed for a lethal attack on two foreigners in a shop in Peking.

What in the West would be considered ordinary crimes, such as theft, violence against persons and murder, are punished with prison sentences, but are considered to be due to wrong attitudes of mind, an inevitable carry-over from the old oppressive society. Thus the view is held that by a period of working for the community, although in a position where it is not easy to commit further anti-social acts – for instance, on a penal farm or in a city prison run as an industrial enterprise – the person concerned can usually become reformed. So little stigma is attached to having served a sentence in the Peking prison that a number of people have continued to work in the prison workshops after completing their sentences, coming in each day to work. Crimes committed by those considered to be class enemies, such as ex-landlords or ex-capitalists, are considered more serious and taken to be evidence that such people are not making sufficient efforts to break away from their past. Sentences are reduced when there is evidence of a change of attitude – an attitude judged to be one of genuine contrition, and a positive social attitude to work and fellow prisoners.

As with all activity in China, a premium is put on participation. To a large extent the prisons are run by the prisoners. I visited the Peking prison in 1959. Not only the hosiery factory, which constitutes the foundation of the life of the prison, but also such work as cooking, gardening and medical work were carried out by prisoners.

Criticism and struggle are quite separate from the legal system, although they may be connected with it through a given action. A person may be struggled against for something they have done and then subsequently committed for trial. This distinction is very important. Law, crime and punishment are the product of the old class society – both the concepts and the institutions – whereas criticism and struggle are both a revolutionary negation and a socialist counterpart of legal proceedings. The purpose of law is to perpetuate a given form of society; the purpose of criticism and struggle is to transform society.

The idea at the root of criticism and struggle is the Marxist idea of social contradiction – the idea that in every social phenomenon there lies a contradiction, and that through the solution of such contradiction society progresses. Lenin applied this idea in the Bolshevik Party and there arose the practice, which to a greater or lesser degree was adopted by all Communist Parties, of meetings of criticism and self-criticism. In Marxist terms, every social contradiction has a positive side, and a negative side; however, it is never just a matter of the positive side defeating the negative side, but the struggle itself is essential to social change, and in the process of this struggle the whole situation is transformed.

Mao Tse-tung has developed this theory of social contradiction further, and given it a greater degree of precision. He has advanced three major formulations in this connection. The first is that there are two kinds of social contradiction; antagonistic ones, that is, contradictions in which the contenders have predominantly conflicting interests so that a given solution will favour one side and be against the interest of the other side; and non-antagonistic ones, in which, notwithstanding various conflicting interests, overall there is a common interest, and there exists the possibility of finding a solution which will be favourable to all those involved. Chairman Mao called the first contradictions 'those between us and the enemy', and the latter he called 'contradictions among the people'. He qualified this first formulation by saying that, if not properly dealt with, contra-

114

dictions among the people might become transformed into antagonistic ones; while in certain circumstances, if properly dealt with, contradictions 'between us and the enemy' might be transformed into non-antagonistic ones. An example that he used to illustrate a favourable transformation is that between the Chinese capitalists and the working class after 1949. Following the establishment of the People's Government and the defeat of the landlords in the land reform, Chairman Mao said that the main social contradiction in China was between the bourgeoisie and the proletariat but, as has been outlined in an earlier chapter, from Liberation to 1956 this contradiction was largely dealt with as a contradiction among the people—the capitalists becoming transformed into salaried, administrative and technical staff members.

A classic example of the latter kind of transformation has been that of the contradiction between the Chinese Communist Party executive structure and the Chinese workers and peasants from 1961 to 1965. Chairman Mao has pointed out that contradictions always exist in varying degrees between the Party executive and the people, but in general remain non-antagonistic – a contradiction among the people. The necessity of the Cultural Revolution arose because this contradiction was transformed into an antagonistic one – 'between us and the enemy'.

The second major formulation of Mao Tse-tung on social contradictions is that any phenomenon is made up of many contradictions, but there is always one that is more important, and by identifying and solving this major contradiction correctly, other minor contradictions can be easily resolved Mao Tse tung's third formulation is that the contradictions that exist in a given society permeate throughout the whole of that society – they influence the thinking and actions of the whole people and, in particular, they are reflected inside the revolutionary party, at every level.

Wherever people join groups, for one purpose or another, there is likely to be criticism of others and some self-criticism. However, in the West, criticism is mainly thought of as a response to mistakes and therefore incidental to normal activity. Further, as the correction of mistakes is considered a function of authority, most criticism is pointed downwards – those in authority criticising those under them. In China the need for criticism is considered to arise from the inevitable occurrence of social contradictions. Thus it is thought of as an essential and central part of social action. For Mao Tse-tung, as in general, social contradiction shows itself in oppression and resistance to oppression, the most important criticism is that which is pointed upwards – criticism by the masses of those in authority.

It follows from the existence of two kinds of contradiction that two forms of activity are required to solve them. Criticism and self-criticism is used to solve contradictions among the people; struggle is used to solve contradictions between us and the enemy. The purpose of criticism is to clarify the situation so that those involved will see their predominating common interest and, in the light of this common interest, resolve their differences and thus become more united. This is summed up by the phrase, 'unity – criticism – unity'. The purpose of struggle is to clarify the conflict of interests, thus to defeat and demoralise the class enemy, raise the morale of the people and advance their social consciousness.

An important difference between a struggle meeting and a criminal trial is that the purpose of the latter is usually to deal with the person being tried, and to reinforce authority, whereas the main purpose of a struggle meeting is to affect everyone taking part, and to destroy some of that authority. A very important aspect of such a struggle meeting is to defeat in oneself the anti-social tendency which one is denouncing in the person being struggled against. This aspect of the nature of criticism and struggle, and its importance in the eyes of the revolutionary leadership in China, is indicated by Lin Piao's statement, 'We should regard ourselves as part of the revolutionary force and at the same time constantly take ourselves as targets of the revolution. To make revolution demands that we revolutionise ourselves too . . . Otherwise the revolution will not be successfully carried out.'

In the early part of the Cultural Revolution, large numbers of people in positions of authority in government, industry and other fields of social life were severely criticised, and many were 'pulled out', and struggled against, including many who have subsequently returned to positions of responsibility. Some negative features of this were that much confusion was caused and many people stopped being active in their jobs for considerable periods of time. Also, many people were embittered and had their feelings hurt, and much antagonism was created. Positive aspects, though, can be seen in relation to these negative features. The collective efforts to restore the smooth running of the country have liberated a new flow of creative initiative – as in the Shanghai Clock Factory, where production figures far surpassed previous records. Cadres who became embittered have come to realise that making socialist revolution demands the humility to take criticism and even 'struggle'. Important here is the fact that the harshest struggle was mainly reserved for those who had acted in an arrogant manner towards those they had authority over. Positive advance arises from the need to dissipate hostility between groups or individuals. The unity of the Party membership and the rest of the people is the cornerstone of socialism. In the early sixties, tension and hostility developed between the Party leadership and non-Party people at all levels, such as that between many of our students and their political instructors. The Cultural Revolution broke up the institutional relationship through struggle, but only a long process of criticism, and especially self-criticism, could create a new unity.

Struggle meetings are usually carefully prepared. Detailed enquiries are made, and, generally, the meeting centres on one major criticism. However, in contrast to courtroom proceedings there is no code, and anyone may speak their mind. The following two accounts of meetings we attended illustrate both the formal and the spontaneous aspects.

When news came to our shop at the factory where we worked during the early months of 1967 that there was to be a struggle

116

meeting against the factory manager, we went with our section to the canteen-cum-theatre, and sat down on some cable reels near the front. The hall was already nearly full by the time we arrived – half sitting on the normal benches and the half at the front sitting on reels, like ourselves.

Around the stage there was considerable activity. Some PLA and militia men, and about a dozen young men and women workers were coming and going. As was usually the case, two young women sat at a table at the side, almost out of view of the auditorium, with writing pads preparing to take notes. By the side of their table was a standard microphone which a young worker was using in his attempt to get the audience to sing revolutionary songs.

Three middle-aged men were brought onto the platform and seated on cable reels by a group of young worker Red Guards, amidst loud shouting of slogans and 'Da dao so-and-so' ('Down with so-and-so'), led by the worker at the mike. Su, our factory manager, was then led onto the stage in the same way, amidst louder denunciations. He was strongly built, in his fifties, and looked healthy and self-assured. One young PLA man and about half a dozen workers and Red Guards took seats at the back of the platform, and a young worker opened proceedings from the table at the front. A previous meeting had been held to hear the charge against Su, at which he had also been present, but he had not been called upon to speak.

Prior to coming to our factory, Su had worked as head of the city treasury department. He was a probationary Party member, having been demoted from full Party membership in the Socialist Education Movement in 1963. A major part of this meeting was devoted to his activities while at the treasury. As they were implicated in these activities, we had at our meeting a vice-mayor of Canton, the Provincial Party Committee member responsible for the treasury work, and an official of the Electric Motor Production Bureau that our factory came under.

All four men were struggled against in the meeting, but Su was the main target of attack. He stood throughout the meeting and was frequently called to the mike to answer questions. The other three only stood up when answering questions during the latter part of the proceedings. All four men spoke humbly and quietly, and only when spoken to. They joined in all the quotation reading and slogan shouting – including denunciation of themselves – except on the one occasion the vice-mayor refrained. When he was asked why he had done so, he said he did not agree with that particular criticism of him. This appeared to be accepted as valid. The three men from the city offices looked very gloomy and humbled, with bowed heads, but Su looked more at ease. They all took notes throughout. At the end, a young worker went up to Su, took his notebook out of his hand and scanned through it. He objected to the names of the accusers being written down, saying, 'I suppose you want to write down the names so that you can take revenge later?' (Revenge taken against previous critics was one of the things he was charged with.) Su scribbled out the names.

These were the charges made against Su: That he had put

production before politics. It was said that he had neglected his own and his staff's political study, and had said things indicating that he had no respect for it. One of his staff said he had often gone dancing when he should have been at political meetings. That during 1964, when there had been a national philosophical controversy concerning conflicting views which were summed up in the two expressions, 'one splits into two' and 'two joins into one', he had upheld the counter-revolutionary idea of 'two joins into one'. That he despised cadres of working class and poor peasant origin, and had taken revenge on those in subordinate positions who had criticised him. A long part of the meeting was taken up with an argument about Su having at one time checked up assiduously on the use of travel permits, after having neglected the matter for ten years—allegedly because he wanted to collect incriminating evidence against certain members of his staff. He was charged with having committed adultery, both before and since Liberation. It was alleged he had procured a house near his own for the use of a mistress, and had given her public property to sell. He admitted to having been adulterous before Liberation. Another charge was that he had taken over a department, while he was at the city treasury, which dealt with confiscated smuggled goods and had embezzled many items, including one hundred and sixty watches. At the shop where the goods were normally sold he had arranged for his friends, including the vice-mayor, to buy valuable goods very cheaply. The vice-mayor came to the mike and admitted to having been given a bottle of something and an object made from a small piece of wood – he indicated the small size of this article with his hands, and there were shouts of, 'What would a vice-mayor want with a small bit of wood?' and much laughter. The vice-mayor was also denounced for having connived at Su sitting on the Municipal Party Committee whilst on probation. Another charge against Su, which the meeting obviously felt very strongly about, was that he had failed in his responsibility as the director of the apprentice middle school which was attached to our factory. It was said that he had neglected the welfare of the students and recruited an excess number over the available accommodation, in order to keep his wage bill down. It was added that he had suddenly started to take an interest in the students when they became Red Guards and, therefore, an influential force in the factory.

A young worker, who was a member of the Provisional Factory Committee and was the first critic to speak, staying on the platform throughout the proceedings, broke in a number of times when other people were speaking. Several times he walked over to Su and pulled him towards the mike when he was not properly audible. Once, when the three city officials were standing up to answer questions, he went over to where they were standing and kicked the cable reels away from them, as if to say, 'We're not going to have you sitting down to rest any more, you scoundrels!' Also, he went over to Su several times and shouted at him to answer when he appeared to be hedging.

Towards the end of the meeting, a young woman from Su's

office ran onto the platform and made a passionate denunciation of him. She said she had not intended to speak, but she felt so strongly she felt that she just had to. She spoke in such a torrent that Huang Pao-ti could only translate a fraction of what she said, but the main point of her criticism was that Su's behaviour had had a demoralising effect on his staff, particularly his victimisation of those who had criticised him. A young man in the middle of the hall, who shouted his criticisms from where he was, made a similar impassioned attack.

The meeting ended with the four men being led away as they had come onto the stage, followed by the shouting of some slogans and the singing of 'Da Hai Ha'.

In Su's case, although the criticisms of him were serious and his behaviour had strongly antagonised people in his office, in general, the factory had quite clearly been a happy place to work in and, if our section was anything to go by, the relations between workers, foremen, technicians and section managers was easy going, informal and co-operative, so there was not a very intense feeling of condemnation of the leadership. In the university, though, the situation was quite different.

President Li had roused intense feelings, throughout the university, by his efforts to divert criticism from himself in the summer of 1966. This chapter ends with an account of a struggle meeting carried out by the Red Flag Commune against President Li. There were many other such meetings organised by both sides, which together covered his whole life of work in the Communist Party. In the next chapter, on the cadre question at Zhongda, the main criticisms of Li are outlined. The following report is set down here to convey something of the pattern and feeling of a university struggle meeting. Elsie wrote it up while we were still in China, and we have left it in the context of her remarks because we believe both the meaning and the feeling conveyed by them are relevant:

Just as in the days of land reform, when struggle meetings were a means by which the peasants freed themselves from the oppression of the landlords, so the struggle meetings of the Cultural Revolution helped the students, workers and peasants emancipate themselves from bourgeois intellectual and Party bureaucratic domination.

The struggle meeting has more than one function, however. In the process of the meeting, through questioning, a person shows where he or she stands. But it is not a legal process conducted in a non-emotional way. It is a dramatic process in which everyone present becomes emotionally involved, and in so being, expresses his anger against the person who has done wrong and, at the same time, rids himself of his own ideas which have developed under the influence of this wrong leadership.

There were two preludes to struggle meetings we heard about. Thorough investigations were made into the life and work of the person who was thought to have pursued a line in opposition to the Cultural Revolution and the policies of Chairman Mao, the Party and socialism. The material collected was usually written up in posters and discussed by small groups. The members then decided whether the person was someone who has been taking the capitalist road and, therefore, should be struggled against, or was someone who had merely made mistakes, and whose case could be looked on as reflecting contradictions among the people. The second prelude to the meetings was that the person was given the opportunity of making self-criticism. He or she might write posters to explain his actions, or make self-criticism at a mass meeting, or both.

It is as if the people said, 'Look, we've collected all this evidence together: here it is in black and white for anyone to read. But now let us take it out of the print; let's bring it to life; see how this has all come about by listening to those concerned. It must mean something to us. If we keep it all in print, we will not be able to understand why this person acted in the way he did. Or we may understand it intellectually but then, through time, forget and so in the end have learnt nothing.'

The meeting to struggle with President Li was held in the Large Auditorium. The seats had been removed some months before so that it could hold more people, and on this day it was packed. There were perhaps two thousand people present. Everyone sat on the concrete floor on pieces of newspaper or leaflets from their pockets, or on stools they had brought with them. Most of them were students, but there were also teachers, kitchen workers, gardeners, plumbers, electricians, office workers and, as always, children, some sitting quietly with their parents, others coming in and out to see what was going on.

Above the stage hung a slogan, black characters painted on red paper. More slogans were pasted onto the front of the stage, on pillars and high up on the walls – red, purple, blue and yellow sheets of paper, covered in black characters, against the white of the wall.

A passage way had been left down the centre of the floor, from the entrance doors at the back of the hall to the stage. There were two microphones on the stage – one for the use of the person to be struggled against, and one on a desk for the speakers. A third microphone was held by a student who stood at the side and came forward at frequent intervals to lead slogan shouting.

The meeting began:

'We must criticise Secretary Li's policies of hitting at many to protect a handful, and directing his criticism against the rebellious students. We are sure that all the revolutionary cadres, students and teachers, who had been deceived by Li will soon return to the correct line of Chairman Mao. We call on all revolutionary cadres to draw a clear line of demarcation between themselves and Li. If Li continues to be stubborn he will come to no good end.'

The student with the hand microphone stepped forward and

shouted, 'Da dao Li ('Down with Li'), the top Party person taking the capitalist road!'

Everyone turned round as Li was brought into the hall. He was pale and looked thinner than when I'd first met him a year previously. At that time he had been very confident, now he walked with his head down, in front of five or six students who had brought him. One of the students pushed him in the back from time to time as he walked, which made him stumble a little. People who had been sitting got up and raised their fists at him and shouted, 'Down with Li! Down with Li!' The shouting continued until he was standing in front of the microphone, the students behind him and beside him. Several people shouted 'Bow your head, bow your head!' and one of the students pushed his head down further.

'Reactionary revisionist Li is the top Party person taking the capitalist road in our university. At the beginning of the movement he followed the instructions of the Provincial Committee. Did you oppose Chairman Mao?'

'I have admitted a lot of very serious mistakes since the beginning of the movement,' said Li.

'Did you know the directive from the Central Committee?'

'Yes, but I did not understand it well.'

Here the student leading the slogan shouting came forward. Nearly everyone was shouting, 'Down with Li!' It was obvious from the roar of anger from the assembly that they did not believe this.

'Do you remember what you said on June 4th? You said then, "You can criticise anyone from me downwards." You directed the spearhead against the teachers. Why did you oppose Chairman Mao's directive?'

'I did not know the directive from the Central Committee was a guide to the Cultural Revolution.'

More shouting from people on the stage and in the hall. The students standing beside Li brought their fists right up to his face as they shouted.

'At the beginning of the movement you tried to shift the target to some of the reactionary professors. Did you follow the "February Outline" (of Peng Chen), or the "May Circular" (drafted by Chairman Mao)?'

'I understood the directive politically, but did not know it was a guide to the movement.'

Li's words were followed by shouts from many parts of the hall. The speaker banged his hand down on the desk and pointed at Li.

'You listened to Peng Chen, not Chairman Mao. What did you say in your report?'

'I called on all of you to criticise anyone from me down.'

One of the students who had been standing beside Li came forward to the microphone and shouted into it, looking accusingly at Li as he did so.

'Li said: "This movement is without precedent, so we don't know how to lead the movement. . . . Listen to the radio and read People's Daily." He also said: " All questions, any questions, can be brought up." Did you say this?'

'No, I didn't say this.'

Shouts of, 'Answer, answer!' from the assembly.

'Why did you say that all questions could be brought up? The circular said quite clearly that the point was (and here he read from it), "To criticise and repudiate Wu Han and the considerable number of other anti-Party and anti-socialist representatives of the bourgeoisie (there are a number of these in the Central Committee and in the Party, government, and other departments at the central as well as at the provincial, municipal and autonomous region level)." '

Turning to Li, 'Why did you leave this out of your report? Why follow the Provincial Committee before the Central Committee?' To the assembly, 'Li followed the report of Peng Chen and rejected the Central Committee circular. Li had read the directive from the Central Committee and it stated everything quite clearly. But in Li's speech in June 1966 he said he didn't know how to lead the movement. It is clear that the reactionary line was being carried out by a few leaders, and Li was one of the leaders of the Provincial Committee.'

Shouts of, 'Down with Li, down with Li!'

'In his report, he said that the main orientation of this movement was to criticise all the words people spoke and all their actions that were against socialism. Why did you say this? Li was telling lies. He is the same as Liu Shao-chi. Li was leading the criticism of literary works in the Provincial Committee. The guiding idea was the "February Outline".'

A great deal of slogan shouting and shouting of questions came at this time. The pace of the meeting was terrific, and it was impossible for anyone to translate all that was being said, so a lot has been missed here.

Obviously a question had been put to Li and he answered as follows:

'I was only one of the group leaders, the plan was made at the Central South Bureau (of the Party). After reading the directive of the Central Committee they did not understand the aim of the movement.'

'What stand did you take? You understood well, but took the reactionary stand. Why did you try to shift the target?'

'All reports since the movement have been guided by . . .' (interruption).

'Come to the point. Which document did you follow?'

Li did not answer. People in the hall shouted, 'Answer the question!' But he did not.

'You could see clearly which document was right.'

'The "February Outline" was wrong.'

'Did you mean to follow the "February Outline" by shifting the target?'

'It was the spirit of the directive to criticise all people who were against the Party.'

Again Li had refused to answer the question of which policy he had followed.

'I followed the Provincial Committee, and the Central South Bureau.'

122

'If you are not carrying out a revolutionary policy you are carrying out a reactionary one. Were you a leader in the Provincial Committee?'

'No, an ordinary member. I did not work according to the "February Outline".'

Again everyone was shouting, 'Down with Li!' The noise was tremendous.

'In a poster put up in June, which was approved by Li, the target was shifted from the leading Party members to the reactionary professors outside the Party. It said that all words and actions against the Party should be opposed and criticised. Ordinary teachers were also criticised. When the students of the German department wrote their poster, Li was afraid, and spoke to Lo (a departmental Party secretary). He said that Zhongda was not like Beida (Peking University).' Turning to Li, 'Why were you so afraid when they put up the poster against the Party Committee? If you had no bad plan in mind, why say at the meeting that you did not know how to lead the movement?' The student with the hand mike came forward and the assembly shouted, 'Down with Li!' 'When Li heard that a poster criticising the Party Committee was going to be put up he spoke to the political group saying, "There are some misunderstandings that I must clear up." When Li was at a meeting of the Central South Bureau someone phoned to tell him that a poster had been put up saying, "Down with Secretary Li". He said that the position was very critical, even he was being criticised. He asked the militia at Zhongda to find out who had written it, and to take a photo of it. Then he made a "black report" about the student and said that he was a doubtful person.'

Much shouting, 'Down with Li! Down with the top Party person taking the capitalist road! Long live the Great Proletarian Cultural Revolution! Long live Mao Tse-tung's thinking! Long live Chairman Mao!'

'... Li used the militia to suppress the students. All the reports he made at the beginning of the movement showed his policy of directing the spearhead at many in order to protect a handful. He protected leaders at all levels. Since the beginning of the movement about three hundred teachers have been criticised. Over a hundred in the Physics department have been mentioned in posters. The Physics department Party secretary reported this to Li, saying that too many teachers had been criticised in posters. Li said that it was all right, and that the department was doing quite well. Did you make a plan to attack the academic authorities in accordance with the lead given by the Central South Bureau?'

Li would not answer. There were shouts of, 'Answer! Answer!'

'I did not understand the Central Committee's circular clearly. I did carry out the spirit of the "February Outline". I've admitted many mistakes, but did not understand the circular clearly enough then.'

'Why can you understand the "February Outline" well but not the directive of the Central Committee?'

More questions and answers followed, but anger was mounting, people were shouting at the same time as the speakers were talking, and it was impossible to hear what was being said. Then Li was told to get out.

He left the hall as he had entered, through the crowd of people shouting, 'Down with Li! Down with Li!' People moved closer to the middle to show their condemnation of him.

The meeting was brought to a close with everyone joining in the shouting of slogans:

'Down with Li!

Down with Liu-Teng-Tao!

Long live the Chinese Communist Party!

Carry the Great Proletarian Cultural Revolution through to the end!

Long live the invincible thought of Mao Tse-tung!

Long live our great teacher, great leader, great supreme commander, great helmsman!

Long live Chairman Mao! A long life to him!'

12 The Cadre Question

During the Cultural Revolution it was generally the Rebels who criticised and struggled against political oppression. The Conservatives, in the main, focused their attention on cultural oppression. Thus, although Party cadres were singled out for attack by both sides, and other Party cadres united with by both sides, in many cases those who one side chose to oppose the other united with.

However, by April 1967, the line of Party authority responsible for the implementation of the rightist educational policy, which continued up to June 1968, from the national level down to that of the University Party Committee, had already been identified. It ran from Liu Shao-chi and Teng Hsiao-ping in the Party Central Office, through Peng Chen, Lu Ting-yi and Chou Yang, who were responsible for education and culture, through Tao Chu, secretary Central South Bureau, to Chiao Tzu-Yang, first secretary of Kwangtung Province, to President Li, the Zhongda Party Committee and vice-president of the university. Therefore, there were people who constituted focal points for criticism at each level, whom both the Rebel and Conservative sides recognised as those in authority who had taken the capitalist road. However, at the level of the University Party Committee the situation became complicated, and these complications focused, from early 1967 until summer 1968, on a vice-secretary of the University Party Committee called Yang, and to a lesser extent on President Li and Secretary Liu.

Secretary Yang

Much in the conflict over the person of Secretary Yang is of general significance, which is why it is worthwhile considering his case in some detail. Yang was given support by the Red Flag, and became very closely connected with their activities. On the other hand, the Rebellious Committee, although they denounced and held struggle meetings against President Li, characterised Yang as the 'top person in authority taking the capitalist road in Zhongda'. I outline the question of Yang, first by relating the main points of his career, as more or less agreed to by all, then outlining the charges brought against him by the Rebellious Committee and his defence by the Red Flag, and finally setting down his own self-criticism which he made at a meeting in the Cinema Field, which we attended.

Yang came from a peasant family in North China. After leaving school his family was growing in prosperity and he was able to enter a teachers' training college. In 1928, while still a student, he applied to join the Kuomintang, and worked in a Kuomintang office. After graduation he became a primary school teacher, and taking a general interest in education, wrote articles for educational journals. Later, he left his family and went to Yenan where, in 1939, he applied to join the Communist Party. While in Yenan he continued to write articles on education. After Liberation he worked in education in Sinkiang Province and subsequently in the Ministry of Education in Peking, where he assisted in the preparation of educational texts. He was sent to Zhongda in 1960, presumably in connection with the ill health of Liu, the then first Party secretary and vice-president of the university. He became acting first Party secretary until, in 1965, this post was filled by Li who had been the Provincial Committee member responsible for education. From 1961 until 1965, Yang was directly responsible for carrying out the educational policy handed down from the Ministry of Education and the Provincial Committee at Zhongda. In 1965 Yang went to the countryside to join in the Socialist Education Movement. There he worked not as a leader of a work team, but as an ordinary rank and file member. He returned to Zhongda in the autumn of 1966, after the Eleventh Meeting of the Central Committee and the publication of the 'Sixteen Points'.

On his return to the university he was 'pushed aside', and spent his time studying the works of Mao and material on the Cultural Revolution, and taking part in physical labour under the supervision of Red Guards. In November, when the Rebels raided the Party offices for 'black material', he praised their actions and criticised those who had opposed them. In March 1967, when the Red Flag was under attack, he again gave them some support. The Conservative Red Guard of Bingtuan organised criticism meetings against him in November 1966, but did not denounce him as a reactionary. He put up a poster supporting the Red Flag on the 4th of March. The Rebellious Committee first denounced him and organised a struggle meeting against him on the 8th of March. During 1967 both the Red Flag and the Rebellious Committee sent investigation teams to the various parts of China where Yang had lived and worked, including Peking and his home area in Hopei Province.

The Rebellious Committee alleged that Secretary Yang had, throughout his career, shown anti-socialist tendencies, and had on various occasions misled the Party about his activities and his family background. At the meetings held to struggle against Yang a great deal was said about him. The following is a summary of Yang's activities as indicated by the reports made at these Rebellious Committee meetings.

Yang joined the Kuomintang in 1927, and in 1928 worked in a Kuomintang party office. He had been put in charge of an educational course for Kuomintang members, and this was proof of the trust that the Kuomintang had in his political attitude. Later he wrote articles in which he praised Chiang Kai-shek. He had written an article for a Peking youth paper that was controlled by the Chen brothers (extreme right-wing supporters of Chiang, who were responsible for hounding left-wing students and others during the thirties and later). When he joined the Party he had lied about his family background, saying they were poor peasants or middle peasants, when in fact they were either rich peasants or landlords. While at the Ministry of Education he had taken part in the preparation of a book on education which was anti-socialist. In 1960 he had criticised Chairman Mao, and criticised Party policy on the communes and the Great Leap Forward. He claimed to have criticised the bourgeois professors when he first arrived at Zhongda in 1960, and alleged that he had been citicised for doing this by an investigation team sent in by the Provincial Party Committee; there was, in fact, no evidence for this. After 1961 he had taken a leading part in setting up groups of scholars to run the university departments, and at the same time had persecuted students from worker and poor peasant families, in one case having had a student removed from the university and sent home at night.

In November 1966 when some groups had raided the Party offices and certain other groups had opposed the raids, he had 'set the masses against the masses' by denouncing those who had opposed the raids. Finally, he was still intriguing to set the Red Flag against the Rebellious Committee.

The Red Flag's defence of Yang parried all these attacks, mainly in terms of his own self-criticisms, but also to a considerable extent from the information that their investigation team had gathered in their work. Their view of Yang's career was roughly as follows:

Yang had admittedly made serious mistakes from 1962 until leaving Zhongda for the countryside in 1965, but he had made full self-criticism, and since his return to Zhongda had acted as a revolutionary cadre. He had explained to the Party the nature of his family background when he had applied to join in 1939, but as land reform had not at that time been carried out his family had not been assessed. Yang had certainly applied to join the Kuomintang in 1927, but immediately after he had put in his application, the son of an oppressive landlord had become the leader of the Kuomintang in the area, and he and some other students had decided not to join. On the question of his writings in the thirties, the Red Flag maintained that the youth paper he had written for in Peking was run by students and was not directed by the Chen brothers, and that his articles had been in line with the policy of the national front which was the Party's policy at that time. His claim to have been criticised by a provincial work team for condemning the rightist professors in 1960 when he first arrived at Zhongda was correct, and he himself had made a full self-criticism of the way he had carried out the 'black line in education' from 1961 to 1965. When he had gone to take part in the Socialist Education Movement in 1965 his work had been highly commended in a PLA report. On his return to Zhongda in the late summer of 1966, he had been 'pushed aside' and had immediately set out to make self-criticism to study Chairman Mao's thought, and do physical labour so as to remould his world outlook.

When the Rebel students had raided the Party offices for 'black material', Yang had come out in support of them and had condemned their critics. This showed that he was a genuinely revolutionary cadre. The Red Flag added the assertion that, at first, the Rebellious Committee had tried to enlist Yang's support, and had only come out against him after he had himself come out in support of the Red Flag on March 4th.

It should be noted that on two of the matters raised in the argument, his response to the raids on the Party offices and his activity at the time of the argument, the differences between the Red Flag and the Rebellious Committee were not so much about the facts, but rather how the facts should be assessed. As their assessments were diametrically opposed, there could be no solution to the argument in the context of hostility. If Yang's very support for the activities of the Red Flag were to be held against him, then clearly the Red Flag had to strongly desire *rapprochement* with the Rebellious Committee before they could settle the question concerning him.

Another, but related problem, was Yang's behaviour at Rebellious Committee meetings. He is a very powerful and assertive character, and considering the tremendous difficulties which have faced the Chinese people over the last thirty years and the extent to which these difficulties have been born and dealt with by the leading cadres of the Chinese Communist Party, it would be surprising if there were not many leading cadres with such powerful and assertive characters. When the Rebellious Committee held their struggle meeting with Yang which we attended, it was quite different to other struggle meetings we went to. Yang not only argued back, but on several occasions got angry, shouted and thumped the table at which he was being interrogated. The reaction to this behaviour was similar to that following his criticism of the Conservatives at the time of the raid on the Party offices. The Red Flag applauded him, and asserted he was quite right to fight back against the criticisms of the Rebellious Committee, as by so doing, he was showing he was a revolutionary cadre who could stand his ground against false criticism. The Rebellious Committee argued that his lack of humility at their meetings showed he was not genuinely contrite for his past mistakes, and that he was not prepared to humbly accept sensible criticism.

We attended the self-criticism meeting of Secretary Yang in November 1967, and since it dealt with matters that took place before April and the nature of the quarrel about Yang between the two sides continued in much the same form right up to the summer of 1968, it is appropriate to relate it here.

The meeting was held in the Cinema Field. Secretary Yang was alone on the platform, except for the occasional child wandering across the stage as was their wont at all meetings, and delivered his self-criticism as he might have delivered a lecture. The meeting was interpreted for us by a teacher colleague, Hu Chou-yu. The following is taken directly from Elsie's notes of Comrade Hu's translation of Yang's self-criticism.

'In the years leading up to the Cultural Revolution the university was basically dominated by old intellectuals. In 1962 apologies were made to teachers who had been criticised in 1957 and 1959. Historian Liu wrote an article against Chairman Mao. The students criticised this and turned to me for support, but I turned them down. I thought it was wrong to criticise the teachers. A biology professor openly held up his 'white flag' (the Kuomintang flag, *J & EC*). The general branch of the Biology department wanted to make a criticism of him, but I did not allow them to do this.

I made mistakes in the plan for training young teachers. Our university should train successors to the revolution, but only bourgeois intellectuals could be trained according to my plan. Only the 'Mei Lan-fans' (old opera star much lionised in the 1950s, *J & EC*) would have the right to speak in the country. Only these people would have privileges and be allowed to study abroad.

I also made mistakes in connection with the promotion of cadres and teachers. Their promotion was based on achievements in research and teaching. Political level was neglected. As a result, many teachers, professors and administrative cadres were only interested in vocational questions and research, and neglected politics. This was the result of my wrong policy. During the seventeen years since Liberation, bourgeois ideology spread.

In 1956, during the formulation of the plan for raising the scientific level, many bourgeois intellectuals were placed in high positions and accorded preferential treatment – given red tickets to hospitals and barbers shops, and special seats in buses.

Rightists rose to attack the Party in 1957 and were struggled against. In 1961 when the "Sixty Points" directive for education came out, bourgeois ideology again spread unchecked. I admit I carried out the "Sixty Points" faithfully. I have been a tool for the restoration of capitalism in the university.

Now I will deal with mistakes in education policy in the university. I understand now that education should serve proletarian politics, include productive labour, and follow Chairman Mao's teaching. I acted against the Party's policy. The fundamental task should be to train proletarian successors to the revolutionary cause. I forgot this and only remembered the mechanics of teaching and research. Five-sixths of the time was devoted to teaching and research, to the exclusion of politics. I propagated liberalism.

Liu's article was written at the same time as Chairman Mao was writing on literature and art, but I spent little time on Chairman Mao's article, and in 1964 the biology professor raised his "white flag", but I failed to oppose these bad things.

I overstressed the three fundamental trainings – knowledge, technique and experimentation – and stressed that all students must reach a high educational level. This resulted in a low political level. Thus, after graduation, they appeared as "mental nobles", and many ideological weak points began to show themselves.

I made mistakes in my treatment of students from worker and poor peasant families, and practised bourgeois distatorship. We should try to increase the proportion of those from worker and poor peasant families among the students, teachers and cadres. This proportion among the cadres and teachers rose very slowly, and I failed to pay attention to training. The case of the students was worse. In 1961 the proportion of worker and poor peasant students rose rapidly in the middle schools, but the reverse took place here. The following figures give the picture (Secretary Yang's figures have been put in the form of a table for clarity, *J & EC*):

Year	Percentage of students from worker or peasant families	Percentage from exploiters' families	Percentage of CYL members
1960	69	8	60
1961	73	8	—
1962	40	30	30

This was the bad result of bourgeois dictatorship and I am ashamed of it. I apologise to the students of worker and poor peasant origin.

In running the university, instead of following Chairman Mao's policy I was carrying out the policy of Liu-Teng-Tao. According to statistics, over sixty students were dismissed from 1960 to 1965, and over two hundred were kept back. Among those dismissed was one called Liu. I decided to send him home by force, and sent him away like a criminal. Another cadre, who came from the army, was made to leave the university and go to another job.

The marking system was unreasonable. Sixty per cent – pass, fifty per cent – fail, but what is the difference between the two?

Superficially I appeared to have neglected to put politics first – I admitted to this earlier this year in a self-criticism. But recalling Chinese history, the Northern Warlords and the Kuomintang rulers always put politics first, only it was bourgeois politics. Why under conditions of proletarian dictatorship should we put vocation first? Why dismiss students in great numbers, and Party members and League members in such great numbers? I was putting politics first, but it was bourgeois politics. It is true that I gave up the proletarian stand and forgot proletarian dictatorship, and exercised bourgeois dictatorship. I will sincerely bow down to the masses and admit my crimes.

I would like to say something now about my wrong ideas concerning the Great Leap Forward. I was greatly stimulated by the slogan of "Changing the countryside in three years" (A slogan of the Great Leap Forward of 1958 based on the view that with hard work in the communes the problem of food production could be finally solved, *J & EC*) and by the communist spirit of "Dare to think, dare to act, and dare to make a revolution!"

I once attended a training class for cadres given by our Provincial Party Committee under Liu-Teng-Tao. There I expressed wrong ideas concerning the Great Leap Forward. In the class some leading cadres wildly attacked the "Three Red Banners" and Chairman Mao. A report by Liu Shao-chi said the communes had been set up too early. Liu said the difficulties of 1959 to 1962 were due to calamities – thirty per cent natural and seventy per cent human. At the time those attending the class did not know there existed two groups inside the Central Committee. In the class a vice-secretary of the Provincial Committee and another member of the committee took a lead in exposing the mistakes and the shortcomings of the Great Leap Forward and tried to encourage others to do the same, promising not to expose them.

I also expressed the doubt whether or not the communes had been set up too early. I thought that the communes did not seem very satisfactory and made investigations in Hunan Province. I thought that the achievements of the communes were seventy per cent, and the shortcomings thirty per cent. The Party said combine enthusiasm for work with seeking the truth through facts. I neglected enthusiasm for work, and emphasised only truth through facts, even before coming here to Zhongda.

Before Liberation and up to 1958 there were only a thousand students and three hundred teachers and cadres here. After 1958 there were six thousand students and others. So the achievements of the Great Leap Forward occupied the first place. At the time I was not sure of this, and so had many wrong ideas. Once the masses become their own masters and have their own destiny under their control something very wonderful takes place. This is a period of great change and Great Leap Forward. Shortcomings are inevitable and natural.

One mistake I made in 1964 even had a bad influence throughout the country. The Ministry of Higher Education called a conference on natural and engineering science, which I attended. That year was the year that Chairman Mao made his call for educational reform in schools and colleges. During the Spring Festival, Chairman Mao called for discussions on teaching reform, and talked to leading cadres about this. At the conference the "Sixty Points" directive was discussed and I defended it. During this upsurge in education I did not act as a revolutionary but as a royalist. At the 1964 meeting, many leading cadres made criticisms of the "Sixty Points", and of the rightist tendency at the Ministry of Education. This aroused the attention of the revisionist leaders at the Ministry, and they called urgent meetings to defend the "Sixty Points". At one meeting (at the conference) I was appointed to take charge of a study group of leading comrades from science teaching institutions. I reported to Lu Ting-yi. He gave instructions that the "Sixty Points" should be treated as basically correct, and said that if something in the directive was found that did not

131

comply with present reality it could be changed. I passed this on to my group. At the last session of the meeting two of us spoke. The other man spoke of the achievements and the problems arising from the "Sixty Points", but I only praised it highly, saying it was a glorious socialist document. This idea came from Lu Ting-yi.

My mistake was that I overlooked the struggle between the two lines in education. I thought that the 1958 educational revolution was directed by the united Central Committee of the Party. Also that both the "Sixty Points" directive and Chairman Mao's Spring Festival instructions in 1964 were similarly directed. My wrong idea was expressed at a meeting at the national level, so this was especially bad.

Now I come to the question of my actions during the Cultural Revolution. My family was a landlord family. I put down everything about my family's economic affairs. I thought that they were middle peasants, economically, when I filled in a form of self-criticism. Later I wrote that my family were small landowners. At first they had had fifty *mou* (8 acres). They rented this land to the peasants and bought more land, and rented that also, so they were landlords.

Concerning Kuomintang (KMT) membership: I admit I filled up a form applying for membership. I should not have argued about this. As I had done this, I should have made self-criticism. I did not know whether or not I was accepted. After some time I did work for a Kuomintang party branch, copying documents. I admit that at that time my thoughts were those of the KMT. After 1929 the reactionary nature of the KMT became clearer and I had more understanding, but still did not come over completely to the revolution. Later I began to study the Soviet Union, and gradually began to support the Communist Party and the Soviet Union, and oppose Chiang Kai-shek and imperialism. I admit I should not have said at a Rebellous Committee struggle meeting in April this year, "If I am shown to have been a member of the KMT I should be beheaded".

In my diary written earlier in the movement (autumn 1966, *J & EC*) I expressed opinions about some organisations – this one was wrong, that one was royalist – and people I thought to be royalist or reactionary. This was also imprudent.

The final question I want to deal with is the historical and ideological origin of my mistakes. Before the Cultural Revolution I did not know that the "Sixty Points' was against Chairman Mao's thought. Before the Cultural Revolution my proletarian world outlook had by no means been established. Before going to Yenan I was a primary-school teacher and a follower of a bourgeois educationalist called Tao, who believed China could be saved through education. After I came to Yenan there was a rectification campaign, and the problem of education was raised, and I began to think about it. When I myself heard about the revolution in education in primary and middle school, Tao's ideas were basically destroyed in my mind.

After Liberation the question arose of whether to reform

education on the basis of the experience in the old liberated areas, or to copy the Soviet system. Chairman Mao teaches us to take the first road, but somehow we accepted that the slogan, "All after the Soviet Union!" meant revolution in education. Before 1961 and the "Sixty Points", my educational opinions were to learn from the Soviet Union. Even though Chairman Mao had said, "pay more attention to modern and not ancient, and make use of foreign things to help China".

When the "Sixty Points" came out I began to make further mistakes – both subjective and objective. I was criticised by Tao Chu for not having enough respect for the old specialists, and not paying enough attention to teaching as the first priority in the university.

My ideology was still bourgeois, my world outlook had still not been remoulded. I failed to pay enough attention to the study of Chairman Mao and his instructions, and paid more to the old regulations and systems.

Concerning the period after 1935 when the leadership of Chairman Mao was established in the Central Committee, I never dared to think that there existed two headquarters and two lines in the Central Committee. But after the Cultural Revolution started, I began to realise this was so, and also to realise my mistakes which were being proved. Although I had been a communist for thirty years, my ideology had not been remoulded, it was still bourgeois.

It is not strange to find people in the Party taking the capitalist road. So it is wrong to carry out whatever policy comes from the Central Committee without judging whether or not it conforms to Chairman Mao's thought.

My final remarks are these: before I joined the ranks of the revolution all my family and relatives were poor and lower-middle peasants. Afterwards my family became wealthier. I have been in continuous contact with people in education – at first in primary education, then as director of middle-school education in Sinkiang Province, and finally at Zhongda. Here I have been in constant contact with professors. Ideologically I was influenced by the old intellectuals. My ideology was changing for the worse. I had to deal with these professors, who were basically bourgeois intellectuals. I admit that after the issue of the "Sixty Points" I committed the error of orientation and line, so I owe the people a debt. Also I'm sorry for what I did in relation to cadres and students of worker and peasant origin. I promise to accept criticism until my shortcomings are thoroughly overcome.'

President Li

It has been said earlier that both sides had denounced President Li as a Party person in authority taking the capitalist road, that both the Rebellious Committee and the Red Flag had organised meetings to struggle against him, and that these parallel activities presented common ground on which to unite. However, the position of Secretary Li was more complex than this, and further consideration of the question of his case will help to make clear both the positive aspects of the cadre question, and the contradictions inherent in it.

The general case against Li was as follows: It was said that from the time he arrived at Zhongda, in 1965, to become first Party secretary and vice-president of the university, he had neglected to push educational reform and political rectification so that the domination of the university by the bourgeois scholars had remained. He had defended the bourgeois professors by saying that there was no longer class struggle in the university, and that '. . . now all these intellectuals are members of the union, and they support the Party, so they are part of the workers and the peasants . . .'

In the spring of 1966 he had carried out Peng Chen's 'February Outline', causing the Cultural Revolution to be diverted into academic criticism. In May when the 'May Circular' opposing the 'February Outline' had been issued, he had minimised its impact and continued to follow the 'February Outline'. To this end, he had brought an old teacher of his to the university, to give lectures on literary criticism.

When news of the poster denouncing the Peking University set up had roused the students in Zhongda, Li had asserted that the situation in Zhongda was different to that in Peking, and had instructed the class political instructors to suppress criticism of the Party Committee, and collect dossiers on the Rebel students. Later, in June, failing to dampen down the criticism of the students, he had first tried to turn them against the old professors, then against many of the political instructors, and finally, it was alleged by the man concerned, had engineered the dismissal of a Party vice-secretary so as to placate the Rebel students.

A group of students in the German department, who had written a poster suggesting the situation in Zhongda was similar to that in Beida, was charged with being anti-Party and anti-socialist and told to keep to their dormitory, make self-criticism, and study Chairman Mao's works and Liu Shao-chi's *How to be a Good Communist*. It was further stated that Li had directed the work of the work team sent in by the Provincial Party Committee, which until it left the university in August had suppressed the movement.

He was criticised for having used the car, put at his disposal for official duties, for his personal use, and for having frequently taken his family to see films, brought in from Hong Kong, at a cinema in Shamien (an island in the Pearl River, previously occupied by foreigners but where their consulates still remain). It was stated that on 4th of June he had leaked the news of Tao Chu's promotion to the leadership of the Party's propaganda department to defend his own position, as it was generally known that Tao Chu had had close connections with Zhongda.

The Rebellious Committee's struggle with Secretary Li started after that of the Red Flag, and was less intensive. Whereas the Red Flag put the main emphasis on Li's adoption of the 'February Outline' and his suppression of the Rebels, the Rebellious Committee emphasised his defence of the intellectuals before June 1966, and his attack on Party cadres after the beginning of that month. Added to this, by their attack on Secretary Yang as 'the top person in authority in Zhongda taking the capitalist road', they effectively removed the main focus from Secretary Li.

As was clear from the previous chapter, Secretary Li admitted that objectively he had implemented the policy of the 'February Outline' and had oppressed the Rebels in June and July. He attributed his actions to his not being clear about the Cultural Revolution and, with great insistence, to the fact that he had merely carried out the directives of the Provincial Party Committee and the South Central Bureau of the Party.

Thus, it may be seen that while there was common ground in the criticism of Li by the two sides, the criticism was also to a marked degree complementary, and, to some extent, contradictory. Considering the struggle against both Li and Yang together, its complementary and contradictory nature comes out even more clearly.

Criticism of Li put the emphasis on political oppression, bureaucracy and authoritarianism, whereas criticism of Yang put the emphasis on the condemnation of professionalism and and the oppression exerted by the 'scholar tyrants'. Through the conflict between the two sides over the cadres, both main anti-socialist individualistic tendencies were being criticised – authoritarianism and professionalism. This was one of the most important aspects of the whole movement, and clearly reveals one reason why the movement could not have been successful without the two sides coming into being.

The negative features of the differences concerning Li and Yang were also very pronounced. Firstly, they constituted an obstacle to forming an alliance and, secondly, they resulted in emphasis being drawn away from the main issues, for in order to try and defeat the other side over the question of the leading cadres, both sides made great efforts to unearth damning evidence which would decide the issue finally. The Rebellious Committee went to great expense of time and money to prove Yang's complicity with the Kuomintang before Liberation, and the Red Flag made similar efforts in relation to Li, and to find evidence to counter that of their antagonists in relation to Yang. Both sides were, to a considerable extent, successful. The data unearthed was political education for all concerned and, no doubt, in general, such investigation was important in helping to weed out enemies of socialism from positions of authority. But, at the same time, in the summer of 1967, it certainly distracted attention from the main issues of the Cultural Revolution, the conflict between the capitalist road and the socialist road in the period of the People's Republic, and the suppression of the Cultural Revolution by Liu Shao-chi and his following in the summer of 1966. More specifically, their defence of Yang inhibited the efforts of the Red Flag to seriously come to grips with a criticism of the 'black line in education' and those responsible for its implementation from 1961 to 1965.

We may say that the conflict over the cadres in the long run was a necessary and important factor in the development of the movement, but in the short run, during 1967, it was a major obstacle to the formation of the 'great alliance', the necessary prelude to the setting up of new revolutionary leading committees.

Secretary Liu

In January 1968, the Red Flag attempted to break the impasse over the question of cadres by turning their attention to ex-First Party Secretary Liu. The 'pulling out' of Liu by the Red Flag is described here, anticipating the events in later chapters, because the criticisms of him are of greater relevance to the general cadre question than the timing of his 'pulling out' or the fact that he was pulled out by the Red Flag Commune.

We attended three struggle meetings against Liu, but at one of them we had very little of the meeting translated, and left in the middle. There were at least three further meetings which we did not attend, and one of which we were specifically asked not to attend as it was expected that information was to be divulged which 'foreigners should not hear' (this was presumably the view of the leadership of the Red Flag Commune). Therefore this account of the criticisms levelled against Liu is clearly incomplete. The following notes of Elsie's, taken at one of the meetings we attended, contain most of the criticisms we heard, although repetitions have been left out of the later speeches:

Chairman of Red Flag Commune

'Liu is a representative of the "black line in literature and art in the thirties" – a right opportunist who had close connections with the Kuomintang. Shortly after Liberation he came to Zhongda, and faithfully carried out the sinister directions of Liu Shao-chi. He has been defending ghosts and monsters in our university, and has built a solid foundation for bourgeois intellectuals to dominate it. If we do not overthrow him, we cannot overthrow the bourgeois reactionary line. He is sabotaging the "great alliance" in our university. It is important to overthrow Liu. We must help those cadres who were influenced by him. Help them to draw a clear line of demarcation between Liu and themselves.'

Representative of 'August 31st'

'If we do not expose Liu we cannot smash the old bourgeois educational line in Zhongda. He is the obstacle in our way. If we do not overthrow him we cannot carry out the Cultural Revolution to the end. . . .

Why can't we realise the "great alliance"? Because Liu is still manipulating some people to undermine the Cultural Revolution in our university. He is not a dead tiger, he is a living tiger. Liu and his followers have been sabotaging the Cultural Revolution here since it began. . . .'

Representative of the university workers

'Comrades and friends, Chairman Mao has just taught us that

136

the situation of the Cultural Revolution is not just good, it it is excellent. In the New Year we are facing an arduous and glorious task. . . . We must completely eliminate the bad influence of the revisionist educational line and the "black" political line. . . .

The lid of class struggle in the university office cannot be lifted because Liu's influence is still there, and his followers are still dominating the office. People of worker and peasant origin are looked down upon. There are two trades unions in the office – one for the intellectuals with high salaries, another for the ordinary workers with low salaries. This is the result of Liu's revisionist policy. Liu showed great concern for the bourgeois intellectuals.'

At another meeting Liu was charged with responsibility for the criticisms of Secretary Yang by a high-level investigation team which came to Zhongda in 1961 – similar teams were sent in to Peking University and other universities at the same time. The main criticisms of Yang by the team were that he had been guilty of the following mistakes:

Neglecting teaching, and putting too much emphasis on physical labour ; neglecting the welfare of the old intellectuals ; placing too much emphasis on class analysis (it was said that he had prepared lists of Party members, one with good class origin (dependable) and one with bad class origin (shaky) ; not taking sufficiently seriously the annual meetings of the leading scholars, which were given the traditional name of 'meetings of the immortals'; or 'meetings of the superior men' ; and trying to get rid of some of the old scholars on the grounds that they were highly reactionary.

Liu was alleged to have been a member of the Kuomintang for five years after 1930, and to have kept this secret from the Party.

In the fifties, he is alleged to have recruited to his staff a number of very reactionary professors. Notable among these was a professor in the German department. In 1953, the Canton security office had attempted to have the man arrested and charged, but it is alleged that Liu managed to resist this and keep the man on the university staff.

The final charge we heard against him was that he had continued to be active during the Cultural Revolution, and was responsible for directing struggle against the Rebel students from behind the scenes.

We are not concerned here to assess the degree to which Li, Yang and Liu were truly revolutionary, vaccilating or counter-revolutionary. They all joined the revolution in the thirties, at a time when it was courting death at the hands of the Nationalist government. As they joined in very diverse circumstances, and came to play very different roles in the Cultural Revolution and the various stages of the Chinese revolution which led up to it, for us, as for the various sections of people at Zhongda, consideration of these three cadres helps to clarify the revolutionary process.

Secretary Li can be seen to represent the regional bureaucrat, who through his local origin and years of high level administration work had developed an authoritarian élitist, yet demagogic, attitude.

Yang represents the son of poor peasants who, together with his family, started on the road towards privilege and security in the traditional Chinese way – his father acquiring more land, and he himself going to school and acquiring education. He broke with this life to join the revolution in Yenan, but through years of high-level educational work among teachers, scholars and officials, he lost touch with the masses. When in 1961, Party authority rapped him for being too revolutionary, and three years of intense difficulties threw doubt on the whole revolutionary process, he regressed to his youthful convictions that only through orthodox, élitist education could China achieve prosperity.

Liu, by his Kuomintang background in Shanghai, followed by a movement to the left to the Communist Party in the late thirties, one may conclude was a cosmopolitan intellectual caught up in the nationalist struggles, which had their centre in Shanghai. Whether the high proportion of repatriated Chinese who had studied abroad at Zhongda was due to Liu's influence, or merely coincidental to his own cosmopolitan background, is not of great significance; what is clear is that these two facts would necessarily result in the strengthening of bourgeois cosmopolitanism in the university.

As we have already observed through criticism and struggle focused on Li and Yang, both authoritarianism and bourgeois professionalism could be countered and exposed, but within this pattern of criticism it might be that Party leadership is weakened. Thus, by shifting the focus of attack to Liu, it might be that a more balanced understanding of the whole cadre question could result. However, in the cultural revolutionary situation of 1967 and early 1968 there could be no solution to the cadre question, only alternating periods of intense struggle and periods of self-criticism. For struggle required emphasis on Li, the suppressor of the movement in 1966, and criticism required emphasis on Yang, the director of the 'black line in education' in Zhongda from 1961 to 1965. A premature focus on Liu might have resulted in an anti-foreign orientation, which would have weakened the whole movement. Chou En-lai's anger at the sacking of the British Chargé d'Affaire's office in the late summer of 1967 is indicative of the seriousness with which the revolutionary leadership took the danger of the development of just such an anti-foreign orientation to the movement.

13 Call for Unity and Mass Criticism

The 'January Storm' achieved three things. The mass of the workers and large sections of peasants were drawn into the struggle ; the structure of political power that was directed down the road towards capitalism was disrupted, both at national level and in the provinces ; and 'revolutionary bases' had been established in the four provinces and two major cities. In a sense, the 'January Storm' culminated in the setting up of the Provisional Revolutionary Committee in Peking on April 20th, and thus overlapped succeeding stages in the struggle. From April, the strategy adopted by the Centre was the traditional Mao Tse-tung strategy of rolling up the enemy, sector by sector, by concentrating your forces. Struggle was continuous throughout the country, but the issue was settled province by province. There were many delays and reverses but, over the following year, revolutionary comittees were set up in all China's provinces and municipalities (except Taiwan), and in most lower units.

February had seen struggle giving way to criticism and review, and in March this had led on to a measure of retreat and the 'counter-current'. April saw the beginning of fresh advance. If one thinks of the whole Cultural Revolution as consisting of 'struggle-criticism-transformation', and remembers that all three processes were interwoven and continued at the same time, then April 1967 may be thought of as the time when the emphasis shifted from struggle to criticism. The criticism was built up until it covered every aspect of social activity – distinguishing that which was socialist from that which was capitalist in industry, in agriculture, in education and culture, and in international affairs. The criticism was focused on those in authority in the Party who had taken the capitalist road, but to concentrate the attack, and to make it concise and vivid, it was particularly focused on 'the top Party person in authority who had taken the capitalist road', Liu Shao-chi, chairman of the Republic and vice-chairman of the Party. From this time, there poured forth a stream of articles contrasting the two lines of Mao Tse-tung and Liu Shao-chi, covering the whole period of Chinese revolution from the twenties up to August 1966, and covering every field of social activity.

The other aspect of the new initiative starting at this time was the emphasis on unity. In the 'Sixteen Points' it had been said that (we must) 'win over the middle and unite with the great majority so that by the end of the movement we shall achieve the unity of more than ninety-five per cent of the cadres and more than ninety-five per cent of the masses'. To do this, it was now proposed that, taking the Rebel groups as the core, all the mass organisations should form alliances. These alliances should, in turn, unite with the PLA and most of the old leading cadres to create a 'triple alliance', forming a basis for the setting up of 'three-in-one' combination revolutionary committees – the new organs of political power. Editorials in the national press and innumerable speeches asserted that, as the overwhelming majority wished to carry the Cultural Revolution through to the end, if everyone applied themselves to repudiating the handful of 'capitalist roaders' and the 'top Party persons' in particular, they could overcome their sectional differences through the process of criticism and self-criticism, and come to a deeper understanding of their common interest in the good of the collective.

Already, in late March, Liu Shao-chi's major published work *How to be a Good Communist*, critically referred to now as the 'The Book on Self-cultivation', was being widely denounced. Three main criticisms were levelled against it. Firstly, that it ignored class struggle and the dictatorship of the proletariat – and before re-issue in 1962, had edited out of it quotations from Lenin concerning the dictatorship of the proletariat. Secondly, that it promoted a slavish attitude among communists of accepting uncritically orders from higher levels. And, thirdly, that it subtly encouraged individualist ambition by suggesting to Party members that by being loyal and obedient they could expect to achieve positions of authority. In April, the all-out repudiation of Liu Shao-chi was commenced with a powerful attack on him in *Red Flag*, under the heading 'Patriotism or National Betrayal? (On the Reactionary Film, *Inside Story of the Ch'ing Court*)'. This dealt with a film which started production just before Liberation and was completed just after, and shown throughout the country in 1950. Mao Tse-tung had denounced it as a film of 'national betrayal', whereas Liu Shao-chi had said it was patriotic. The film deals with the period of the Boxer Rebellion and the attack on China by the European powers in 1900. The weak hero is the young Emperor who is foiled by the Empress dowager in his efforts to initiate liberal reforms, and prevented by her from marrying his favourite who, instead, becomes one of his concubines. Chi Pen-yu, a member of Wen-ge, attacked the film for whitewashing the imperialist aggression against China, for expressing contempt for the Boxer Rebels (the Chinese masses who fought against imperialism and the Ch'ing Empire), and for extolling the liberal bourgeois reformers.

By launching the criticism of Liu Shao-chi in the form of this film criticism, it lent it a drama which was deepened by having the film re-shown all over the country. It also put the Cultural Revolution in its widest historical setting by relating it to the fight against feudalism, imperialism and bourgeois reformism, and took the question of the struggle between the two lines – the struggle between Mao Tse-tung and Liu Shao-chi – back to 1949 and Liberation.

We went to a showing of the film at Zhongda. It was introduced by a short speech about how it had been criticised by Chairman Mao and defended by Liu Shao-chi and others, who were under fire. Several times, while the film was showing, reactionary aspects of the film were pointed out over the loudspeakers.

Other films were criticised and shown in the same way during the following weeks. At the same time a number of dramatic works dealing with the revolutionary struggles of the workers, peasants and PLA soldiers were staged in Canton, and the dramatic groups of the mass organisations, called propaganda teams, put on performances denouncing Liu Shao-chi and other capitalist roaders, and depicting the struggle of the peoples – particularly the Red Guards.

The return to classes, as was to be expected, varied greatly. Even within a given school or college it varied from department to department and from class to class. The infant schools or crèches mainly returned to full-time working. The junior end of the primary schools returned to regular hours, the senior end remaining more unsettled. Most of the middle schools failed to return to settled classes at all. In Zhongda the science departments held the most classes. But throughout the return was not to the old routine.

The infants like everyone else learnt and performed revolutionary songs and dances, and even in the case of the very young there was a new spirit of rebellion and argumentation. In the primary schools there was dissention between students supporting different groups, and uncertainty about the reliability of the teachers and about what should be taught. In general, mathematics and science kept more to the old texts and methods, whereas language focused on the texts of Mao Tse-tung and academic arts subjects were not resumed. In the middle schools, where classes were resumed, the work was centred on studying Mao Tse-tung's thinking, and taking part in militia training with the assistance of small groups of PLA men, but there was intense dissention between members of opposing organisations and, again, a lack of confidence in the teachers.

The teachers themselves were very uncertain as to what they should do, except that they should join their students in studying Mao Tse-tung's thought and adopt an attitude of democratic equality with them on the principle that, 'teachers should not only teach and students learn, but they should learn from each other'. There was no doubt that many teachers were intimidated by the thought of returning to face classes of students who, a year previously, they had left as obedient children possessing the traditional Chinese respect for the teacher but who, in the meantime, had not only 'pulled out' and struggled against teachers and school directors, but in many cases high state and Party officials too.

The 'black line in education'

At the beginning of June we stopped working at our factory because there were so many meetings which we wanted to attend in college.

The Red Flag students of our department focused their criticism on four people. One was the Party secretary of the Language department, and the other three were professors – the Dean of the department, the Dean of the English department, and the Dean of the French department.

A general meeting of the Language department of the Red Flag was held in the students dining hall. After some speeches concerning the 'black line in education', with emphasis on the way students from poor peasant and workers' families had been oppressed, and the reactionary nature of the texts used, it was decided that we should divide into five groups, each of which would make a detailed study and criticism of one of the four people who were being criticised. We joined the group of sixteen who were to deal with Professor Lung the Dean of the department. It was agreed that a student of the German department should be the chairman of our group. Apart from us, there were two young teachers in the group. Our sixteen members were divided into four sub-groups – one to study the Dean's written works (Elsie and I joined this, together with Comrade Wu, one of the teachers), one to study his diaries, notes and self-criticism, another to study his record in past rectification campaigns, and the last group to study his work in the Language department. Our group of sixteen met twice in the following weeks, but attention was switched to making arrangements to help with the summer rice harvest so there were no further meetings after that. In these two meetings we started from the need to approach the problem by applying Mao Tse-tung's *On the Correct Handling of Contradictions Among the People*, but this led on to discussion and argument concerning our relations with the Rebellious Committee. One reason why we didn't really get down to our criticism of the Dean was the need to first collect and study the material concerning him, which had yet to be done. However, with student's minds so taken up with the struggle between the two sides, and particularly the problem of Secretary Yang, it was quite clear that conditions were not ready for this part of the movement to be carried through.

The choice of people through which to criticise the capitalist road in education seemed to us to be entirely sound. Professor Lung, from our experience of him, was cynical, had very little contact with his students, did not take seriously the question of the students taking part in manual work, nor their making close contact with the workers and peasants. In 1965, his department had wangled things so that his students went to the countryside for a shorter period than those of other departments and, contrary to the purpose of their going, were encouraged to take language textbooks with them and keep on with their studies in the villages. A student, to illustrate Lung's attitude to the students, recounted how he 'came into our class-room, looked at the ceiling and recited some lines from Shakespeare, and then

142

left the room without looking us in the face'. From contact with him, it seemed that he avoided serious discussion and spent a lot of his time telling jokes. As a comic turn, at a small party, he had sung one of the most moving arias from the *White Haired Girl* in a quivering falsetto voice. When he was out with the students and teachers doing physical labour, he spent most of his time leaning on his hoe chatting, and nearly always left early. A Rumanian woman, an old revolutionary, who was professor of the German department, recounted how when she had written articles before the Cultural Revolution, the Dean had tried to persuade her to leave out mention of revisionism by saying that this should be left to higher authorities.

The Dean of the French department stood out for his arrogance and contempt for his less able students. He had spent some years in Europe and spoke several European languages. Among the students in our department he was clearly the most resented of the professors. He had been classified as a rightist in the fifties, but rehabilitated in 1961, and it was said later (in January 1968) he had even been co-opted into the Party Committee. Two criticisms of him were the following. That he had concentrated on the more advanced students and neglected those who were having difficulty in their work – who were mainly those from poor peasant families – and when this resulted in many failing their exams and being held back, he had refused to give them lectures, and had assigned to them the less experienced teachers. The second criticism concerned a student who had become his favourite. This student was apparently strongly disapproved of and disliked by his classmates and eventually, when he had been found to be stealing things from them, they had demanded that he be expelled from the university. The department branch committee had upheld the demand of the students, but the Dean had dug in his heels, and eventually had threatened to leave Zhongda and take a post elsewhere if his protégé was expelled. By doing this he won his point.

The Dean of the English faculty was criticised for working closely with her departmental head in carrying out the 'black line', but we heard of no personal criticisms against her. She had struck me as a forceful, old-style teacher with a lot of the attitudes one might expect from someone who had grown up in the Anglo-Chinese middle class of Hong Kong, while at the same time dedicated to her job and anxious to be a good Party member. Her main view of teaching was the need to keep driving the students and keep correcting their every mistake. She and her husband lived with their three children, who were old enough to help with the housework, yet they had another woman in to do it. She assumed that we would want someone to do our housework, and when I said Elsie had always done her own housework, and we would rather do it in China, she at first thought I was just being polite and then, when she realised I was serious, remained very dubious. The point here is not that she had a servant, or that she expected us to want a servant, but her regarding this situation as satisfactory. The acceptance of the vestiges of bourgeois culture patterns of this kind by those in authority is a major factor, constantly dragging a revolutionary socialist society towards the capitalist road. Miss Wei appeared to feel the criticism of her very deeply. In autumn of 1966 she had been thrust aside and allocated physical labour by Red Guards. When we saw her cleaning the department building, she looked very sad and lonely. At the struggle meetings, where she, Lung and two other language professors had been denounced, she had looked in a state of inner struggle, and had cried a number of times, especially when accounts of poor peasant students being victimised were recounted. Miss Wei was treated differently to the others at the meetings, being permitted to sit down when not actually being criticised herself or answering criticisms. Later, in July, she came to the countryside with us to harvest rice.

The departmental Party secretary was, as it were, a career Party worker. She had graduated from Zhongda in philosophy and had gone straight into full-time Party work. She was criticised in the same way as Miss Wei — for 'slavishly following President Li's lead and carrying out the 'black line in education' — but, in her case, she also faced strong criticism for having suppressed the students of our department at the start of the movement. She had attended most of the social gatherings arranged for us, so we had seen her quite often, but we had hardly spoken to her. At the struggle meetings, she had looked at the beginning as if she was bored, or even contemptuous of the proceedings, but had soon become involved, at times arguing firmly, at others, looking contrite or crying as Miss Wei had.

To place the criticism of these four people in fuller perspective, it is worth considering two other people in the department. The first is Comrade Sung, who was the most prestigious of the young teachers, and was already an assistant professor. Before the Cultural Revolution he had been engaged on preparing texts. He was a Party member and clearly looked upon in the department as well versed in Marxism. He had studied in Wuhan and been abroad to Indonesia and India, acting as interpreter. He had been the person in the department most prepared to argue, and the person most knowledgeable about world politics. Comrade Sung was clearly working closely with the Dean, Miss Wei, and the departmental secretary early in 1966. He was severely criticised and spent some months — probably from about September 1966 to April 1967 — 'pushed aside' and studying Mao Tse-tung's thought in a small group of people who had all been criticised. The group made self-criticism and discussed it, mainly cut off from participation in the general activity. Sung had made self-criticism which was generally accepted in the department, and was now taking an active part in the criticism of others. At one meeting he lead the criticism of the departmental secretary.

To my mind, Comrade Sung had a particular importance. If he was repudiated and branded as a rightist, then the position of Marxism would be weakened in the department. If he were left in the university atmosphere to propound Marxism and live cut off socially from the workers and peasants, then it was likely he would become an academic bureaucrat. That he should be criticised, yet also lead criticism, seemed to us a good thing; that he should work for a long spell with the peasants as he had been planning to do, seemed just as necessary.

Professor Hsieh had been educated in the States and had been an important person in the department as a director of studies. Yet, if he had been criticised, we had heard nothing about it and it could not have been very much. At this period he was already a supporter of the Red Flag, but not it seemed, criticised for this by the Rebellious Committee. Why this was so was clear – Professor Hsieh was loved and respected by the students. He had contact with them, he was concerned with their difficulties and most important, he was concerned to help students from poor peasant families who had the most difficulty. When he took part in physical labour he took it seriously, and when he went to the countryside he behaved as someone who had come to work and to learn. Furthermore, he was enthusiastic about his sons' involvement in the struggle.

The focusing of criticism and repudiation on such people as the French professor and Lung meant that the students were attacking people they really felt had been oppressing them and were anti-socialist. The situation of people like Sung and Hsieh indicated the need to radically transform the educational system. Although they were clearly dedicated to serving China and supporting the Communist Party and advances to communism, their very liberal, easy going and friendly attitude to the students, coupled with their isolation and that of the students from the workers and peasants before the Cultural Revolution, had been a very powerful factor weaning sons and daughters away from their worker and peasant background and transforming them into individualistic professional intellectuals.

When I had been at university in England, I had known a steel worker in my class, who had come from trades union work. I became aware that the strongest influence on him, changing his class attitude from that of a militant worker to a liberal intellectual, was not the arrogant reactionaries, who merely intensified his working class feeling, but our exceedingly humble and considerate conservative professor. Hsieh's liberal humility with Sung's academic Marxism were a more deadly 'sugar-coated bullet' than the cynicism of Lung and the egotism of the French professor. The answer to the latter was criticism and struggle, the answer to the former would need the total transformation of education.

Struggle meetings at the university included, besides those at a department level against professors and cadres of the department and those at university level against leading cadres and professors, meetings to repudiate city and provincial leading cadres. One such meeting was of particular interest because it presented a very clear example of the opposed policies that arose in the Socialist Education Movement and then again in the Cultural Revolution in the summer of 1966. The Vice-Mayor of Canton was criticised for his leadership of the Socialist Education Movement teams which were working in the suburbs of the city. Before these teams started their work, the members were called upon to take part in meetings of criticism and self-criticism, so that they could straighten out their own political position before helping the peasants to resolve their problems. The tradition of the Chinese Party in such work was that, if the work teams were going to give a strong lead to the masses to express freely all their criticisms of those in authority, then it was necessary for the team members themselves to have a good political understanding of the situation. But even more important, it was necessary that they should have clear political consciences for if they went into action having doubts about their own position, they would be inclined to smother criticism of those in authority, lest they themselves get into trouble. The Vice-Mayor was criticised for having negated this policy, by 'hitting at many to protect the few'. It was said that he had encouraged a thousand team members—who included teachers and students from Zhongda – to make self-criticism, and had then used this self-criticism against them. It was alleged that a hundred team members had been denounced and four had had very serious charges brought against them, with a result that the teams, instead of having had their political morale raised, had been demoralised and intimidated, and thus brought to a state of mind in which they were reluctant to encourage criticism by the peasants of people in positions of authority.

During this high tide of criticism there were also many meetings concerning events outside China and in Hong Kong. Earlier in the year, when the Americans had commenced their bombing of Hanoi, the focus had been mainly on Vietnam. In April, it had shifted to Indonesia where the widespread attacks on the Chinese living in that country had culminated in the return to Peking of the Chinese ambassador. In May, with the beginning of the strike movement which ushered in the period of struggle in Hong Kong, the focus had come to rest on that question. There were not only mass demonstrations against the British occupation of Hong Kong and the brutality and arbitrary arrests by the Hong Kong police, but also a campaign of collecting and despatching material to Hong Kong, particularly the works of Mao Tse-tung. One day we arrived at our factory shop to find that half our section was going to a meeting in the city. When we asked them where they were going, they replied, 'To a meeting about Hong Kong. You are good people, but the Hong Kong police are very bad'. Towards the end of June, we marched with the Red Flag students to an all-city demonstration in Yueh-hsiu Park linking the denunciation of the British authorities' actions in Hong Kong with denunciations of the United States imperialists' actions in Vietnam, and their support for Israel against the Arab countries in the June War. Prior to the meeting, Chou En-lai had sent a telegram calling on the students and workers of both sides to unite.

The return to study by classes above the level of primary school could not get properly off the ground until there was enough unity and stability to allow for settled discussion on the new forms that education should take. This was not really to begin for another year, but it was from then that many secondary schools created their unity and developed the struggle and criticism which was the essential basis for working out the new forms. In the universities and colleges, departmental struggle and criticism was developed in some units, such as Tong Chi Civil Engineering College in Shanghai, to the extent that new patterns of organisation uniting study with productive labour and bringing about closer relations between students and workers were formed. But, in general, the antagonism between the two sides, the contradictions concerning the cadres, and the Rebels' relations with the PLA, absorbed the students' attention and inhibited organised activity or clear thinking in relation to education. From our point of view, the central difficulty was reflected in the contradiction facing the Red Flag: while it was criticising and struggling against many professors and the Party secretary in our department, it was at the same time defending the leading cadre who, at the university level, had been most responsible up to 1965 for the 'black line in education'.

Premier Chou's visit to Canton

Following the *Red Flag* editorial re-asserting the correctness of the general orientation of the Rebels and calling on the PLA to support the left, the commander of the Canton Command, Huang Yung-sheng, went to Peking for consultations. In Peking he made a self-criticism of the way he had handled the situation and, in particular, for the way he had treated the Rebel organisations. On the 14th of April he returned to Canton accompanied by Chou En-lai. The Premier stayed in Canton for less than four days, most of which time seems to have been devoted to listening to representatives of all sections of the people. Chou En-lai said that Commander Huang had reported to Peking because the situation in Canton was very complex and, whilst he was there, invited him down. Premier Chou put a lot of emphasis on the International Canton Trade Fair which opened on the 15th of April.

We had part of the proceedings of one meeting translated for us from a leaflet, which was of special interest because it dealt with the question of Liu Shao-chi, and we listened to and had translated for us a report which Premier Chou made to the student representatives. This report was made in the Sun Yat-sen Memorial Hall, the largest in Canton, and was taped and played back at meetings in colleges and schools. We listened to the recording in the Cinema Field.

Apart from the speeches of Premier Chou, we had recounted to us a number of things he had said at other meetings. These indicated his purpose of taking the students down a peg, encouraging them to deal with problems through discussion rather than coercion, at the same time as asserting the general correctness of the Rebels. At one, a peasant woman had made a report of the situation in her village. Chou En-lai and others had applauded her report but a group of our students had sat in stoney silence. Chou had turned to them and said, 'Why didn't you applaud the comrade's report?' One student said, 'I didn't think it was so good. They only became active after they had been helped by the PLA.' Premier Chou said, 'It is very good to learn from the People's Army.' He turned to another student,

147

'Why did you sit silent after the comrade's report?' the second student replied, 'I come from the North, I couldn't understand the woman's dialect.' Chou said, 'How long have you been in Kwangtung?' The student replied, 'Five years.' Chou said, 'You should be ashamed of yourself – I only lived down here for two years, and that was thirty years ago, but I could understand her report.' At another time, late at night, some Rebel students were complaining to Premier Chou about the activities of the Chu-yi-bing – the Conservative school organisation, mostly led by the sons and daughters of cadres who had been criticised. Chou said, 'We have a similar problem in Peking. Are there any Chu-yi-bing members at this meeting?' Having been told that there were none, he asked what sort of trouble they caused, and when told that they created disturbances at night, he said, 'Some of you go out now and see if you can find any of these boys. If you can bring them back and we'll hear what they have to say.'

The following accounts, given the conditions under which they were taken down, should certainly not be read as documents, but they probably give a fairly good idea of his view of the situation at that time.

At one of his meetings Premier Chou was asked, 'As it is now clear that Liu Shao-chi is a counter-revolutionary, how is it that he was not exposed earlier?' Chou's answer to this question was printed as a leaflet, which was translated to us as follows:

This question indicates that the questioner has not looked at the matter fully, from every angle. Liu's mistakes developed over many years. Marx and Lenin taught us that the proletariat, as the leading class, must be strict in principle but lenient with people. Marx co-operated in the First International with the anarchists, while at the same time struggling with their wrong ideas. In the October Revolution two leading Central Committee members betrayed the date of the insurrection, yet Lenin agreed to their remaining in the Central Committee. Chairman Mao has developed the organisational line of the Party, which is 'unity-criticism-unity'.

There are very few people who were able to hold high the banner of Mao Tse-tung's thinking from 1935 to 1945. Most leading cadres made serious mistakes, but the Party encouraged them to correct their own mistakes in practice, and in this way to develop themselves. During this period neither Liu Shao-chi nor Teng Hsiao-ping made very serious mistakes. Liu was a leading cadre in the area held by the Kuomintang. In assessing Liu we must particularly consider his whole record since 1945. I have not time to give you a complete report, but I will deal shortly with five mistakes of principle made by Liu Shao-chi:

In 1945, when the Japanese imperialists surrendered, many people were afraid of the atom bomb and thought that the Third World War was about to start. Even Stalin was anxious. Liu had this fear that the Soviet Union would be attacked, so he put forward the policy of 'peace and democracy' in China. He did not recognise the objective reality of Chiang Kai-shek's huge army, and Chiang's claim to maintain this army. Chairman Mao saw that the United States war threat was bluff – that there would be no war at that time between the United States and the Soviet Union. He also saw clearly that there *would* be war with Chiang Kai-shek. Therefore he gave us three instructions: to build our army; to increase production; to advance land reform so as to widen the field of battle. After Chairman Mao had made this position quite clear, Liu made a report in which he put forward his policy of 'peace and democracy'. That was Liu's first mistake of principle.

In 1949, Chairman Mao said that with the fulfilment of the bourgeois democratic revolution we would now go forward to the socialist revolution, so that the main contradiction now was between the working class and the capitalist class. This was very clear throughout the Party, but just at this time, in a speech to businessmen in Tientsin, Liu praised the capitalists and told them to extend their industry. He said, 'In China now, we need not fewer capitalists but more capitalists.'

The third mistake of principle was in 1953. Chairman Mao proposed the setting up of co-operative farms, but Liu Shao-chi opposed this saying that we should consolidate 'New Democracy'.

The fourth mistake related to the situation as it developed in 1955. At this time, after the co-operatives had been set up in the countryside, Liu Shao-chi said that production was not keeping pace with the new social organisation, and therefore we should reduce the number of co-operatives. He stated that the main contradiction in China was that between the new social relations and the low level of production (Liu Shao-chi maintained that agricultural mechanisation should precede collectivisation), that is, between co-operative socialist ownership and the low output of grain. Chairman Mao wrote a book refuting this line – not mentioning Liu Shao-chi by name – but showing how production would advance with social ownership, which should therefore be pressed forward. He reiterated that the main contradiction was between the working class and the capitalist class. (Hence the main danger in the countryside was the emergence of a Kulak class of rich peasants which would be assisted by every remnant of private enterprise, *J & EC*).

Liu Shao-chi's fifth principle mistake concerned the 'Four Clean-ups' movement from 1963 to 1965. Our aim was to raise the general level of the peasants by criticising and exposing the few leading cadres who were taking the capitalist road. Liu Shao-chi organised work teams to go into the countryside to criticise all the lower-level cadres and suppress the poor and lower-middle peasants by picking on their petty faults.

These are Liu Shao-chi's five most important mistakes of principle. He made many other mistakes which will be fully exposed later. We must assess him in the light of his complete record.

Chairman Mao is very disappointed in Liu Shao-chi, who

he had chosen as his successor. Comrade Lin Piao has shown himself to be an outstanding leader who is able to hold high the red banner of Mao Tse-tung's thinking. It is correct therefore that we regularise his position as successor to Chairman Mao.

Premier Chou held two all-night meetings at which he listened to reports and arguments between students and other representatives of mass organisations. He also held several other meetings. On the day of his arrival he made a report about the situation, and on his last day he made a five-hour summing up. The following is the translation of Chou's report that Elsie took at the meeting in the Cinema Field on the 14th:

I greet you on behalf of Chairman Mao, the Central Committee, the Military Commission, and the National Committee of the Cultural Revolution (slogan shouting) . . . comrades, be quiet please.

Today I have taken the opportunity to come to Canton, and now I am going to tell you my reasons for coming. We are holding the Commodities Fair. It is a big event, and the Central Committee has shown some concern about it, and therefore decided to send me here to make some arrangements.

The Central Committee has made decisions concerning the fair which you may have read. However it is necessary for me to talk about them. The decisions are addressed to the PLA, the Red Guards and the revolutionary workers.

Our economy is progressing and the fair will show our political and economic development.

The Central Committee hopes that all concerned will make the fair a great success. The last fair took place during the first stage of our Cultural Revolution. This fair is taking place in a new stage, one in which we have achieved economic advance.

Last May the decision was made to launch the Cultural Revolution. In June, the first Marxist-Leninist poster appeared in Peking. Immediately after this there was a great upsurge of the Cultural Revolution throughout the country. Unfortunately during June and July, while Chairman Mao was away from Peking, Liu Shao-chi and Teng Hsiao-ping, who were in charge of the Central Committee work, put out a reactionary bourgeois line to suppress the Cultural Revolution. They practised a white terror, which caused a great set-back. At that time Chairman Mao was visiting universities and schools outside Peking. (Wuhan and Shanghai, *J & EC*). As soon as he heard of the situation in Peking he returned to correct the mistakes. After his return he initiated the Red Guard movement in seven middle-schools in Peking. The Red Guards spread to all corners of the country. Since then the two lines, the working-class line represented by Chairman Mao, and the reactionary bourgeois line represented by Liu Shao-chi, have been struggling. Those persons taking the capitalist road are not reconciled to criticism by the masses so the reactionary bourgeois line has stubbornly persisted, and our Cultural Revolution entered the second stage.

The character of the second stage was shown when the

150

workers of Shanghai rose up to criticise the city Party Committee, and fought against economism. Now we are waging an all-out struggle against those persons in authority who have taken the capitalist road.

The first stage aimed at mobilising the masses, popularising the Red Guard movement and bringing about the exchange of revolutionary experience. This was the mobilisation stage. In the second stage, our main task is to criticise and repudiate the reactionary bourgeois line headed by Liu and Teng.

The reasons for taking this as the second stage are as follows: firstly, the leaders Liu Shao-chi and Teng Hsiao-ping are not reconciled to defeat, nor are they admitting their mistakes – they want to make a come-back. Secondly, many people are still deceived by the reactionary line, and some fail to realise the harm of this line.

Since our present task is to denounce this line we should stop visiting different areas. All comrades should return to their own units. Our task determines the form in which we should work. All revolutionary comrades should take part in this movement and should understand the effect on their own unit of the reactionary line. These are the reasons for Chairman Mao's instructions. Owing to these reasons Chairman Mao made the decision that visits should stop in early March.

Our central task in the present stage is to wage a campaign of revolutionary criticism. We must rely on the left in every unit and, using this as the nucleus, unite the masses. The PLA should also take part in this criticism.

Last year the Military Commission took the wrong decision that the PLA should not take part in the Cultural Revolution in each area. The PLA *should* join with the masses in each area.

What forces must we rely on? Chairman Mao teaches us that we must rely on three forces during this Cultural Revolution: the revolutionary masses, the PLA, and the revolutionary cadres of each unit. If we rely on these three forces we can make a success of the Cultural Revolution.

We must have confidence in the revolutionary masses – they are the real creators of human history. The PLA is the mainstay of the proletarian dictatorship, created and nurtured by Chairman Mao and now personally led by Comrade Lin Piao. PLA men are the models for studying Chairman Mao's works creatively. The participation of the PLA men in the Cultural Revolution has been very important. The PLA's control of some local areas has helped the Cultural Revolution go more smoothly. PLA control can safeguard victory and prevent the class enemy and secret agents undermining the Cultural Revolution.

In 1949 we seized state power from the Kuomintang reactionaries. In 1952-3 we had the land reform movement in which we seized power from the landlords. After land reform we had the 'Three and Five Anti's' movements, in which we seized power from the capitalists. In 1957 we had a movement against right deviationists, in which we criticised agents of the capitalist and landlord classes within the Party. Now the class struggle is still continuing. We are confronted with the task of consolidating and developing the proletarian dictatorship. We must have a thorough socialist revolution to defeat the class enemy on all fronts. To fulfill the present tasks we must have proletarian unity. But how can we achieve this proletarian alliance? The most urgent task is to thoroughly criticise and repudiate the reactionary bourgeois line. It constitutes the main obstacle to the alliance. The left should educate those who have been deceived by the reactionary line, and should do political work to win over such people. Unity can only be achieved through struggle. Conservatives are also deceived by this reactionary line (*laughter*). Conservatives have made mistakes during the movement, but they should be given the chance to correct their mistakes. All of us are victims of this bourgeois line.

Our unity is not a unity without principle. It is based on Marxism-Leninism and Mao Tse-tung's thought. All revolutionary masses should recognise the main target. Conservatives must rise up and rebel against our common enemy. It does not matter when one rebels. We must welcome them.

The comrades in front of me are right, left and conservative (*laughter*). Our aim is to unite the majority and isolate the handful of rightists. The left should unite to fight the class enemy. In no case should we take the masses as the main target for attack. We should direct our spearhead against the top Party person who has taken the capitalist road. Our spearhead should be directed upwards and not down. An important aspect of the bourgeois reactionary line is that it attacks the majority and protects a handful. We should reverse this.

The majority of cadres are good or comparatively good, but most have made mistakes of some kind. These cadres should thoroughly criticise their mistakes. So long as they make sincere self-criticism the revolutionary masses will pardon them. Genuine revolutionary cadres should dare to stand out. Of course some cadres who have been corrupted will be dismissed at the end of the movement, but genuine revolutionary cadres are the treasures of the Party.

We must have absolute faith in the PLA men. By and large the military control is good and effective. However, it is understandable that some units have made mistakes, but this does not matter so long as they recognise their mistakes. Chinghai Province is a bad example, but there are few such examples. One or two commanders in Chinghai were revisionist and ordered the PLA to suppress the students. This happened about two weeks ago. We must always guard against class enemies who direct their spearhead against the PLA. Don't fall into their trap. As soon as the Central Committee learnt what had happened they took measures to restore order. One PLA leader was arrested.

In short the Cultural Revolution is going smoothly. The second stage is going fine. Our production targets are being over-fulfilled. The Cultural Revolution has not hindered production. Last year we had seven months of the Cultural Revolution, yet production was increased not decreased. In the first quarter of this year in Canton production increased rapidly.

Under these circumstances the trade fair should be better than ever. The fair is in fact another battlefield of the Cultural Revolution. Revolutionary workers and cadres must work hard to make the fair a success. Through this Cultural Revolution we will put power in the hands of the genuine revolutionaries, the hands of the working people.

Chairman Mao and Lin Piao are both in good health. Should US imperialists attack us, we shall defeat them under the guidance of Chairman Mao.

Last year, a hundred Red Guards went to Vietnam without permission to take part in the struggle. This action could not be accepted. All Red Guards would be ready to follow this example. This was a courageous action.

In South Vietnam there are a million soldiers, including 400 thousand American soldiers. If Vietnam can resist one million – how many could China resist? The number of US soldiers in Vietnam exceeds the number that was in Korea. Twenty-five per cent of US soldiers fall ill – some physically, some due to fear of war and death.

In the future the Americans may be driven out, or the war may spread to other countries, even to China, but we are not afraid, as we have made every preparation.

Let us make every effort to make this fair as successful as possible. The Central Committee has made a five-point decision concerning the fair. This will be given to you later, but I will discuss these questions with you now.

During the period in which the fair is open for foreign visitors revolutionary organisations should not arrange visits. You will be able to visit the fair after May 15th.

Last year social order was not satisfactory, so this year we must pay more attention to it. This is making a higher demand on you. The units concerned (the people working in the fair, *J & EC*) should stop making their Cultural Revolution for the duration of the fair – they should stop writing posters, arguing and debating. They can make up time later. They should not visit other units. Some people working at the fair will have come from other cities – they must not go off on visits, but must concentrate on their work. Posters should not be put up in the fair or in hotels (this referred to Cultural Revolution posters expressing the ideas of individuals or groups, not to the many inscriptions, slogans, etc, which were part of the fair decor, *J & EC*). Some Red Guards would very much like to put up posters and stage performances specially for foreigners – but they must not. Western papers rely very heavily on Japanese journalists who can read our posters, but there are so many posters that even they get confused (*laughter*).

Two ballets and two Peking operas will be provided for our visitors. *The White Haired Girl*, the *Red detachment of Women*, *Raid on the White Tiger Regiment* and *Sa Jia Village*.

Liu Shao-chi is a bourgeois democrat. During the period of the democratic revolution he could be a revolutionary leader, but he is not prepared to carry the socialist revolution through to the end, therefore he has committed errors of political line many times. After the founding of the People's Republic of China, Liu wanted to develop capitalism in China. He said, 'Exploitation is not a crime . . .' and, 'The working class will benefit from exploitation'. He said, 'In China, capitalism is not too much but too little'. Liu's guiding thought is wrong – he has in fact become an agent of the capitalist and landlord classes. Since 1949 we have entered the stage of socialist revolution, and must get rid of all ideas of exploitation. The struggle between the two lines has been long and complex. Liu and his followers passed the test of capitalist revolution, but not of socialist revolution.

After Liberation, Liu visited one of the biggest Tientsin capitalists and encouraged him to extend his exploitation of the workers.

Revolutionary cadres will be the backbone of the future leadership, as they have the greatest revolutionary understanding and experience, and we hope that those who have been deceived will rejoin us.

Later we should hold various congresses of peasants, workers, students and teachers up to provincial level, but we should not hold congresses at national level during this stage. This will lead to the formation of the triple alliance of revolutionary rebels, revolutionary cadres, and PLA or militia groups, in all units.

How do we assess cadres? We examine his or her words or actions now, and his record during the Cultural Revolution. Practice the mass line to determine whether a cadre is good or not. The way to form the great alliance of revolutionary organisations is to form an alliance in the basic units and then form alliances from there up to higher levels.

The Cultural Revolution in Kwangtung is not lagging behind, and I'm sure you will not lag behind. I'm sure through criticism of the bourgeois line you will form your great alliance soon.

Long live the Great Proletarian Cultural Revolution!
Overthrow the top Party person in authority taking the capitalist road!
Long live the proletarian dictatorship!
Long live the great Mao Tse-tung's thought!
Long live the Chinese Communist Party!
Long live our great leader, great Chairman, Comrade Mao!

When Premier Chou flew back to Peking the steps required to continue the Cultural Revolution were clear, not only objectively, but subjectively in the minds of most people we talked to. Everyone should return to their own units ; there they should study the two lines represented by Chairman Mao and Liu Shao-chi. The Rebels should criticise their own mistakes and set an example in criticising the wrong line, and through these actions allay the fears of the Conservatives and enable them to play a full supporting role in the movement. The Conservatives through studying the two lines would come to see the correctness in principle of the Rebels' initiative and their own wrong attitude. Both sides, through joining together in criticising and repudiating Liu Shao-chi, Teng Hsiao-ping and representative 'capitalist roaders' in their own units and at intermediate levels, could overcome their previous opposition to each other.

With the mass organisations united, the majority of the old cadres who had opposed the Rebels during the earlier stage of the movement, or had merely been pushed aside, or had stood aside through timidity or confusion, could become active again. By joining in the movement of criticism they could play a vital role in the process of transformation which could not be carried out effectively without their experience and generally high political understanding.

Groups of PLA men joining in the activity of criticism would help to break down sectarianism and localism because they would be free of the sectarian interests of the units where they worked, and because they had been reviving their revolutionary traditions under the leadership of Lin Piao ever since 1959. Indeed, their way of life is conducive to the attitude of 'serving the people' – strengthening collectivism as against individualism – which was the essence of the whole movement.

In much of the industry of Shanghai and some other cities, considerable progress was achieved along these lines at this time. It meant the return to productive work, which was straightforward and conducive to co-operation. Although many cadres had been severely criticised, most had stayed at their production posts, and those who had stopped work had, in a return to production, a comparatively easy first step to a return to full activity. In Shanghai, the Conservative organisations had mostly been identifiable under the leadership of the now discredited old committees, and had thus now largely distintegrated, so that the conflicting groups were not so much Rebels and Conservatives as competing Rebel groups. When we visited the city in August, although it was clear that there were still intense struggles going on and only a few units had set up new revolutionary committees, nevertheless much progress had been made.

In Canton the situation was different. In the factories, although April saw the re-emergence of the Rebel groups and renewed criticism of those in authority, the schism between the two sides intensified rather than the reverse. In the middle schools, the return to classes mainly foundered on the intense antagonism between students who belonged to different groups, but also because there was great confusion as to what to do in the schools. Any tendency to return to the old pattern was strongly resisted by the Rebels, and there was very little idea about what school education for the future should be like. Where classes were recommenced, study was limited to the works of Mao Tse-tung and a little mathematics and language.

At Zhongda the combined effect of the new line being followed by the Military Commission and Premier Chou's visit was considerable, and showed itself clearly in relation to our Red Flag Commune. The Red Flag rapidly regained most of its old membership, including many who had joined the Rebellious Committee in March, and from being completely on the defensive, it once again took the offensive. The Rebels were jubilant and full of fight. The Rebellious Committee members were not so happy. They now publicly recognised that the Red Flag was a genuinely revolutionary rebellious organisation, but at the same time insisted that their organisation was also ; they admitted that they had made some mistakes, but insisted that those of the Red Flag had been more serious.

Both on the surface, and deeper down, there were many factors which were conducive to the unity which was being called for from Peking – but there were also those factors which stood in the way of unity. With the appearance of struggle in Hong Kong, and the developing attacks on Chinese in Indonesia, coupled with the continuance of the war in Vietnam, the international situation was conducive to unity and, in fact, it was during the campaign to support the people of Hong Kong that the greatest degree of unity was achieved. Then again, both sides were taking up the campaign of the repudiation of Liu Shao-chi and holding study sessions of all kinds to apply their study of Mao's writings and national editorials to understanding the two lines of policy, especially in education. To a considerable extent there was agreement about who were the most reactionary professors in the various departments. Both sides were denouncing Tao Chu, first secretary of the Central South Bureau – who played a dominant role in Kwangtung and personally in university affairs – Chiao Tzu-yang, provincial first secretary and his vice-secretary, O Mun-jei, and most important, President Li, first secretary of our University Party Committee. Taken separately, it looked as if the Red Flag and the Rebellious Committee were running parallel, and therefore it would only need an organisational change to integrate them.

However, while all these parallel activities were going on and were recognised by most people as representing a real basis of the eventual unity which was strongly desired, a considerable proportion of the energies of the people on both sides was devoted to opposing the other side, and this was particularly true of the leaderships. This conflict, besides having gained passion from the struggles of the preceding year, which were kept burning by the current recriminations, more importantly had a real social basis. There were all sorts of people on both sides – students, both successful and backward from peasant, workers, ex-landlord, and urban ex-capitalist and professional backgrounds, teachers of all kinds of background from pre-Liberation Kuomintang officials to post-Liberation peasant graduates, and Party members and cadres. Overall, the Red Flag Commune contained more of the able students and young teachers, and northerners and Kejia people (mainly hill peasants from the North who settled in the South several centuries ago and still retain their own dialect), and the Rebellious Committee a higher proportion of Party members, Party cadres, Cantonese and peasant and worker students who had had most difficulty with their studies. Thus, the most active members of the Red Flag had reason to oppose the influence of the Rebellious Committee leadership, which was conducive to the re-establishment of the old Party structure, whereas the militants of the Rebellious

Committee had equal reason to resist the influence of the Red Flag, which leaned towards being anti-Party, professional and anarchistic.

The campaign which was focused on Liu Shao-chi, 'the top Party person in authority taking the capitalist road', the stream of articles in the national press analysing the two lines of policy during the whole period of the Chinese revolution, and the emphasis on Mao Tse-tung's writings, met the revolutionary aspirations of both sides, while at the same time exposing their sectarian shortcomings. That this campaign was unable to bring about unity in the summer of 1967, was mainly due to two contradictions which faced those desirous of it. One concerned the problem of assessing the old cadres, the other concerned the PLA.

If the campaign to repudiate the line of Liu Shao-chi was to affect the students deeply, then it was necessary that they analyse fully the situation in the university leading up to the Cultural Revolution. In this case, those cadres who had been most active in the years from 1960 to 1965, when the rightist line had been most pronounced, would come in for the most searching criticism. If, as was equally necessary, the majority of leading cadres was to be united with in relation to the Cultural Revolution, then cadres would need to be assessed (as Premier Chou had recommended) firstly, on their current attitude to the movement, and secondly on their activity over the previous year. These two requirements came into conflict in a particularly acute manner in Zhongda over the question of Secretary Yang, whose case was discussed in the last chapter.

The contradiction concerning the PLA was that on the one hand, the whole movement forward of the Cultural Revolution rested on the trust that the mass of the people had in the PLA — for it was the army that held the ring, and the army that was playing a leading role in propagating Mao Tse-tung's thought — while on the other hand the PLA was an integral part of the Chinese people and contained within it both the conflict between the two lines and the schism between the two sides. The movement of criticism was proceeding in the cultural and service units of the PLA, but not among the operational troops who had to maintain military order and discipline. The Rebels were being called upon to trust the PLA in general, but in particular cases had to resist a Conservative or counter-revolutionary lead being given by specific commanders or PLA groups. Within this situation an ultra-leftist line, aimed at disrupting the whole leadership of the PLA developed among the most militant Rebel groups such as our 'August 31st' and within the revolutionary leadership at the national level. This ultra-left line had marked repercussions in Canton and at Zhongda in particular.

At the end of June the students went harvesting. Students and teachers, including some who had been severely criticised, joined in a harvest which was made the more joyous because it included the best lichee crop anyone could remember. All groups went, but the two sides went separately.

The next chapter describes our experiences helping with the harvests in three villages. This was our main direct experience of the Chinese countryside and agriculture, and therefore represents only a small proportion of the book. However it is important to stress that the peasants were in every way as actively involved in the Cultural Revolution as students, workers, intellectuals and cadres. Experience of the often harsh conditions in the countryside has always been seen as a crucial part of the socialist formation of intellectuals and cadres in China, and this factor was even more important during the Cultural Revolution. The accounts of our experience show something of the impact of student groups on peasant communities and, more important, the effect of the peasants and their working conditions on the students.

14 Making Revolution and Promoting Production

Changsha Village harvest

On the 30th of June we travelled with a group of language students and teachers to assist with the harvest at Changsha. Our expedition had been organised by the Red Flag Commune, and about forty of us went, ranging in age from twenty to fifty. The first arrangement made to go to a commune to work broke down because of the obstruction of the leaders of that particular commune, although the brigade had been co-operative.

Changsha village itself lies about twenty miles north of Canton. The population of 1300 is divided into four teams, which together form a brigade. The brigade is one of eighteen making up the commune, whose headquarters are at the town of Zhonglotan, about a mile away, numbering a total of 20,000 people. It owns a brickworks, employing fifty people, and raises geese. It also ran the lichee drying plant, the primary school, the clinic and some shops. The teams organise farm work and, after paying state tax and levies to the brigade and commune for investment and social services, distribute the value of their produce among their members. Our team – Number 2 – of eighty families and some three hundred people owns a pigsty of about a dozen pens and a threshing machine. They raise fish, ducks and geese.

The village is in the flood plain of the Pearl River where the plain enters the hills, so low hills lie within a few miles to the east and west. A large river runs at one side of the commune's lands, dividing it from the neighbouring commune. The day we arrived it was about a hundred yards wide, but after a heavy downfall of rain it rose two feet, and became twice the width. It was flowing at swimming speed between ten-foot banks, covered with bamboo groves, lichee orchards and many other trees. In flood years the village may be under several feet of water, the river, from its lowest ebb, rising by something in the order of thirty feet.

To the university group we were with, this expedition was an integral part of the Cultural Revolution, but it was also an event in the general tradition of the Chinese revolution, that of linking all social movements to the livelihood of the poor peasants. From the first setting up of communist-led revolutionary bases in the countryside in 1927, a tradition has been developed of the revolutionary army and the revolutionary cadres sharing the lives, work and hardships of the poor peasants. This tradition was spread to the whole country after Liberation in 1949, but in the succeeding years its success was gradually weakened. In 1957 it was again emphasised by the Central Committee as an important aspect of the Great Leap Forward policy and the formation of communes.

Since 1958 it has been the policy of the Chinese Communist Party and government that all intellectuals, cadres and army personnel take part in physical labour and give assistance to the peasants by working, eating and living with them for some weeks each year, while receiving no material return. This, too, lapsed in the middle sixties.

Our reception, at Changsha, was very cool at first. We unloaded our things and most of the party went into a long, low building to rest and wait further instructions. The remainder of us stood or sat about in the entrance of an old temple, now used for drying lichees. Some village people came up and chatted in a friendly way, and lots of children crowded round the foreigners. No one in our party seemed to know what was going to happen. We waited about an hour and were then taken to a primary school at one end of the long terrace of houses at which he had arrived.

The terrace was about a quarter of a mile long, divided by alleyways leading into the middle of the village. In front of the houses of the terrace were concrete drying-grounds and a dust roadway, then a low stone wall and a fish pond running almost the length of the terrace. Our school was at the west end of the village and consisted of single-storey buildings on three sides of a courtyard measuring, perhaps, thirty yards across. A well stood at one corner outside a peasant's house. We occupied rooms facing each other across the courtyard. The third side was occupied by a PLA unit consisting of three commanders, recognisable by their age and comparative corpulance, two girls – a nurse and a primary-school teacher – and fifteen soldiers. They were also at the village to help with the harvest.

After we had unpacked, a very friendly, middle-aged woman came in with buckets of food. This was Mrs Fong, with whom we were to make friends later.

After dinner we went out to the threshing floor, very near the school, where two men were threshing rice with an electric machine owned by the team. Another man was removing and weighing the filled baskets and then emptying them onto the threshing ground to dry the rice. He entered the weights in a notebook. A crowd of small children were having a great game tossing the sheaves towards the machine from a large pile, and two young women were cutting the sheaves loose with small curved knives. About eight women forked the straw ten yards yards or so to a pile, thus gleaning the last grains.

160

The political instructor of the team was working with us. A very strong and active man of about fifty, with rounded shoulders and a body almost burnt black by the sun. He wore a pair of black wide-flowing peasant trousers but nothing else. He looked very serious most of the time and made no effort to talk to us. We weren't asked to do anything, but just joined in where there was something to do. I joined the weigher, helping him to lift the full baskets on and off the scales and spreading out the grain. Very soon we got into a smooth rhythm of work together. A couple of hours after we started there were some drops of rain. The electric thresher was stopped and everyone set-to to sweep the grain into large heaps which were then covered with reed 'capes'. A wooden board pulled by ropes, wooden scrapers, bambo rakes and willow brooms were all used. The spread rice, perhaps thirty yards square, was raked up and covered in a matter of minutes – then came the downpour. This arduous operation was repeated once a day during our stay in the village – both with rice and peanuts. As the peanuts were mostly covered with dry mud, sweeping them up in a rush resulted in getting eyes, ears and nose blocked with dust.

We returned to our rooms, washed at the well with our buckets, and had our supper brought to us by Mrs Fong in the same way as our dinner. In Changsha the peasants only have two meals a day. Supper was the same as dinner. Mrs Fong, who also cooked our food, was in charge of feeding the team's pigs, so she cooked all our food in the 'sty kitchen' where she cooked the pigs' food. This time she stayed a little longer and chatted. She and her family were poor peasants. Before Liberation she had lived most of her life in poverty and hardship in Hong Kong. Her husband had been a farm labourer with no land or home, and had worked all his life in Changsha for the landlords. To this day he has not been to Canton. When he rented a little land he had to pay half of an average harvest to the landlord, so at times he had to work his rented land the year round for nothing. The Fong's have five children, and are now a very important family in the village.

In the evening we gathered for a meeting. We read several quotations from Chairman Mao on the need to learn from the masses, and to serve the needs of the poor peasants. After this Wang, our student leader, read a statement to us, to the following effect: a student, who had worked for some months in the village in 1965 had been here just before our arrival and had told the peasants that the Reg Flag would cause trouble between different peasant groups. The commune cadres appeared to be hostile to us and, it was reported, had arranged that the young men of the village should be working away from Changsha on some commune project, as they were mostly in Rebel groups. Thus we would not be able to meet them. Further, it appeared that previously some students had come to the village to pick lichees and had eaten so many that the peasants considered their help not worth the cost. In view of these facts we were called upon to work very conscientiously, and not to start political arguments concerning the opposing groups. Posters would be written and put up to explain our position, and to emphasise our

161

wish to help the poor and lower-middle peasants, and promote production. The main emphasis would be on studying the works of Chairman Mao and learning from the peasants. Any slanders that had been made against us would be answered. During the rest of our stay, members of both groups were busy writing and pasting up slogans and short articles to these ends. Many people did this during our dinner break, and in the evenings, but one or two were assigned to the work each day when we went to the fields.

Finally, we were also told that arrangements had been made for us to eat with individual peasant families – which is the normal situation. It was quite clear that our eating separately had been arranged because at first we were distrusted. This was a significant step forward.

During our visit we learned something of the village economy, of its background. Up to Liberation, a few landlords owned more than half the land. One landlord owned 1000 *mou*, which was roughly the area worked by our team of eighty families. There are about a dozen different family names in the village. Thus the old clan unity of the traditional South Chinese village, with its one family name, had already been lost. Three large private schools in the terrace facing the pond, each previously owned by a single family, but now used for housing and storage, were evidence of the wealth of the old landlords.

At land reform, in 1950, one family had been particularly widely denounced for having oppressed the poor peasants and causing brutalities and deaths among them. The father and one son were shot. The other son committed suicide by throwing himself off a roof. Absentee landlords were not brought back to the village, and were thought to have escaped to Taiwan. There are now no landlord families in the team, and only two rich peasant families that are still classified as class enemies. They have full economic rights in the team and the commune, but they are still denied political rights. Of the remainder of the team more than half are upper-middle peasants, the rest poor and lower-middle peasants.

The large proportion of middle peasants means great emphasis has to be put on the need for the poor peasant association to combine with them. In our team, one middle peasant who had shown up well in the Socialist Education Movement had been given a post of responsibility and trust.

Our Number 2 Team had seventy acres of paddy, which in 1966 produced 160 tons of grain: fifteen tons paid the total tax to the State; a further 25 tons was the quota sold to the state co-ops; about another 15 tons went to increase the brigade stocks of food and seed, and those of the team; the remaining 105 tons was distributed to the team members according to their family needs. This works out at about two pounds per person per day.

Rice prices were as follows (these have remained very stable over the years since 1952): peasants buy rice from the team at 0.8p per lb; the State buys rice from the teams at 1.4p per lb; the retail price in the towns is 2p per lb. Thus each family of the team would have received in 1967 an average of about £10 for

162

the state quota of rice, have been able to eat rice for every meal, and put some aside as a reserve.

The team had 40 acres of peanuts and gathered 25 tons of nuts in 1966. Most of his harvest was sold to the co-ops, according to quota, at about 6p per lb, giving a return to an average family of about £30. The surplus nuts were again sold to the peasants at a lower price.

The previous year was a very poor one for lichees, but 1967 proved to be outstanding, with a harvest of 18 tons. The fruit is sold to the State fresh at 2p per lb, or dried, and also sold to the State at about double this price for export (as wet fruit). Thus, each family will have received about £10 to £15 from the sale of lichees that year.

We did not get data on the production of pork, but as most families raise at least one pig, and the team pigsty must have raised at least one pig per family, I would reckon that the income from the sale of pigs would be of the order of £20 per family. Income would be received from the raising of fish and poultry, but we learnt too little about this even to get a rough idea of what this would amount to.

Apart from their rice, peanut oil for cooking and a little fat pork, probably eaten only twice a month in most families, nearly all the peasants' food and tobacco are grown on their own individual plots or, as in the case of eggs and chickens, at home.

The total income of a family, based on our figures would be in the order of £1.50 per week per family. This squares with the overall figures for income we were told.

All income, apart from that produced on the individual plots or at home, is distributed on the basis of work points, which have a money value, whereas the allocation of the rice – although paid for – is on the basis of mouths to feed. Welfare-fund distribution to those in need (mainly large families with only one worker, or families suffering from illness) ensures that all families are able to buy their allocation of rice, cotton cloth and cooking oil.

Family plots were fixed at thirty-five square yards per person. In Changsha the main crops on the plots seemed to be peanuts, sweet potatoes, beans and cabbage, as well as tobacco. Other crops grown were aubergines, all kinds of marrow, melon and cucumber, onions and leeks. They were very intensely planted and, with a twelve-month growing season, irrigation, a subtropical sun and night soil fertilisation, were highly productive. In communes where pig husbandry is highly developed the family pig may be eaten at home and meat given to urban cousins or friends (it may not be individually sold), but in Changsha, I understood that the home-raised pigs were mainly needed to fulfil the state quota, so were sold back to the team after raising for about ten months.

The first morning at Changsha we gathered at 6 a.m., after washing at the well and sweeping out our rooms. We recited several quotations from Chairman Mao, and set off for the lichee orchards. On arrival we found two young couples already at work. The two girls, in bright check shirts, were up a tree picking, and the two men, in khaki slacks and white shirts, were

163

picking from the ground. I took the men for soldiers and the girls for students, but although right about the latter, it turned out that the girls were PLA too.

The team member who was responsible for this orchard explained the job and showed us how to pick the fruit, and away we went, picking lichees. After we had enough for several basketfulls we settled in the shade of a tree to strip the fruit from the branches.

At about 10 o'clock it started to rain, so we packed all the fruit into the baskets and took them to a nearby cottage. We crammed ourselves into the little entrance. Two young women and several children pushed in after us. There we settled down to strip the rest of the fruit, while waiting for the rain to stop, before returning to the village for our breakfast/dinner.

In the afternoon we went to another orchard which was near the brick kiln. A group of middle-aged women were working with us. They were very animated, and chatted away gaily as they worked, sitting up in the trees picking off the bunches of fruit. Since our schedule was to work until 5.30 we usually started to clear up at about 5 o'clock.

Each morning the PLA group paraded before setting out to work. On the few occasions that I watched these parades, a young soldier (not one of the three commanders) took the parade, the latter parading as ordinary soldiers. They sang 'Dong Fang Hong', recited the eight rules of behaviour that had been devised by Mao, after 1927, as a basis of creating close bonds of comradeship between the revolutionary army and the peasants, read several quotations, and ended up by shouting, 'Long live Chairman Mao!' The parade was performed before a framed picture of Mao that was leant against a tree.

For the remainder of our stay we ate at the Fongs' house, usually outside the entrance on a little concrete drying-ground, but inside when it was wet. The home consisted of a covered entrance leading to a tiny patio about four yards square; a kitchen on one side of the entrance-way containing a huge iron cooking-vessel fitted like an old fashioned English wash boiler; a bedroom opposite the kitchen; and finally, a third room with no wall on one side which was open to the patio. There were no windows nor a chimney for the kitchen.

Mrs Fong was a first grade worker which means she was employed on work which is rewarded at the top rate, such as caring for the pigs, and was capable of carrying a full load (perhaps 150 lbs!) on her carrying pole. She was also the team's representative on a county advisory committee. Mr Fong was greatly trusted in the village, so had been given the job of looking after the team's stores. The twenty-two-year-old son was on a tractor driver's course, in anticipation of the arrival of a tractor that had been ordered by the brigade, but was back during part of our stay to help with the harvest work. He looked handsome in his smart pair of slacks and spotlessly clean, light-blue shirt, although he was rather shy and retiring. Ai-ling, the twenty-year-old daughter, was obviously a chip off the maternal block, very conscientious and capable. She was leader of a shock team of young women, and was being trained hy the present man to take over the job of political instructor of the team. On two occasions she addressed team meetings while I was there. A son of about fifteen did one and a quarter 'days' work one day we were there, picking peanuts. The youngest son of twelve helped his mother a great deal in the home and, according to his mother, had grown fat sampling the food she was cooking. A chubby bright-faced little girl of nine completed the the Fong family. It was not difficult to see that besides being a great asset to the village, if private enterprise were to be encouraged, the Fong family could quickly develop into members of a new 'Kulak' class.

One evening we turned out for a village meeting that was held in the space between the terrace and the wall by the pond. One rather dim bulb hung at the entrance to the lichee drying 'temple'. Clustered in and around the entrance way and against the walls of the terrace houses, sat women, some with their babies, and many children.

A circle immediately in front of the light was more or less clear. Around this circle were mostly children, sitting or lying on mats or on the ground. Amongst these were a few old people. Sitting on the wall by the pond were the men of the village and ourselves.

When we had settled ourselves on the wall, a man next to me rolled me a cigarette out of his home-grown tobacco and asked me a few questions about where I came from, and praised me for coming to help them. Throughout the meeting, people came and went, chatted and generally behaved in an easy going, relaxed manner. The children wandered about, played, or went to sleep. A baby cried, a child shouted to a friend, someone would walk through the middle of the meeting as if it were not taking place. The speaker went placidly on with his or her speech.

Our political instructor, Chou, read an editorial from *Peoples' Daily* calling for the study of Chairman Mao's works and the repudiation of the 'top Party person taking the capitalist road'. He referred to the hard life of the poor and lower-middle peasants before Liberation, to their security and good life now, and to the fact that so many people had come to help them with their harvest without reward, and emphasised that if Liu Shao-chi had had his way they would have lost these benefits. He went on to talk about immediate production problems. They must work hard to get the lichees picked and stored before the threatened typhoon arrived, and should be inspired by the help they were getting from students, cadres and PLA men. This led on to some criticisms: some people did not turn out for work on time – the women had their homes and children to attend to, yet they were often in the fields, working, before their men-folk. (The women in the factory where we worked, in the main, worked harder than the men. Traditionally the southern Chinese men put much of the hardest work onto the women – like many other peasant communities throughout the world.) ; some of the buffalo boys were neglecting their animals ; in order to earn more work points, one group had planted rice shoots hurriedly, and badly, in the middle of the field, but had planted the side near the road very neatly so that people passing would think they had worked well. Chou then turned to the principles involved. They must root out selfishness, which had been encouraged by the political line of Liu Shao-chi. This had encouraged free markets, had called for larger private plots and had aimed to base production quotas on the individual family and not the team collectively. He emphasised again that all the free help they were receiving was only possible under socialism. They, the poor peasants, must watch the rich peasants and landlords because they were always on the look-out for ways of weakening the collective. He warned, 'Sometimes the rich peasants will invite you in for a meal, but this is only to win you over to their side. We must always remain vigilant!'

One afternoon we were working near some Communist Youth League cadres, and got talking to them about their work. They were part of a group of eighty that had come to the village to help with the harvest like ourselves. An advance party of five had come to see to accommodation and so on, and we had met them at the Fongs' house where they also came to eat. The Canton office of the Communist Youth League is responsible for recruitment, for organising political courses, and for propaganda work. At present the CYL branches don't meet, and their normal activities are suspended. They carry out the Cultural Revolution in their own office, not among the general membership. They told us that they had come to help with the harvest and learn about the Cultural Revolution in the countryside, but not to try and influence it or to carry out propaganda.

The following day we had a chat with a group from the general headquarters of the trades unions in Canton. This office is the nearest thing the Chinese have to our trades councils. We mostly talked to a woman cadre who was there with her two sons of about twelve and fourteen, and a jolly, bespectacled, middle-aged man who, like most of the students, just wore shorts, vest and sandals. Their office is responsible for welfare, the political education of the workers and various evening classes. They also make the transfer arrangements for people from other spheres of life who wish to work in the factories, as for example the students. (All our students had worked in factories for several weeks during the time of their courses.) These trades union comrades emphasised that it was their main responsibility to find cases of hardship in the factories by making regular, on-the-spot investigations. Often workers who were in financial or other difficulties would keep these to themselves, and it was their job to try and find out where help or advice was needed. I raised the question of disputes between the mangement and the workers. One of our party said there were no such disputes because in China the managers were all workers. I reminded him that in the factory where we worked the manager had been denounced for having concentrated on production problems and neglecting politics, for having cut himself off from the workers and taken the capitalist road. One of the trades union cadres said that normally disputes were settled by negotiation in the factory, but that their office could be called in if difficulty was being experienced in settling the matter. The three cadres more or less repeated what the CYL group had said, to the effect that they had come here to work and not to interfere in the peasants' Cultural Revolution. They had a propaganda team with them who put on song and dance shows concerning the general issues of the Cultural Revolution, and to encourage people to study Chairman Mao's works better.

The two sons of the woman trades union cadre seemed to keep aloof from the peasant children. During the three days I saw them around, I never once saw them talking or playing with any of the village children. At first they helped a little, stripping peanuts but very soon went off hunting locusts and generally playing about – as I would expect boys of their age to do in England under the same circumstances. They wore rather smart blue shorts and tee-shirts that also marked them off from the village boys. I got a strong impression that here were a couple of incipient bureaucrats.

Saturday evening the CYL cadres put on a performance for the village. The troupe marched on the 'stage' and we all sang, 'A ship can't sail without a Helmsman'. A smaller group came on and sang some songs, to the last of which one of the girls danced. This was loudly clapped and encored. Next, three lads appeared with two large poles representing ink brush and paste brush, and a bucket, followed by a fourth carrying an imaginary ladder. They wrote imaginary posters, and pasted them on an imaginary wall with the aid of the 'ladder'. After each 'poster' was pasted up they recited its contents to the rhythm of a drum. The acting was in the style of Peking opera and was exceedingly well done and very amusing. The main themes were, 'Down with Liu Shao-chi', 'Carry the Cultural Revolution through to the end', and 'Learn from the workers and poor peasants'. The audience was very enthusiastic and shouted for an encore. We ended up again singing the 'Helmsman' song. The whole thing went off with great enthusiasm and high spirits.

Sunday was our last day so I decided I must get some photos taken. We walked away from the village towards the brick kiln. On the way I took a shot of some peasants cutting rice. At the brick kiln we were taken into the office where several people were talking, two of them were introduced as leaders of the yard. The workers are paid wages by the brigade, and these are fixed so that they earn rather more than the average peasants income. The director offered us seats and hot water to drink, but I explained our mission and our shortage of time, whereupon he insisted on taking us on a quick tour of the yard and kilns. The yard makes bricks, tiles and floor slabs and several other odd things, such as pots for putting over leeks and onions. They also sell a special earth they have which is used for making a rough glaze, and buy high-quality clay from Fushan, a pottery town. I succeeded in taking pictures of several groups and also of the kilns.

We arrived back at the threshing floor, where the PLA men and commanders were working together with some from our group and some from the peasants. When we got out to the fields where the reaping was going on we found that in the cleared fields ploughing had already commenced. People from all groups were cutting and carrying the rice sheaves.

The next morning, I was able to have a short talk with the PLA commanders before leaving Changsha. They were quite willing to answer my many questions about the PLA and how it is organised. Regardless of the position held, the mode of address in the PLA is normally the person's name followed by 'tong-zhi' (comrade). Knowledge of who is in charge is established by the soldiers knowing all the people in their unit. The general principle in army life is the 'three togethers' – work together, eat together, live together. University graduates who join the army to become regulars spend their first year doing physical labour, such as irrigation work, land reclamation, road building and so on. Wherever a unit is stationed all its personnel will take part in farm work as required by the needs of harvesting, transplanting of rice, natural disasters – floods, droughts and the like. Enlisted men, who are in the main from peasant families, also do a year of *lao-dong* during which time the emphasis is put on learning to serve the people. The daily routine is based on an eight-hour day of work, and eight hours of other activities – political studies, meetings, criticisms, sports and self-study. Men usually remain in one unit, except where military requirements dictate otherwise. I also answered questions about where I came from, what I was doing in China and how I liked living here. The youngest commander, who turned out to be in charge, said he thought it was a good thing from the point of international solidarity that we should be working in the village.

After we had been talking for half an hour or so, most of our university people had collected and some more of the PLA men. We stopped to hold a farewell meeting. Wang gave a short report of our work saying that, on the whole, it had been satisfactory. He thought we had developed very good relations with the peasants, and had overcome the difficulties we had faced on arrival. The meeting was thrown open for discussion, but to my disappointment no one else wanted to add to what Wang had said. We then formed up into lines and were addressed by the young brigade leader, then Wang again, and finally the young PLA commander. The brigade leader thanked us for our work, and said it would inspire the people of the village to work better. He emphasised the leading role of the poor and lower-middle peasants, and said it was important for them to unite with the revolutionary workers and students. The commander congratulated the students and teachers on their work, and for thereby carrying out the policy of 'making revolution and promoting production'. All three speakers referred to the need to study Chairman Mao's works and apply them in a living way, and also to the importance of carrying through the Cultural Revolution to the end.

We were to journey home in a chartered coach from the nearby town, so after reaching it we had an opportunity to look around. It was market day, which I was told happens every three days. Hundreds of people were buying and selling fruit – mainly lichees – vegetables, all sorts of poultry, and various handicraft products, such as baskets, brooms, rakes and wooden household articles. The three basic commodities – grain, edible oil and cotton cloth, are strictly controlled by the State to guarantee smooth supplies, facilitate sufficient stock-piling and maintain basic price stability, so these are kept off the free market. Pork sales are also controlled to ensure that the urban population has a steady supply at moderate prices. The produce of private plots and the home, such as vegetables, poultry, and eggs and handicrafts made by the teams, are freely sold in these local markets.

Hsin-chen, the 'New Village'

A week after returning to Zhongda we again set off for the countryside. This time we were to work in a different village, but still in the same commune. Hsin-chen ('New Village') grew the same main crops – rice, peanuts and lichees – as Changsha, but in a number of ways presented a very different picture. It is for this reason that it was of considerable interest.

The people of Hsin-chen had had their village destroyed by the Japanese, and forced to scatter to villages in the hills. After Japan was defeated they returned and built themselves a new village on a new site – hence the name.

Hsin-chen is altogether more prosperous than Changsha. I was told that a man can earn 0.9 *yuan* for one day's work, as against 0.6 to 0.7 *yuan* in Changsha. In Changsha, although the older children look healthy, many of the younger children have skin sores somewhere on their bodies – but it did not prevent them from being lively and cheerful. Here, perhaps only one child in five had such a sore. In Changsha as soon as we turned the lights on in the evening, large numbers of small white moths, mosquitoes and various other insects collected (the moths lay their eggs in the rice flower and cause considerable loss of grain). In Hsin-chen the evening air was quite devoid of insects. A final, very marked, difference was the atmosphere when we worked in the peanut fields. In Hsin-chen, the first morning we went out, the women who were working wanted to talk to me and ask all sorts of questions about how I came to be there and where I came from, as well as the usual questions about my family. Even when groups were working at some distance from each other there was a good deal of shouting and joking between them. In Changsha the peasants, in the main, kept more to themselves: on the threshing floor and when picking lichees there was some talking and interchange of jokes, but in the peanut field almost none.

Hsin-chen provided a reminder that the Chinese peasant has lost none of his canniness. Some time after my return to Zhongda I met one of the friends who had been with us. Having left before the rest of the work party to go on a tour in the North, I asked him if they had stayed in Hsin-chen to finish collecting peanuts. He said no, they hadn't, as there was a large area still to harvest. I said, 'But surely, when I left, there were only a couple of days work still to do?' My friend replied, 'So we thought. You will remember that when we started, the peasants told us there was just 50 *mou* to harvest. Well, when we had finished these we were told that there was still 100 *mou* to do. When we queried this they explained, "We told you that there was only 50 *mou* to harvest because, we thought, then you would feel this was an amount you could easily do and you would work hard to get it finished, whereas if we told you at the beiginning there was 150 *mou* to harvest, this would depress you, and you would not work so well." ' 'Did you criticise them for this deception,' I asked. 'Oh, yes,' said my friend with a broad grin.

Lung Gong

Our visit to Lung Gong with another group of students took place some five months after the visits to Changsha and Hsinchen. Although geographically quite close, Lung Gong was very different in a number of ways, not least in the fact that its members were predominantly poor peasants. In view of these contrasts, it seemed most appropriate to include the account of this visit here rather than later in the book.

The front of Lung Gong is a terrace of concrete, arcaded buildings, some two hundred yards long, with a four-storey building sticking up at one end, the brigade headquarters. In front of the terrace is a wide concrete drying-floor, and two rectangular fish ponds. The village of 4,500 people, about 900 families, is divided up into fourteen production teams, each of which run their own fields and are more or less economically autonomous, although they must fit their cropping plans into that of the brigade and the commune. The day after we arrived we were shown into a theatre with a large stage and a sloping empty auditorium, the floor of which was being used to dry rice. We settled at the front, sitting on the floor or, more comfortably on the rice, and the brigade leader gave us a short speech of welcome and some instructions:

'Half the brigade's rice has been harvested. Some teams can finish in three or four days, others may take a week or more. We have 1300 acres of rice. After the rice is in, we will lay down 600 acres of green manure and 250 acres of wheat and beans. We have a labour force of 1800. The harvest did not increase last year nor this summer, due to insect pests and drought, but this is a bumper autumn harvest and will exceed last year's total.

It is true that there are two competing revolutionary organi-

170

sations in our brigade. There are more people belonging to the 'East Wind' side than to your 'Red Flag' side, but there is no deep division between them, so you do not need to worry about our struggle. We will soon form an alliance between the two sides. You are welcome to join us in studying Chairman Mao's thinking, but you should not be sectarian here. It is better you don't roam about after dark because we have more bad elements (ex-landlords, rich peasants, ex-capitalists and law-breakers) in our brigade than there are in some others, so at night our militia patrols the village.

Yesterday we had a mass meeting at which the cadres and the masses expressed their welcome to you. Our only difficulty was to decide where you should eat. It was thought best you eat on your own, as the peasants say they have so many children and their houses are not very clean. If you meet any difficulty let me know, and our brigade will do its best to find a solution. We study Chairman Mao's thinking every three days – 3rd, 6th . . . of the lunar calendar. We have persisted in carrying out this policy, and from eighty to ninety per cent of the village attend the meetings.'

The brigade leader was followed by our student leader, Cde Wang.

'In our propaganda work we should put the Party spirit above all – above sectarianism. Our task may not be very heavy, but we want to complete it before time. We must be modest and try to learn from the poor and lower-middle peasants. We should practice the 'three togethers' with the peasants.

Do not speak foreign languages so the people do not know what you are saying.

We have a representative discussing with the team leaders where we should eat and sleep. The peasants say their houses are too crowded and dirty, but we would like to eat and live with them.

By sectarianism, I mean criticising the "East Wind" side. We must be careful what leaflets and posters we distribute. We must not antagonise the people belonging to the other side.

The team leaders will do their best to arrange for us to stay with the peasant families.'

We had been divided into groups of about twelve, and now our group was led off by the young leader of the production team we were to help. He was called Jong, but as nearly everyone in his team was also called Jong and I did not learn his personal names, I refer to him as the team leader. He led us to the other end of the terrace, where he distributed the group among the households of his team. I and Chen Fu-biao were to eat with him and his family.

The team leader is twenty-six, and has had his job for about two years. They have elected three different leaders since 1958, and hold an election annually. He has a vice-team leader to help him and they, together with the political instructor, the team accountant, the young girl cashier and one or two others, form the team committee. There is also an association of poor and lower-middle peasants, with a chairman and committee, which wields the political power of the team. Of the sixty-five families in the team, only four are upper-middle peasants, and one ex-landlord, so the rest belong to the peasant association. The chairman of the association has the right to attend all meetings of the team committee. In the team we worked with in Changsha more than half the members were upper-middle peasants, so the political situation was quite different here. The team leader's father had been a farm labourer before Liberation. If he was lucky enough to have had work, he would have lived and eaten in the landlord's house, but would not have been able to support his family. His wife made trips to the hills with her baby (the young 'team leader') on her back to collect fire wood. With luck she was able to earn two pounds of rice in a day. When he was nine the boy did this work himself. Now they grew all their own vegetables on their private plot, as did all the other families, raised two pigs a year, kept their own chickens, and received more than enough rice to eat from the team, together with peanut oil, and fish from the team's ponds. In the evening, the political instructor wrote down the results of the day's work on a blackboard. For the first four days of the harvest the team had brought in 150, 170, 230 and, that day, 250 cwt of rice. The rising total was explained by the fact that they started with the most distant fields, and each day made an effort to improve on the previous day.

At about 6 o'clock the next morning loudspeakers started playing music and songs, interspersed with speeches. Soon after, people started getting up. After washing again at the well and rolling up our beds, most of us assembled, and more or less lined-up, on the instructions of our group leaders. This formality seemed to be forgotten after the first morning. We arrived for breakfast a little later, but had to wait until about 7 o'clock because our host was not up. The meal consisted of individual bowls of rice, which were all filled before the meal began, and several communal dishes – a little dried fish, pickled cabbage and boiled cabbage. These were the basic dishes during our visit, although various others were added, particularly on our last day.

After breakfast we were given tiny six-inch sickles with sharp saw-edged blades, and off we went to the fields. Some people were carrying the rice baskets on bamboo poles. We arrived to find many people already at work, including Elsie and Lu Tsu-min who were cutting rice. There are several slight variations on the method, but usually it is the practice to cut along a row in front of you, consisting of about six clusters. If you don't put the clusters down neatly, or put down too much in a pile, it makes the work of the threshers difficult.

Several times the team leader came along and criticised my method. First, I was leaving the stubble too short, then I was making my heaps too scattered, and finally he said I was endangering my hand by cutting upwards instead of downwards.

The weather was like a good English summer day, and everybody was very cheerful. Chen comes from a peasant village near

172

Swatao, and could cut about three times faster than me, but he was very tactful and merely made a few helpful suggestions.

About mid-morning, a girl brought out two large wooden buckets of hot, boiled water for drinking, and a bucket full of little china bowls. We took a few minutes break and sat on the narrow field dike. A group of young boys came past with a dog. Several had steel rods with small, spade-shaped ends, which they used for digging out harvest rats from their holes in the dikes. Round about us were about a hundred people, working with twenty threshing 'tubs'. Harvesting in numbers like this, even a large field of rice soon turns to stubble, and apart from the feeling of accomplishment, there were always people chatting, joking and laughing, and a stimulating feeling of bustle.

We carried on working until 11 o'clock. The threshing tubs were emptied into sixty-pound baskets, and we set off along the narrow dikes for home. Most of the carrying was done by the peasants themselves, but several of the sturdier students took up the carrying pole.

Just outside the village we stopped for a wash in an irrigation channel, then went straight in to dinner. After dinner we talked, and returned to the dormitory for a short rest before going back to the field.

Elsie continued cutting, but I changed to threshing.

The wooden threshing bucket is about 4 feet long by $2\frac{1}{2}$ feet wide, and about 2 feet deep. A bamboo screen is fitted into it, which is about 5 feet high, and open at one end. Against the open end of the bucket, sloping down to the bottom centre, is a wooden frame, not unlike a washing board, against which one beats the grain heads. One grasps the 'sheaf', raises it over one's shoulder, and brings it down hard against the frame. If the rice is very ripe and dry a couple of hard swipes and several small ones suffices to get the last grain into the bucket, but if the rice is under-ripe or wet, it is much more work. Having a skilled cutter to work with makes a considerable difference.

Towards the end of the afternoon we were getting near the end of a field, and many harvest rats were running out of the remaining clump of rice. Dozens of children had gathered, and were rushing in all directions, hitting, stamping and falling on scuttling rats. As the excitement grew we adults joined in the chase.

On the second day, Elsie went to help on the threshing floor. She worked with a first-year student and a group of village women. They spread the rice out, turned it, swept it up, and then loaded it into baskets to take into storage.

On the third day, we finished cutting rice for our team, and the next day, which was rather overcast, we joined another team that still had quite a bit left to do. The rice was dry and ripe, and the threshing very good. We had expected to take two or even three days, but in fact took only one. At knocking-off time there was still a couple of acres to do but, with about thirty tubs and over one hundred people, we closed in very quickly. At the end, as the tubs were dragged along they were jostling each other, and threshers were lining up four or five deep with their sheaves swung above their shoulders. Children chased the last

few harvest rats and everybody was in high spirits. As the peasants rolled up the threshing screens, filled the rice baskets, and
shouldered their poles, the sun came out for a brilliant minute
from behind the clouds.

On our last evening, we gathered at the house of my host
to meet the other team leaders. They all had the village family
name of Jong. We visitors sat one side of the little kitchen, the
team leaders sat facing us – all on tiny wooden stools, except
our host who sat on the low brick fuel enclosure by the great
cooking pot. There were, as well as our team leader, his deputy –
an older man – the political instructor, the team accountant,
the chairman of the poor and lower-middle peasant association, and the young woman cashier. Our host's father completed
the adult party. Occasionally one of the boys came in to listen
for a bit, and once or twice the door, shut against the cold
wind, was opened to let the two pigs in or out.

No one seemed very sure how we should start the proceedings,
so I said, 'People in Britain are very interested in what is happening in China, but there is not very much information in our
papers, so we are anxious to learn as much as possible to tell
people at home. We would like to know something about the
history of your village since Liberation; how you formed co-
operatives farms, and communes, and how you are making
progress.' When the discussion got underway, the vice-team
leader spoke most, and the team leader least, but everybody
said a good deal, including the old man. The young cashier had
her turn in the middle of the 'meeting', and then went off with
our host's sister since she had some work to attend to.

The following is roughly how the discussion went. I have not
made any indication which of the team leaders spoke, except for
the cashier:

'In 1952 we carried out land reform. We had no very big
landlords. The worst was a man who made money dealing in
in opium, and lending money at high interest rates to the
peasants. In 1953 we solved many problems connected with
our land reform. In 1954 we began to form mutual aid teams
so we would carry out our work better. Co-operatives began
to be formed in 1955. At first only the poor and lower-
middle peasants joined, but later the other peasants realised
the benefits and came in too. We had three co-ops in the
village, and in 1956 these were joined together to form one
advanced co-op (where income is solely paid according to work
and rent is no longer paid, nor for hire of animals or equipment, *J & EC*). We formed our commune in the winter of
1958 from twenty co-ops with a population of 60,000. The
commune was found to be too big to administer properly so
it was divided into two in 1961. Our Shang Yang ('Facing
Sun') Commune is divided into twelve production brigades.
Our brigade has 14 production teams (these constitute more or
less autonomous farms, and organise their own work and
income distribution, *J & EC*).

The majority of us were eager to form co-operatives and
work collectively mainly for two reasons: our small plots of

land were awkward to work, so by joining together we could organise the work better and have more manpower for building dikes and dams for irrigation. After land reform, we all worked individually and very soon some got richer and others poorer. Mothers with several children found it difficult to improve their livelihood.'

'When this happened,' we asked, was it the old rich peasants who got richer, and the old poor peasants who got poorer?'

'That happened before Liberation. At first we didn't encourage the richer peasants to join the co-ops. Later they saw the advantages and wanted to join.'

'How many of you in your team are poor or lower-middle peasants?'

'Nearly all of us. We have only one ex-landlord. He did not have more than fifteen acres of land, but he dealt in opium. We haven't any rich peasants in our team, and only three families are upper-middle peasants.

'What do you think has been the main advantage for the poor peasants since Liberation?'

'Before Liberation, none of our daughters got educated. We had one primary school with 200 students for two villages, and most of the students were from landlord or rich peasant homes. Our boys, at most, got one or two years schooling. Now our village has a primary school with 900 students. We have twenty-five teachers – half from the village and half from outside. (Primary school age is normally from seven to thirteen, *J & EC*).

'Before Liberation many of our people were beggars. Not full-time beggars, but begged when they could not get work as farm labourers.'

'What did labourers earn?'

'Boys from 13 to 16 years got 3 or 4 *yuan* a year . . . that was about 60 pounds of rice. From 16 to 19 years they got 4 to 6 *yuan*. The men . . . it is difficult to say, they earned their keep, and perhaps 120 pounds of rice. They could not support a family.'

Turning to the girl we asked, 'You look very young, when did you become cashier for the team?'

'Nearly two years ago . . . I'm twenty-three years old.'

'Are you paid by the brigade or the team?'

'I only work part-time as cashier. I get work points like any other member of the team.'

'Was anyone who made money from the peasants by dealing in opium or usury treated as a landlord at land reform?'

'Several things were taken into consideration. How much land they owned; how much they exploited the poor peasants; whether they worked on the land themselves, and so on.'

'When was the peasant association formed?'

'During the land reform period. We revived the association again at the time of the Socialist Education Movement in 1965 among the poor and lower-middle peasants. The association has three main functions; (1) to voice the opinions and aspirations of the peasants; (2) to help cadres in their work – the leading members of the association attend meetings of the team committee, and check on their work; (3) to supervise the cadres. If cadres make serious mistakes, the association reports them to the higher authority.'

'Before your new irrigation system was completed, how often did you have a serious flood?'

'Most years the land was water-logged in the summer, and suffered drought in the autumn. If there was no rain for three days we had to get water from the wells. They were from three to ten metres deep, and we ladled the water out in little buckets. (Everyone laughed when the size of the buckets was indicated by fetching a small basket from a corner). A man couldn't irrigate as much as one *mou* in a day. We had an old saying – "Three fairly good harvests in ten years".'

'Last year our income was, on the average, 125 *yuan* per person. Everyone got 50 lbs of rice per month for their quota, and strong workers got 70 lbs.' (A man will eat about 1½ lbs per day, *J & EC*.)

'Have you reached the limit of rice production on your land?'

'We produce about four tons per acre from our two harvests. On similar land near Swatao they produce half as much again.'

'Is the main factor the supply of fertiliser?'

'The main factor is man. We must study Chairman Mao's thinking to revolutionise our people. We must learn to utilise our irrigation better – get just the right amount of water at the right time. There are insect pests, and rats. We can select better seed, and grow more green manure. We use some chemical fertiliser, but we can use more. We can collect more pond mud.'

'What production is run by the brigade?'

'There is a kiln for making bricks, tiles and floor slabs. The brigade runs the machines for winnowing and polishing our rice. They raise geese. Our team owns our piggery. We used to raise some cows, but gave this up.'

'Apart from rice, what crops are grown on the team's land?'

'Peanuts, yellow ginger, which is exported for medicine and dye, and beans. This year we gathered 26,000 lbs of lichees, and we grew persimmons, pears and plums. We also grow wheat in the winter on the rice land.'

'What is the population of the village compared with 1949?'

Some conferring went on following this question, amid laughter. 'We don't know what the population was at Liberation, but it is increasing rapidly. A hundred babies are born every year – so each year we have a new production team (much laughter).'

'How much land has the team?'

'We have 290 *mou* of arable. We harvest about 220 *mou* of rice twice a year. This year we have 60 *mou* of peanuts, and 10 *mou* of yellow ginger. After this harvest is cleared we will plant wheat and beans.'

At about 9.30, because we had been going for over two hours, Elsie and I felt we had taken up enough of the team leaders time, and suggested it was getting late. No one seemed in any hurry to break up the meeting, but after we had conveyed our very warmly felt appreciation, and everyone had said a number of polite and pleasant things, we did disperse.

We had two very pleasant surprises during our stay in the village. On the Wednesday, as we were on our way to our dormitories for the after-dinner rest, we ran into four people we knew from Changsha.

Young Fong had ridden over with the political instructor on their bikes, with their team leader and Mrs Fong riding pillion. After warm greetings all round we found out they had come expressly to see us. A group of Conservative Zhongda students had been harvesting in Changsha, and had told them we were at Lung Gong. We made our way back to the brigade head-quarters and found a room where we could sit and talk. We spent the rest of the dinner-break hearing news of Changsha, and exchanging family news. The following day Mrs Fong's son cycled over with some of his friends and some middle-school students from Canton who were in Changsha harvesting.

On our last morning, with the harvest in, we helped build a stack of straw sheaves. After dinner we packed up our things and got ready for our return to Canton. It was bitterly cold and by the time the lorry arrived to take us home we were chilled to the bone. The two-hour ride back to the university in the open lorry was quite an ordeal, but the students managed a rousing revolutionary chorus as we drove in at the campus gates.

15 The PLA and the Ultra-left Faction

The Cultural Revolution under the overall leadership of Mao Tse-tung was developed through three institutions: the army, led by Lin Piao who headed the Central Committee's Military Affairs Commission; the government ministries led by Chou En-lai as prime minister; and the National Cultural Revolutionary Group (Wen-ge) led by Chen Po-ta. Closely associated with Chen were Mao's wife, Chiang Ch'ing (identified with the Rebel Red Guards) and Kang Sheng, who had played a leading role in the Great Leap Forward. Also in Wen-ge were Yao Wen-yuan, who wrote the key editorials at turning points in the movement; Chang Ch'un-ch'iao, who played the leading role in establishing the new power in Shanghai; and a group of writers on the editorial board of the Party's theoretical journal, *Red Flag*.

While sufficient unity was maintained to allow the movement to press forward throughout the period from 1965 to the Party Congress in 1969, nevertheless the three institutions fulfilled quite different social functions. The leaders of each not only fulfilled the roles of joint leaders of the Cultural Revolution, but also represented their respective organisations and the special interests associated with them.

Chou En-lai not only facilitated the struggle against revisionism in the government structure, he also had the job of maintaining its necessary functions, both internally and in relation to foreign affairs. Lin Piao, as Mao's deputy, had the function of general leadership of the movement, but as head of the Military Affairs Commission he also had special responsibility for the PLA – not only directing its activities but, at times, defending it against criticism and attack. The leadership of Wen-ge led the revolutionary Rebels, it was also largely responsible for the theoretical and propaganda material that developed the movement, and, in particular, produced the detailed criticisms of Liu Shao-chi and those other leaders identified with his leadership. When the Rebels were in difficulties or retreat, Wen-ge sustained their morale.

Up to January 1967 the unified leadership of the movement was comparatively straight forward because there was a single over-riding aim, that of destroying the existing political power as constituted under the leadership of Liu Shao-chi and Teng IIsiao-ping. After January, when new organs of provincial power had been set up in the four provinces and Shanghai, and a temporary halt had to be called to seizures of power because of the degree of national dislocation, the situation became much more complicated and the different tendencies within and between the government, the PLA and Wen-ge became more acute.

In the government a movement developed in February led by Tan Jen-lin, the Minister of Agriculture, to reverse the decisions on a number of government ministers which had been taken earlier. Tan was denounced and 'pulled out', but criticism of the situation within the government by the Rebels developed, focused on Chen Yi, the Foreign Minister. The situation of the PLA was changed when, in the middle of January, it was ordered to join the movement of seizing power, and to support the revolutionary Rebel organisations. Where power was actually seized in January and February, the regional forces did take a part, but over most of the country they did not support the Rebels. In February, the regional forces were called upon to take over much of the responsibility for transport and communication, and in some provinces, local administration. In the main, the regional commanders opposed the Rebels as those causing trouble and dislocation, and supported the Conservatives, who were seen as more constructive.

China's armed forces are divided into regional and main forces. The regional forces are for regional defence and are closely integrated with the local militia. Their command is shared with civilian Party leadership. Usually the provincial Party secretary would be the military commissar for the region or district. The main forces, which include the air force and the navy, also comprise thirty-six army corps. These forces are strategically deployed and centrally directed. It was the regional forces which were drawn into the Cultural Revolution in January. With their close relationship to the provincial Party leadership it is not surprising that in many cases they tended to support the old committees, and when further seizures of power were stopped in February and they had to take responsibility for administration, it is not surprising that they tended to be hard on the Rebel groups.

Wen-ge's role, too, became more complex after Janunary. Firstly, it had the job of guiding the new revolutionary committees, especially that in Shanghai which was led by Chang Ch'un-ch'iao, and secondly, after March, it had the role of developing in depth the criticism of Liu Shao-chi and attempting to guide the revolutionary youth back to their own units in order to carry through this criticism. But its main purpose was still to lead the Rebels and the momentum of their struggle was still directing them outwards, in Peking against the government structure and, in particular, the Ministry of Foreign affairs, and over much of China against the local military commanders who were restricting their activity. In the spring and early summer of 1967 the international situation flared up and fed the ardour of the most rebellious groups. Red Guard activity among the Chinese youth in Burma led to a quarrel with the Ne Win government. The strike in Hong Kong and the brutal reaction from the Hong Kong authorities led to a Red Guard movement there, ranged against the British authority. Most important was the right-wing putsch and related anti-Chinese movement in Indonesia. When the expelled Chinese ambassador, Yao Teng-shan, returned to Peking he was given a heroes welcome at a great rally. He immediately identified himself with the extreme-left Rebels, and took up an active role which developed until August, as the final act in the struggle against Chen Yi, for about a week, he got control of the Foreign Ministry. Yao was supported by Wang Li, a member of Wen-ge. Later both were identified as belonging to an ultra-left clandestine organisation, which probably dates from about this time.

This organisation took the name of the 'May 16th Group' (after the 'May Circular' of 1966 which was made public in May 1967). In September a number of leaders, including Chiang Ch'ing and Yao Wen-yuan, identified the group in speeches.

The ultra-left and the split in Wen-ge

The most serious activity of the 'May 16th Group' was to instigate attacks on the leadership of the PLA throughout the country. In late September, an article appeared in *Red Flag* written by Lin Jei, which included the sentence, 'A movement of mass criticism and repudiation is now unfolding throughout the country against the handful of top persons taking the capitalist road in the Party *and in the army*'. The English edition of the article was abridged, so the full article may have been more explicit and forceful. However, the three last words of this sentence, alone, were no doubt sufficient to galvanise the already serious attacks on the PLA regional command by sections of the Rebels who had been held down by the PLA in March and felt frustrated by their restraining influence during the summer.

These developments were confused in relation to Zhongda. Lin Jei, who was later identified as a member of the 'May 16th Group', had contact with the Red Flag and 'August 31st', and when they went to him for advice concerning Commander Huang, he fobbed them off by saying he worked in a different sphere to Commander Huang and therefore could not help them. Also, when there was criticism of Lin Jei in Canton, the Red Flag interpreted this as efforts to split Wen-ge. In other words, an actual split in Wen-ge, in which the Red Flag was being influenced by the ultra-leftists, was being interpreted by the Red Flag as an effort to split the leadership by rightists. However, as important as it is to see how the schism in Wen-ge was complicating the position among the mass organisations, it is also necessary to see that this schism itself arose out of the nature of the struggle during the summer of 1967.

The policy of forming the great alliance and 'three-in-one' revolutionary committees in April required that the Centre support the rebellious left to counter-balance the Conservative tendencies among the cadres and army commanders, and all the weight of old habits of work, which were tending to drag China back into the situation prior to the movement. However, this left influence operating over several months built up a momentum towards overthrowing all the old leadership in the government and army on the pattern of the January Revolution, and this momentum was very much in line with the state of mind of many of the young Rebel leaders who saw themselves to a considerable extent as a new leading élite, only held in check by the PLA. It was also in line with the interests of the Rebel students as a social group, whose social advancement would be served by clearing away the old authorities, political as much as professional.

The concern about the split in Wen-ge was most pronounced at the beginning of April, and on the 6th we attended a meeting in the Cinema Field attended by representative speakers and groups from many organisations of the Rebels. The meeting was announced as being called to denounce the counter-current aimed at Premier Chou and Wen-ge. There were contingents from about forty organisations present. They included schools, colleges, factories, peasant work teams and security offices.

The following extracts give most of the points made at the meeting:

First Speaker

'Posters have appeared on the campus raising criticisms of Lin Jei, a sub-editor on *Red Flag* who has kept in touch with our representatives in Peking, and wrote a letter of support to us during March when we were being heavily attacked. A poster was put up attacking his letter to us.

It is being rumoured that Premier Chou has been "pulled out", and a poster in the Engineering College attacked Premier Chou. Efforts are being made in Canton to set one revolutionary organisation against another.

It is being suggested that there is a split in Wen-ge. Our Red Flag denies there is a split in Wen-ge; we trust Wen-ge, and we have faith in Premier Chou. We trust the PLA.

We will crush the counter-current, and fight against the attacks on Wen-ge.

Long live the PLA!

Long live the Cultural Revolution!

Long live Chairman Mao!'

Red Flag Commune announcer

'Get ready for struggle.'

(Arrival of delegation from 'East is Red Group' of film studio. Clapping. This group was dissolved in March by order of the Military Commission, but re-established on the advice of Premier Chou while he was in Canton, *J & EC*.)

'Lin Jei's article in *Red Flag* has been likened to Liu Shao-chi's book. This is an attack on Wen-ge, and a reactionary slander. . . .' (The article was about the 'Revolutionary Storm' in Shanghai, *J & EC*.)

Student from Chinese department

'Royalists say Wen-ge is divided, this is a slander. They have representatives in Peking from whom they have received a letter telling them to start this campaign. Royalists criticised Premier Chou for supporting rebellious groups, and suggested that he only listened to one side of the situation here. . . .'

Marxist-Leninist department speaker

'Posters have appeared saying Lin Jei is not the same as Wen-ge. . . . This is an attempt to split Wen-ge. . . . They also say, "We support Kang Sheng and Chiang Ch'ing." This is also to suggest a split. . . . They ask, "Why does Premier Chou support the Red Flag Commune when they only fight and destroy." This is written to discredit Premier Chou. . . .'

7th Institute member of Workers Union

(Quotation) ' "In time of victory we must not lose vigilance. . . ." '

'The counter-revolution is smashed all over the country, but not yet sufficiently. In March they attempted a come-back. My organisation was under pressure to disband, and was subjected to illegal force. The royalists and Conservatives were calling themselves Rebels, then Premier Chou brought Chairman Mao's voice to Canton. There are still attacks on the revolutionary Rebels. . . .'

Member of the Red Flag Commune of the Engineering College

'Our Red Flag and the "East is Red Group" of our college support this meeting.

Premier Chou's visit was a great blow at the reactionaries, but even before he had left they had organised a sit-down strike.

The rebellious students of our two organisations pledge to be the fist of Wen-ge:

The royalists are saying, "Criticise everything. Suspect everything." They will come to no good end. They even say, "Suspect Wen-ge."

All revolutionary Rebels must unite.'

Worker from the Pearl River Film Studio (representing four organisations in the studio)

'At the time when my Commune was banned, the other three left organisations were also under pressure. At that time, your Red Flag together with Rebel workers' organisations supported us. We bring thanks to you.

Rumours are being spread and the counter-current is being launched. We support Premier Chou's directive.

The root of the counter-current is Liu-Teng-Tao.

Some reactionaries say that Premier Chou's estimate of the situation here does not reflect the policy of the Central Committee. We believe that the black wind of March has not yet past. . . .'

Students from 25th Middle School

'The capitalists have been defeated, but it is to be expected that a counter-current should appear.

Each evening after school we used to debate with workers from a Conservative group. On the 23rd of April they put up a poster saying, "Lin Jei is the cruel oppressor of the workers' organisations. Down with Lin Jei!" After this the workers from this group would not debate with us – they were afraid to.'

Student of 'August 31st'
(Following a declaration to the meeting)

'A counter-current is aimed at Wen-ge, hence we prepared this declaration. We revolutionary Rebels are fighting with Wen-ge. Wen-ge is united. Attacks on Wen-ge are attacks on the proletarian headquarters.

Royalist leaders are taking some workers along a dangerous road. The masses should rebel against them. We must smash the counter-current.'

Commander of the PLA group in the university

'This meeting has been very educational for me. I am here only to speak for myself, not for the PLA.

The Cultural Revolution has reached a new stage. The revolutionary Rebels must follow Chairman Mao, they must aim at a small group of reactionaries and seize power from them. Liu Shao-chi is the main obstacle to unity – keep the spearhead aimed at Liu-Teng-Tao. We must reach unity through common struggle.

The *Red Flag* editorial says we must trust the PLA, trust the masses, and trust the majority of the leading cadres.

Carry the struggle through to the end. The PLA supports the left Rebels.

We will fight with the revolutionary workers through to the end.'

Chairman

(Reads letter addressed to Wen-ge)

'Dear Comrades,

Long live Chairman Mao! Long live the leadership of the Party! We members of the Red Flag have held a meeting to smash the counter-current. Our guns are aimed at Liu Shao-chi.

When Premier Chou left Canton, the counter-current began.

They say that Wen-ge has split. The weather is dark. But don't worry, we have been educated by you and Chairman Mao. We will die rather than be defeated.'

(Reads letter addressed to people of Canton)

'Dear Comrades,

The Cultural Revolution is raging, and is smashing the bourgeois rightists. Premier Chou came to Canton and supported the rebellious groups. This deflated the reactionaries. However they do not accept defeat. They fear the support of Wen-ge for the revolutionary Rebels, so they attack Wen-ge.

A counter-current has arisen. It has been suggested that Lin Jei's article on the "Revolutionary Storm" is like Liu's book on "Self-Cultivation", and that he puts down the workers. Royalists say that Premier Chou only heard one side of the case. They covered up the characters on Sun Yat-sen's memorial.

Our three Red Flag Communes (Zhongda, Sun Yat-sen Medical College, and the Engineering College, J & EC) are united.

It is being rumoured that Premier Chou has been "pulled out". His name was crossed out on slogans. The reactionaries hate Chairman Mao's comrade-in-arms, Premier Chou.

The reactionaries say Wen-ge will split, and that the "East is Red Commune" will be dissolved again. They spread the idea of "suspect everything" and "criticise everything".

We have only heard the first note of the counter-current, but we must take it seriously. This is the struggle between the two lines.

All Rebels stand united!

Those who fight Wen-ge, fight us!

All must join the struggle!'

The ultra-left and the PLA

At the beginning of May the PLA group that had been sent into Zhongda at the end of February was withdrawn, leaving only a small liaison group. Throughout the summer the PLA and Commander Huang Yung-sheng came in for criticism from both sides. Chou En-lai had emphasised Huang's trustworthiness to the extent of recalling how he had been a comrade-in-arms of Chairman Mao in the Chingkang Shan in 1927, but in spite of this he continued to come under attack.

In mid-April, after the Military Commission had announced its recognition of the Red Flag as a genuinely revolutionary organisation, the Rebellious Committee sent a deputation to discuss their position with the Commission. It had been said that the Rebellious Committee was going to be divided up into three sections – good, fair and bad. At the meeting, the Commission's representatives assured the visiting delegation that they had no need to worry and that they should continue with their activities as before. This probably gives a good idea of the line of the Commission during the summer. It recognised the Rebels but, in practice, did not come down heavily on either side, and left the PLA group in each unit to make their own assessment. Certainly the PLA group in our factory, which was predominantly Conservative, appeared to be on the best of terms with the workers and staff, and showed no signs of questioning the genuineness of the new leading committee that had been set up at the end of March. Equally, the PLA group at the cement factory we visited, specifically to meet Rebel workers in a factory where they were quite strong, supported the Rebels.

On the 26th May an incident occurred which brought the Rebel criticism of the Military Commission in Canton to a head. A group in the security bureau had seized some dossiers and other material critical of certain individuals and groups, intending to destroy it or hand it over to those implicated. However, other security forces had retrieved the material and locked it away. Arising out of this the Military Commission had issued a circular which included the following points: the PLA and the security forces were the forces of the proletarian dictatorship and should be trusted by the masses; the masses had the right and duty to make reports to the security forces which concerned state security and good order; and such reports should be held by the security organs. 'August 31st' wrote posters to the effect that this showed that there was a 'black line' in the security organs, that the Military Commission and Commander Huang were defending the security forces, and that it was necessary to expose this situation publicly. The Red Flag supported the criticism made by 'August 31st' but equivocated on the question of making public criticism. They did however decide to send a delegation to Peking to report on the situation and get a lead from Wen go.

We went to a meeting of the Red Flag teachers group at which the matter was discussed. There was disagreement, but the predominant feeling seemed to be that the Rebel groups should convey their criticism direct to Commander Huang and abide by the Centre's instructions not to criticise the PLA publicly. 'August 31st' came out with the slogan 'Bombard Commander Huang', which implied public denunciation.

On June the 8th we attended a general meeting of the Red Flag in the Auditorium. There were two speeches; one, a general report in which the attitude to the Military Commission comes out very sharply, while the other continued the polemic with the Rebellious Committee concerning Secretary Yang. The following is from the notes Elsie took from the speech of Jiang, a leader of the Red Flag:

'This meeting is being held to sum up the last few days of discussions.

The struggle between us and the Rebellious Committee is the struggle between the two lines.

We have discussed the international situation with groups at other colleges. We have discussed the situation in Hong Kong, and have paid attention to the class struggle throughout the world.

On June 2nd the Shanghai Revolutionary Committee adopted a resolution strengthening the dictatorship of the proletariat.

There have been meetings in Shanghai to struggle with Tou Yi-tou (secretary of old Shanghai Party Committee, *J & EC*).

The Rebellious Committee have been carrying out the reactionary bourgeois line. The Rebellious Committee is encouraged by Commander Huang, who is also helping Hong-zong and Di-cong. These two organisations have been spreading rumours that our Red Flag is defending Chiao Tzu-yang (Provincial Party Secretary, *J & EC*). . . .

Last year, under the rule of the reactionary bourgeois line, it was all right to raid premises for 'black lists', but now it is not permissible. . . .

We consider that Commander Huang backs the Rebellious Committee.

The "Red Flag Workers" and "Workers' Union" together have a membership of 40,000. This is smaller than the membership of Hong-zong and Di-cong, but they are genuine revolutionary Rebels. . . .

We should not think that we lag behind other provinces and cities, but we must closely follow the line of the Central Committee. In Kwangtung we revolutionary Rebels are repressed because Commander Huang has played many tricks. . . .'

Slogans ending "Long Live Chairman Mao."

The Wuhan incident

As has already been noted, to maintain the effectiveness of the PLA in its three roles of national defence, supervision of communications and civil administration, and propagator of Mao Tse-tung's thought among the masses of the people, there was the need to maintain the confidence of the people in the PLA. At the same time, there was also the need to carry out a rectification campaign in the regional forces which, in so many areas, were opposed to the Rebels and tending to sustain or re-establish the old administration. Because the dynamic for the rectification and criticism of the regional commanders mainly came from the Rebels, and the army was holding the ring in relation to the the struggle between the two sides – particularly the hostility between the most militant, Conservative workers' groups (for example, our Di-cong workers) and the ultra-left Rebel students, and the quarrels over leading cadres – the situation was one of frustration. This exploded in July with the Wuhan incident which was followed by a period of widespread fighting. This in turn increased the polarisation between the regional PLA forces and the ultra-left, which was developing a separate organised leadership centred in Wen-ge and probably, more particularly, in the editorial committee of *Red Flag*.

There had been physical violence in various provinces throughout the movement and this had increased with the 'January Storm'. Particularly violent struggles had been going on in and around Wuhan since April. However, in general, physical violence only became a central problem with the widespread seizure of firearms by the mass organisations from the PLA in July and August, and came to a head in Wuhan in mid-July and, again, in Peking a month later with the burning of the British Legation.

With respect to the two sides, both experienced the feeling of frustration. The Conservative side was held back by the directive of the centre that the PLA should support the left, and that the great alliance of revolutionary rebellious organisations should be formed with the left as the core. The Rebels were held back by the directive that they should stop their wide-ranging liaison activities, restrain their critcisms of PLA commanders, concentrate on sorting out the problems in their own units, form great alliances, and unite with a majority of the old leading cadres. A further factor underlying this frustration of both sides was the decision of the centre to settle the problems in one province after another, thus creating a brake on the developments in other areas while they were concentrating their efforts on one or two particular provinces or cities. The summer harvest in Central and South China gave a respite to this frustration, but its end presented a signal for intensified activity.

Traditionally, the unification of China following a period of turmoil took the form of one side holding the flanks of the northern plain and the other side trying to break its lines of communication by driving through the middle. It was no accident that revolutionary committees had been set up in Shantung and Shansi early in the movement, and with revolutionary committees in Shanghai and Peking, Wuhan became an obvious centre of struggle. Chiang Kai-shek's precipitous withdrawal from Wuhan in 1938 was indicative and historically symbolic of his decision not to actively combat the Japanese invaders.

In June, the intense stuggles in Wuhan had brought north-south traffic over the great Yangtse River to a halt several times, and the numerically stronger Conservative forces were physically attacking the Rebel forces and their premises, with the tacit support of Commander Ch'en Tsai-tao, who headed the Wuhan Control Commission and the armed forces in the area. Shortly before the severest attacks on the Rebels by the Conservative 'Army of a Million Heroes', Tao Chu had been firmly repudiated by the Centre, having been criticised by Rebel groups since the beginning of the year (it was they who had coined the slogan 'Down with Liu-Teng-Tao'). Tao Chu was up to the time of his promotion to the post of director of the propaganda department in June 1966, First Secretary of the Central South Bureau of the Party, so his repudiation may have been the signal for those who had worked closely with him in the past to dig in their heels in this area.

Clearly the order to the PLA not to counter violence with violence was the major factor allowing various mass organisations and groups to acquire firearms. Once a few groups got hold of arms a vicious circle was created, for now other groups armed for self defence, if not for retaliation or aggression.

The situation in Wuhan was brought to a head by the arrival of Vice-Premier Hsieh Fu-chi and Wen-ge member, Wang Li, who were sent by the Centre to sort out the situation, as Chou En-lai had done in Canton in April, and they themselves had already done on this same trip, in Yunnan and Kweichow. In

Wuhan, Hsieh and Wang, after discussions with Commander Ch'en and representatives of both sides, designated certain Rebel organisations as genuine revolutionary Rebels, and designated the largest Conservative organisation – the 'Million Heroes' – as being a Conservative organisation. Commander Ch'en was criticised and called upon to make self-criticism. His response to this was to organise a demonstration of the 'Million Heroes' and to allow the arrest of members of the delegation. Wang Li was so severely treated that he suffered a broken leg. Following this Chou En-lai flew to Wuhan, paratroops of the air force were dropped and naval craft were brought up river. Wang and Hsieh were released and returned to Peking to a heroes welcome at a million-strong demonstration.

Confrontation and violence

An experience we had, at the time the struggle was taking place in Wuhan, indicates the very limited nature of the physical force involved in the struggles in Canton, at least where the workers were concerned.

It was on July 22nd that we went for an interview with the leaders of the Hong-zong and Di-cong, the two large Conservative workers' organisations, at their joint headquarters in Canton. It is a large office building with a number of floors, lying back about thirty yards from the street. When we arrived at nine o'clock in the morning there were many people coming and going, singly and in groups. The area in front of the building was untidy, with pieces of torn posters, stones and half-bricks lying about. When we got inside there was even more bustle and even more mess. We went up several flights of broad, stone steps, and on each landing there were piles of broken bricks, clearly there to be used against a possible attack. The building had very much the air of a battle headquarters, but the piles of bricks strongly suggested that the battle expected was no civil war with military weapons. Most of the people looked like workers in a factory. We were taken to several different rooms and eventually found one which was judged satisfactory for our interview. We sat down on rough, wooden benches on either side of a trestle table.

We did not learn much that was new, but had it confirmed that the two organisations considered that they had the firm support of the majority of the workers in the city. Their criticism of the Red Flag side was first and foremost that it would not recognise their side as genuinely revolutionary, and continued to attack and harrass them. They firmly refuted the idea that they – Hong-zong and Di-cong – were led by people who had been in authority before the Cultural Revolution, and said, 'We here are ordinary workers, and so are our other comrades in the leadership, and we have all been elected by the workers'.

At about the same time as our interview was coming to an end the second major Canton battle was commencing about a mile away.

The Red Flag side had planned a mass meeting to commemorate the death of five of their comrades at a sugar refinery, where the first Canton battle had taken place. The Conservative middle-school organisation, Chu-yi-bing, were in occupation of the grounds of the Sun Yat-sen Memorial Hall. The meeting organisers had wanted to hold their meeting in a park, but the public security had insisted they hold it in the sports stadium. The result was that the march to the meeting passed by the Sun Yat-sen Memorial Hall. As it was passing, the schoolboys attacked the marchers with bricks and various weapons, such as spears and old swords. The marchers were unarmed, with the result that they suffered severe casualties. One estimate we were given was thirty-three killed, and many more injured. The disagreement about the location of the meeting gave rise to the Red Flag side concluding that the security forces had connived in the attack. We were also told, later, that some of the boys who had taken part in the battle had said they were put up to it by Di-cong workers. Our experience was that whenever there was an important event, there were widely differing reports of what had happened, so it was sensible to discount assertions of responsibility. However, what was clearly significant was that many people on the Red Flag side considered this a premeditated attack organised, or at least carried out, with the blessing of a section of the security forces and Hong-zong and Di-cong.

A few days later there was another battle in the middle of the city, but we never heard details of this. The next major encounter took place in the middle of August. Twenty Rebel lorries had gone to an armoury to get weapons. Apparently they had arrived too late, only to find that the other side had taken nearly all the arms. As they drove back into town they were fired on by a machine gun. Many people were killed in the lorries, and several people were injured in two nearby buses. All but three of the lorries were captured and 200 people taken prisoner. The prisoners were taken to a station and locked up in cattle trucks. Two or three days later they were paraded, and questioned to find out which of them were Red Flag members. Some students stepped forward, and a schoolboy was injured. At this stage soldiers arrived on the scene, and took the boy off to hospital.

Apart from these major battles, we heard of several other smaller ones. Chu-yi-bing occupied the trades union headquarters, a large building not far from Hai Chu Bridge. They were in the habit of sniping at a nearby building which was occupied by the Red Flag side. About the middle of August, some Red Flag students blew open the main entrance to the building with a hand grenade and chased the occupying forces up to the top floor. They were about to make a final attack to capture them, when word came through from Premier Chou in Peking that the boys should be allowed to leave the building without being molested. These instructions were acted upon, and the incident was settled without further violence. Another incident also occurred at a sugar refinery. The East Wind side took exception to a film that the Rebels were putting on. Arising from this a peasant lad tore down a poster, and was hit by one of the Rebel workers. This led to a group of peasants coming to the factory to protest, and the thing built up until there were quite large forces assembled on both sides. We did not hear whether or not there had been a battle, but rather got the impression that it had been avoided. Other accounts concerned groups that were entrenched in buildings at various places of work, and were attacked by groups from the other side. This happened at the docks, at the water works, and at a large fertiliser plant that I had visited on two occasions, some miles out of town.

The limited nature of the fighting in China during the month after the occupation of Wuhan by the main forces of the PLA on the 22nd of July can be indicated by a brief outline of our month's tour of the country two days later.

We left Canton by plane on the morning of the 24th and touched down at Changsha. We stopped again at Wuhan where we had lunch at the airport – just two days after the main struggle had taken place. We flew on to Chengchow where we stopped for several hours before taking a train for Sian. In Chengchow, although there were the tell-tale signs of street fighting we were not strongly discouraged from taking an evening stroll in the streets.

In Sian, we were not able to meet up with Rebel groups in the university which we had asked to do, but instead were taken on a number of visits, including one to a large textile mill which was a centre of activity in the movement. From Sian, we went by road to Yenan, where we stayed for several days before returning to Sian and then flying onto Peking. In Yenan, there were signs of tension. People were not very anxious to discuss the situation, but we were taken on the usual tours of places famous in the war against Japan, and again we were free to stroll about the town unescorted.

We landed for a meal in Taiyuan, capital of Shansi, where there were no signs of tension, and met an American couple who had just been on a visit to Ta-chai, which is in the province.

In Peking there was an atmosphere of high activity. But again no signs of widespread violence. We walked along the street near the old imperial city where countless groups, both of Peking and places in other parts of the country, had set up liaison centres. Here propaganda material, including some short acts by propaganda teams of Red Guards, was focused on criticism of the three leaders, Liu, Teng and Tao. There was no signs of fighting or feuding. Elsie and I spent a day relaxing in Peihai Park and, in spite of this being only a few days before the sacking of the British 'Embassy' when it was said that anti-foreign feeling was running high, we encountered no signs of hostility. We made visits in Peking to several colleges and other units, and walked about the city extensively, without running into any signs of fighting.

We next went to Tientsin where we spent several days visiting. Here the situation was very tense. We saw a street blockaded and several lorries filled with workers armed with pick handles, but again we were able to stroll about in the evenings in the centre of the city and along the river side.

The last city we visited was Shanghai. Here we also saw workers' militia armed with pick handles on one or two occasions, and we were told that there was still a serious struggle going on in the city around opposed organisations in a large diesel factory. However, we did not see any fighting and, here again, we were able to walk about the city both by day and in the evenings, without any escort.

When we arrived back in Canton on the 24th of August, after several days delay in Shanghai caused by the situation in Canton, we heard about the fighting in the city and its neighbouring suburbs.

During our absence the situation at the university had become very critical. The Rebellious Committee students and teachers had virtually all left, though not the Rebellious Committee workers. The Red Flag had taken over control of the university and turned the campus into something of an armed camp, with bricked-up windows, pill boxes made of bricks and sand bags, entry by pass only, and regular sentry duties. In August, for over a week, the campus had been besieged and no food had got in. A new PLA group had been sent and after some days had used their lorries to bring in rice. After that, the food situation had improved. The East Wind side had a headquarters in the diesel factory opposite the west gate, and there had been periodic exchanges of fire. One student had been killed when the biology building was fired on. Many of our Rebellious Committee students were staying in the diesel factory.

Up to the July fighting in Wuhan, the main forces of the PLA had been minimally involved in the movement, but when Commander Ch'en Tsai-tao had maintained his support of the Conservative organisations and stood out against instructions from the Centre it was the main forces of the three services that had been sent into Wuhan to take over. In August, a considerable number of regional commanders were relieved of their commands, and main force units became widely involved. In some instances, main force units supported the Rebel headquarters while regional commanders supported the Conservatives. Following the events in Wuhan, throughout China the regional forces tended to be on the defensive in relation to the Rebel headquarters and, in a number of cases, army commanders were seized and struggled against by Rebel groups.

In September, fighting came to an end over most of the country and a second unity movement began. Before passing on to this stage of the Cultural Revolution it is worthwhile to take further stock of the nature of the ultra-left movement that had developed, for it was to grow in importance until it became a central issue in the following year, and remained so for several years after.

In Zhongda, 'August 31st' represented the spirit of the ultra-left. It supported the relentless campaign to 'pull out' Chen Yi, as the focus of a general movement to reject a majority of the old, leading state cadres. It spear-headed the denunciations of Commander Huang, with its implicit condemnation of the general direction of the regional PLA forces. It was most active in the period of fighting in July and August. It was most intransigent in its demands for a share in leadership in the projected revolutionary committees. It was largely through members of 'August 31st' that the ultra-left leadership in Wen-ge influenced events in Canton. Also, with the shift of emphasis from rebellion to criticism on the basis of unity, and the shift of participation in the movement from the students to the workers, the whole of the Rebel side inclined towards the ultra-left.

However, the ultra-left, as a national movement, remained clandestine and the political line of its most publicised expression, the 'May 16th Group', were never made public, although its aim to oust Chou En-lai from leadership of the government and end the influence of the regional commands in the provinces was made clear. The ultra-left did come out in the open in one area in the autumn of 1967 and it was from this source that some idea of their thinking could be seen.

In Hunan, inspired no doubt by the reversal of fortunes of the Rebels in Wuhan with the denunciation of Commander Ch'en Tsai-tao, and encouraged by visits from Mao Tse-tung and Lin Piao in September, Rebel groups set up a headquarters which took a name more or less the same as our Rebel association of January, which was referred to as Sheng-wu-lien. The essence of the political line of Sheng-wu-lien was that revisionism in China, prior to the Cultural Revolution, had developed to a similar extent to that depicted by Chairman Mao as having happened in the Soviet Union. That is, that in China a new class of oppressors had come into existence, of which the leading members of the Party were members. They argued from this that the sweeping away of the great mass of the old leadership in Shanghai in January had been correct, and the setting up of the Shanghai Revolutionary Committee in February and restitution of most of the old cadres had been a retreat. They also argued that the period of fighting, because the masses had taken up arms and the PLA was on the defensive, was a great period of revolutionary struggle. They asserted that the policy of educated youth being transferred from the cities to the countryside had been mistaken, with the implication that they, the Rebel youth of the Cultural Revolution, rather than going to develop the backward areas of the countryside ought to remain in the cities to take over the positions of authority vacated by the old cadres. Finally, Sheng-wu-lien came out most determinedly against Premier Chou En-lai, who it identified as the architect of the betrayal of the Cultural Revolution.

About the beginning of August, representatives of both sides, from many organisations, started discussions in Peking under the auspices of Premier Chou and Wen-ge to sort out the situation in Canton. After a week or two of discussion an agreement was reached, which included the handing over of arms to the PLA, and the release of prisoners. The Red Flag handed in its arms before the final day agreed to, which was to be the 16th August. But all arms were not handed in, and the final date was put off until the 20th.

We were told that the PLA had said they would rather not accept the home-made hand grenades. This seemed to us a very wise decision on their part.

The initiative from the Centre for unity in April had taken the form of calling for a general recognition that the Rebels' actions had been in essence necessary and, in spite of mistakes, their leadership correct. However, it had not succeeded. Firstly, because, given this support the Rebels became arrogant and ultra-left – that is, they demanded submission not only from a few leaders designated as capitalist roaders, but from all those who had opposed them, instead of being prepared to work for unity through mutual criticism and self-criticism. And secondly, because the Conservatives were not, in general, prepared to accept the leading role of the Rebels, partly because of Rebel arrogance, but also because they were usually in the majority. The July fighting both indicated the need for a fresh initiative and, certainly in Canton, created the public mood in which it would be welcomed by both sides. When it came, it no longer emphasised the leading role of the Rebels. Instead it shifted the emphasis from the students to the leading role of the working class.

On the 23rd of August word came through of Chairman Mao's tour of investigation covering the northern, central and eastern provinces, including visits to Shanghai and Wuhan, and his summing up of what he referred to as the excellent situation in the Cultural Revolution. Chairman Mao's summary included the following words: 'There is no fundamental clash of interest within the working class. Under the dictatorship of the proletariat, there is no reason whatever for the working class to split into two big irreconcilable organisations.'

'The revolutionary Red Guards and revolutionary students' organisations should realise the revolutionary great alliance. So long as both sides are revolutionary mass organisations, they should realise the revolutionary great alliance in accordance with revolutionary principles.'

The need for new thinking and a clear break with old ideas in order to achieve the new unity, was emphasised in the National Day editorial of the combined editorial departments of *Red Flag, People's Daily,* and *Liberation Army Daily* by linking these words of Mao Tse-tung with a quotation from *The Communist Manifesto* by Marx and Engels, 'The communist revolution is the most radical rupture with traditional property relations ; no wonder that its development involves the most radical rupture with traditional ideas.'

16 Unity through Struggle

Throughout the Cultural Revolution the Central Committee had emphasised the need for revolutionaries to concentrate their attention on the class struggle, and 'that in the last resort all class struggles are struggles for political power'. Also it was emphasised that contradictions among the people exist among the revolutionaries, but that these contradictions would resolve themselves in the process of carrying out the struggle against the class enemy, and should not be emphasised. Further, it was pointed out that the class struggle had two aspects, the struggle against the external enemy, that is, all the reactionaries and those in the Party in authority who had taken the capitalist road, and the internal enemy, that is, all bourgeois ideas in one's own mind. Only by analysing and reaching an understanding of the two roads through struggling with the class enemy, both externally and internally, could the movement be carried through successfully, and a new and more advanced unity be reached.

Chairman Mao made a distinction between the workers and the students. In the case of the workers he said, '. . . there is no reason whatever for the working class to split into two big irreconcilable organisations', indicating that if the various workers' groups that had been engaged in dispute were to unite, and focus their attention on repudiating those who had been leading industry wrongly, and combined this political struggle with efforts to increase production, then the movement would be advanced. The implication of those being that the issues had been sufficiently clarified to allow the workers to see through revisionist leadership. In the case of the students, however, he said, '. . . So long as both sides are revolutionary, they should realise (the alliance) . . .' Implied in this qualification is the danger that in the schools and universities, if an alliance was formed including an organisation that was directed by those taking the capitalist road, then it was possible that the whole situation might degenerate, and such a school or college fail to transform itself into an institution serving the workers and poor peasants. Another implication was that the Rebel student leaders had adopted the ultra-leftist position, and only by a prolonged process of criticism and self-criticism could the revolutionary alliance come about.

During this whole period in Zhongda, there was a gradual approach to forming an alliance between the two sides, notwithstanding there were several reversals. The obstacles to unity included the two old ones, the question of Secretary Yang and the opinion of the Red Flag side as to the nature of the Rebellious Committee, and two new ones, which were disagreement about the representation of the two sides should an alliance be formed – a question which was never solved to the satisfaction of the membership of both sides – and dispute over where the returning Rebellious Committee should stay, and which offices they should have.

Efforts towards forming the alliance included the following activities: Small group meetings were held for 'Combatting self and criticising revisionism' (Dou-si-pi-siu). The idea of these meetings was that people would relate their own experiences in the course of the movement to socialist principles in the form of Chairman Mao's writings and, on this basis, make self-criticism; larger meetings, such as departmental meetings of one side or the other, or general meetings of either side, or meetings of both sides, at which leaders made self-criticism; meetings of the leaders of both sides for negotiation, concerning day-to-day activity, such as poster writing and broadcasting, or for discussing the conditions for forming an alliance; further investigations, particularly concerning cadres; meetings to hear reports from other units where alliances had been formed; representative discussions in Peking with national leaders, where again emphasis was put on self-criticism; discussions held with the Military Commission, and later the leading group that replaced the Military Commission as the provincial and municipal authority. Our PLA men in Zhongda took part in discussions at all levels in a further effort towards the formation of the alliance.

For the first month after National Day, unity was very much in the air. There was the relief that the fighting was over, and every day there was news coming in of alliances being formed in factories and other units.

A major setback took place on 5th November. An Albanian theatrical party came to Canton. It was decided by the Military Commission that they should visit Zhongda, where both sides would join in welcoming them. After they had performed, it was arranged that they should have a discussion with the students to hear about the Cultural Revolution. It was over this last part of the schedule that trouble arose. The Military Commission decided that it would be fitting that the Albanians discuss the Cultural Revolution with representatives of the Red Flag Commune, as they were the recognised revolutionary organisation. The Rebellious Committee took exception to this arrangement, arguing that the Albanians should meet both sides, as they too were a revolutionary organisation. Negotiations took place, and we were told that agreement was arrived at on the 4th. Nevertheless members of the Rebellious Committee demonstrated at the East Hotel, where there was the office making arrangements for the visitors, and at the HQ of the Military Commission.

We set off from our house on the 5th to go to the Cinema Field to attend the Albanian performance. We had been exceedingly surprised at the decision of the Military Commission, as, it seemed to us, it would inevitably lead to trouble. However, we had heard of the agreement, and hundreds of students had made the campus gay with posters greeting the visitors, and over the radio a well-known Albanian revolutionary song was being played again and again.

On our way we passed a group of people bearing a man along who had been injured. A little further we were overtaken by a man carrying another on his shoulder, who was also clearly hurt. Reaching the car park we saw several lorries and buses full of people. At the Field there was a 'full house'. Some performances were being put on by our students but there was no sign of the Albanians. We learnt that due to the demonstrations they were not going to come. We next heard shouting and a little later a column of 'August 31st' students came marching along. At the front, two students were frog-marching a man who, for some reason, they finally locked up in the cinema projection hut. Apparently what had happened was that members of the Rebellious Committee had held a meeting at which they had celebrated their victory concerning the Albanian visit. 'August 31st' enraged by this, had attacked the Rebellious Committee members.

The general feeling among the Red Flag teachers was that the attack on the Rebellious Committee members was very bad, but that the initial error lay with the Rebellious Committee itself for not accepting the decision of the Military Commission. Some leaders of the Red Flag went to the hospital, where the injured Rebellious Committee members were being treated, to present them with gifts of fruit, but this peace offering was rejected with scorn.

Discussions in Peking with representatives of all the main groups in the province led to the formation of a provisional leading group to take over the administration of the city and the province. This group, which was composed of five members from the PLA and the Central South Bureau of the Party, co-opted representatives of the various mass organisations, and therefore took on the form of a three-way committee, while acting as half-way house between the military administration and a proper 'three-in-one' revolutionary committee.

In November most of the students and teachers went harvesting again. On the 20th November the Red Flag held a day of celebration on the anniversary of their foundation, meetings, sports events, including teams from the army, and theatrical performances in the evening were organised. The Rebellious Committee members tactfully left for the countryside just before the 20th, and the Red Flag members went soon after (our visit with them to Lung Gong was described in Chapter 14).

After returning to the campus, the movement to form the alliance and resume classes while continuing with the Cultural Revolution quickened its pace. Efforts to form alliances took

196

place at all levels throughout the university. The workers on the campus formed their alliance and, from late November on, alliances kept being announced of classes, whole years, and even departments, but it was clear that until there was agreement at the university level, these agreements lower down would remain unstable.

A major effort towards unity in the university was made in mid-December. A university meeting was called under the auspices of the investigation group that had been sent down from Peking by the Centre. The main speeches were made by workers from the city water-works, in the form of reports of how they had managed to achieve unity in most of their departments. A worker from each side spoke, and these speeches were followed by speeches of criticism and encouragement from a member of the investigation group, who was a very jovial man who spoke with authority and much humour, and a PLA man from our resident propaganda group.

The meeting was held in the Cinema Field. The members of the Red Flag and the Rebellious Committee sat separately on opposite sides of the field. The Rebellious Committee group contained a large number of workers, including several friends from our dining-room.

The following is an edited report of the meeting:

Worker from the Red Flag side

'Our Canton water-works administration employs 2500 workers. Five hundred of us are concerned with maintaining the city water supply. Most of our units have achieved a great alliance, but there are still four units which have failed to unite.

Last year, when the movement began, the reactionary leaders played one section of workers off against another. At that time there were no organisations. After Sheng-ge-lien seized power, the rebellious workers in our works also seized power, and those taking the capitalist road were very afraid. On January 27th an opposing organisation seized power from the first group.

After Chairman Mao's call that there was no fundamental contradiction within the working class the workers realised the need to form the great alliance, and groups called upon each other to do this. However, we found it difficult to resolve the differences of opinion between groups because we had not made enough self-criticism. The Red Flag side refused to admit that the East Wind side was revolutionary, and vice versa. Both sides claimed that they were the only revolutionaries.

With the help of the PLA men we held a study class of Mao Tse-tung's thought. The first study group had twenty members from each side who were mainly cadres. The purpose of this study group was to combat self-interest. At first people were reluctant to join the group because of the irreconcilable state of the two sides in the past. The contradictions seemed so great that we had little confidence that they could be resolved through the study class. The key

197

question was whether or not the leaders of both sides could take a lead in making self-criticism. Fortunately, our leaders were willing to make self-criticism. I myself underwent a sharp struggle in my mind. At first, the other side laughed at me, and taunted me with having admitted to serious mistakes . . . After making self-criticism the masses understood and pardoned me, and my standing rose . . .

I will deal with some of the concrete problems which faced us in forming the alliance. At our water-works we pioneered the form of building the great alliance by dissolving all old organisations. The dissolving of the organisations was the first step. The next question was, who should form the nucleus of the leadership of the new organisation? . . . To solve this problem we needed to have faith in the masses – they would know who should be the new leaders. . . .

The next problem was the struggle between the two lines. Some comrades said, "If you dissolve all the old organisations you have obscured the struggle between the two lines." As I understand the problem, the struggle between the two lines will continue to exist in the new organisation. It is wrong to say that one organisation represents Chairman Mao's line, and another Liu Shao-chi's line. The struggle between the two lines does not necessarily mean the struggle between the two organisations. For example, we have only one Chinese Communist Party, but there has always been the struggle between the two lines within it.

The final problem was whether the time was ripe yet to form the great alliance. Some felt it was premature because there were still differences of opinion between the two organisations. On looking at this problem we should distinguish between the major and the minor currents. It is true there are still disagreements on certain questions, but the main current is that the majority of workers desire a united organisation – the masses demand the great alliance. Leading comrades should be aware of this aspiration of the masses. We should be bold and form new types of organisation that suit our revolution and serve production. So long as we hold high the great banner of Mao Tse-tung's thought, the dissolution of former organisations will not hinder revolution or production.

Your university is influential. We hope you will soon achieve your great alliance. As far as I know many workers and students look up to Zhongda. We hope that your students and teachers can live up to other's expectations.'

Worker from the East Wind side

'There is nothing special about what I am going to say, it is just an account of our experience.

The workers in our unit have already realised the great alliance. This is a great victory for the line represented by Chairman Mao. Because of the intrigues of the capitalist roaders the majority of our workers last year formed into two irreconcilable organisations. The new organisation has been formed from these two sides. Each side is on an equal footing. In the new committee each side has three representatives. There are three heads, a chairman and two deputies . . . when we decided who should be head and who deputy head we did not let this question hold up the formation of the alliance. The only criterion was to see who had studied Chairman Mao's works the best, who had applied them best, and who was implementing the Party's policy best. Workers in our unit were concerned with who was most competent to lead, not which side he was on.

Each side had accumulated a lot of material about the capitalist roaders. At first, each side was reluctant to hand over this material, considering it their own political capital. However, the study group did a lot to help in this matter. Finally both sides agreed to hold a struggle meeting together. We have since had more than ten struggle meetings sponsored by both sides.

I will now relate five of our most important experiences:

The first is the exposure of the capitalist roader, Chen. In our unit he incited the masses to struggle against each other. Both sides cited many facts to prove that he was the boss behind the scenes. Some of his previous followers came out and exposed his crimes, describing the instructions he had given them. After a struggle meeting against him the workers started to concentrate their fire on him, and stopped criticising each other. Chen became isolated, and was exposed in his true colours.

Each side learnt how to criticise themselves and not criticise the other side. It is very important to make self-criticism and not criticise others. We found the following quotation from Chairman Mao very valuable, " In the course of these campaigns, the army on its side, and the Party and the government on theirs, should thoroughly examine the shortcomings and mistakes of 1943 . . . there should be repeated self-criticism before the masses of any high-handed behaviour by the troops in the base areas towards the Party or government personnel or towards civilians, or of any lack of concern for the troops shown by the Party or government personnel or the civilians (each side criticising itself and not the other) in order that these shortcomings and mistakes may be thoroughly corrected."

We practised "strengthening the situation through study". Some comrades used to estimate the situation wrongly. They were pessimistic about the situation, and said the Cultural Revolution was far from finished. They said, "The lid of class struggle had not been lifted off, therefore it was not yet time to form the alliance". We must not over-estimate the enemy. Generally speaking the capitalist roaders have been dragged out in the last year of struggle.

Another experience was finding out the importance of study classes. Before our great alliance was formed some comrades did not pay enough attention to editorials in *People's Daily*. In the study class we helped all the comrades to study the important articles in a systematic way. We had a study class in every workshop. After we have deepened our understanding in this way we realise how far we have progressed in our own struggle. This is studying Chairman Mao in a living way.

The last experience concerns the question of grasping revolution and at the same time promoting production. In August and September we could not fulfill our production tasks because of the fighting. Since October both sides have gradually come to realise the necessity of promoting production while at the same time making revolution.

On 2nd November we realised our great alliance. In one workshop there were three organisations – a similar situation to the one here in Zhongda. The workers there spent a lot of time discussing the problems but could not reach any conclusion. This hindered production a lot. This workshop has not realised its great alliance yet – they need help from you. We hope that you can create a new method of forming the great alliance.'

After these two speeches, the following notes which had been handed up to the platform, were read out by the chairman of the meeting:

'By a first year mathematics student of the Red Flag: "We challenge the Rebellious Committee to dissolve all organisations."

From another student: "Have open meetings of negotiations."

From a group of Red Flag Commune members: "Heads of organisations should make clear their attitudes and start negotiations immediately."

Another note: "We demand that heads of organisations have negotiations on the stage immediately after the meeting. Open negotiations at once – we will do without our meals." '

The meeting continued with a speech from a PLA man with a high reputation for political work, who was the deputy leader of the investigation team sent down from Peking. His jovial and humorous manner went down very well with the meeting:

Peng Chuen-chun

' "Dou-si-pi-siu" (Fight against self and criticise revisionism)

Today we have come together to hear about advanced experience in forming the great alliance. This is a very important matter. The water-supply workers' general orientation is absolutely correct, that is, in dissolving former organisations and forming one, new, united organisation. They take "Dou-si-pi-siu" as the key. They make self-criticism only, they did not criticise the other side, this soon led to the formation of the alliance. It is a very good experience. The Preparatory Provincial Committee and the investigation team of the Central Committee have decided to hold an "on-the-spot-meeting" tomorrow in the water-works to spread knowledge of this experience. Revolutionary students, teachers and Red

Guards should follow their example, and realise the alliance as soon as possible. Your university is indeed lagging behind in this respect, but this does not matter much, so long as you can learn from the advanced experience of others. You can quickly catch up with the work of these other advanced units. So long as you are modest and willing to learn from others you can closely follow Chairman Mao's strategy and catch up with the others.

We often say you should grasp the general political orientation. What is it now? It is to resume classes while making revolution. There is one pre-condition, and that is the great alliance. Do you want to resume classes? (This was a direct question to the audience. The students enthusiastically answered Peng with the shout, *"Yes!"*) Do you want to form the great alliance? (Most of the audience shouted back, " *Yes, we do!"* Lots of students rushed enthusiastically from the edge of the field to the middle. There was much laughter and other signs of high spirits.) Very good – it shows that all of you are demanding the great alliance. It is a pity that there is a handful of people who are revolutionary in words but not in deeds. Can you help these comrades to get rid of their wrong ideas?

When you realise your great alliance, our team will come here to congratulate you. Some people are saying, you should realise the alliance and resume classes, but in fact they are struggling for personal fame and representation on the new committee. These ideas are at variance with Chairman Mao's thought, therefore help the comrades to correct their wrong ideas.

The current situation is excellent. We have in the main overthrown the bourgeois headquarters represented by China's Kruschev. We have "pulled out" a bunch of counter-revolutionary revisionists, such as Liu Shao-chi, Peng Te-huai and Chiao Tzu-yang. Our future task is still arduous and glorious. I hope all of you will be staunch, indomitable revolutionary fighters, and make revolution all your lives.

Zhongda is an influential university. Would you like to catch up with the others? (Shouts of *"Yes, we would!"*). If you work out a new way of forming the alliance, the Preparatory Provincial Committee and the investigation committee will also hold a meeting in your campus.'

This speech was followed by one given by a representative of the PLA group resident in the university, who mentioned that the study classes for the leaders of both sides had commenced the previous day and that the best way to form the alliance was for all existing organisations to be dissolved. The Red Flag side had already expressed its willingness to follow this course.

At about this time, our teachers in the Language department formed a united committee, but as the only two members of the Rebellious Committee in the department held firmly to the position of their side, it was not very united, but its formation did result in more emphasis being put on returning to work.

In the discussions about our return to classes, great emphasis was put on the need to break down the separation of the teachers from the students, and it was generally agreed that as well as meeting the students in class, and holding discussions with them towards transforming education and working out new methods, teachers should develop close social contact with the students, visit their dormitories and share in all their activities. It was clear that this was quite straightforward for some of the young teachers, who were already quite intimate with their students, but raised many problems for the older teachers. Arising from this, before actual classes were resumed, a number of discussions were held in the dormitories to which teachers went, and many of the teachers visited the students' dormitories informally in the evenings.

The entry in my diary for 20th December expresses something of our feelings: 'Yesterday we started teaching – *great day*.' (Our teaching, which remained limited to mornings and, except for a few classes, went on in the dormitories, continued with a break of several weeks over the Spring Festival, until early June.)

At the end of December the Canton Engineering College was near to forming their alliance, and the South China Engineering College, the largest in Canton, was preparing to set up their revolutionary committee.

On January 4th Party Secretary Liu was 'pulled out' and struggled against by the Red Flag. As we discussed in Chapter 12, by the assertion that Liu was the 'top Party person in Zhongda taking the capitalist road' the Red Flag was creating the opportunity for the heat to be taken out of the impasse concerning Secretary Yang. The appearance of posters written by Rebellious Committee members supporting the 'pulling out' of Liu in the days that followed and, later, the organisation by the Rebellious Committee of their own meetings to struggle with Liu, increased this opportunity. It is probable that the exposure of Liu helped towards the degree of unity that was finally achieved in February and March, but the rift still had too substantial a basis to be healed by tactful stratagems, however wise and carefully launched. During January and February, though, there was still considerable momentum carrying the movement towards alliance forward.

In this situation, in which there were alliances being formed rapidly in the colleges and, to a lesser extent, in the schools of Canton, serious negotiations were taking place at Zhongda. A particular difficulty now was internal disagreement among the members of each side, so that any compromise on the part of the leaders was denounced by sections of its own membership as a 'sell out'. However, the movement towards the alliance continued, and on the 15th February a turning point was reached when, at a university meeting, leaders from both sides made self-criticism.

Elsie and I arrived for the meeting a bit late. Jiang of the Red Flag leadership, was already speaking. In the audience were about a hundred PLA men forming a column near the middle, and as many teachers and workers. I guessed there were less than a thousand students. As most of the students who were in the university would certainly have been at the meeting this indicated that more than three quarters were still away. The following is an account of the meeting:

Jiang (Red Flag Commune)

'. . . *Red Flag*, in issues thirteen and fourteen, supported what we did, so we felt happy. Now, many articles are published with things that do not suit us. We only took notice of things that suited us, and did not pay attention to editorials that did not.

When Chairman Mao called on the PLA to support the revolutionary left we were overjoyed. Now the *People's Daily* says the PLA should support the left but not factions.

Now the situation is developing fast but we are not keeping up with it. . . . We did not see progress made, especially in September. Chairman Mao says the Red Guards and the two sides should realise their great alliance if both sides are revolutionary. We did not accept that the Rebellious Committee was a revolutionary organisation. We thought, " If the Rebellious Committee is revolutionary, then there are no Conservatives in Kwangtung Province".

When the latest instruction was issued we did not follow it closely; we did not accept others as revolutionary, and were unwilling to unite with them. If we thought carefully, the Rebellious Committee made some progress, especially in September. They have a lot of good points that we should learn from.

Chou En-lai came here last year and said that there was a reverse current of capitalist restoration here, and that we should pay close attention to it. Many revolutionary organisations demanded that the judgement on the workers' organisation called the "August First Workers' Corps" be reversed. At first, some of the Rebellious Committee opposed this: afterwards they supported it, and what the Red Flag was doing.

Chairman Mao inspected the situation in North, East and Central China, and then issued instructions, but we did not organise our members to carry out these instructions properly. This is why the great alliance has not been formed in Zhongda. We must be held responsible for this.

Last November 5th there was fighting here. At that time we thought we had done right because the Rebellious Committee were Conservative, but now I have come to understand that what we did was wrong. Most of the Rebellious Committee members are our class brothers and some of them were injured. We were sorry for this. What we did satisfied our class enemies, such as President Li. . . . We should be held responsible for the fact that we have not formed the great alliance. November 5th made the contradictions sharper than ever.

We also wanted to make the Rebellious Committee disband. On January 1st this year, some Rebellious Committee members went to search the homes of revolutionary cadres with pistols and other arms. The leaders of our Red Flag held a meeting telling members to write posters exposing their crimes in order to make confusion amongst the Rebellious Committee members. We issued a statement demanding that Rebellious Committee members make a public self-criticism. . . .

The January 22nd meeting (to commemorate the seizure of power by Sheng-ge-lien the previous year, *J & EC*) was also a "small group mentality" meeting. Holding this meeting could only do harm to the chances of forming the alliance, and would harm the workers who had already formed their alliance. But some of our members did not agree to its cancellation. . . . On the night of January 21st, Premier Chou rang Comrade Wu (leader of the Red Flag, *J & EC*) up, and told him not to hold the meeting, but Wu thought that because preparations were well advanced, it was better to hold the meeting. Thus Party spirit was not put above "small group mentality". Chairman Mao said, "Both sides should talk less about each others shortcomings." I did very little on this. . . .

On August 20th, some of our Red Flag members were seized by Jiao Ping-liang (an association of poor and lower-middle peasants, *J & EC*) on the outskirts of Canton. They reported this to the Central Committee and Premier Chou, and asked him to take measures to protect our members' lives. Then some PLA men went to the office of our Red Flag Commune to investigate the matter. Because I was excited and the PLA men were very calm, I got very angry. I smashed the telephone, saying, "What feelings do you have towards our members?" I mention this because sometimes I did not take the correct attitude towards the PLA.

Why do we have "small group mentality"? Because for a long time we did not emphasise the study of Chairman Mao's works, especially his latest instructions. . . . We did not make many self-criticism; we shifted the blame on to the other side. When we met with an organisation with a different viewpoint, we did not want to hold discussions with them, and would not accept them on an equal footing. We called them names – called them Conservative – we went to search houses, and destroyed property; in this way the contradictions became sharper and sharper. Last year we said that the showing of a film of Chairman Mao receiving the students should only be arranged by us, not the Rebellious Committee. They prepared to show the film in the Auditorium. Our members broke in and attacked some of them, and some people were injured.

We considered ourselves extremely left; the other side always wrong. For example, we were the first to demand the reversal of judgement on the workers of "August 1st", while others opposed this. Then it turned out that we were right, so we thought that we were always right.

The situation is developing fast, but my ideology remains the same. We cannot follow closely the strategic plan of Chairman Mao, and cannot follow his instructions. . . .

The New Year's Day editorial says, "whether we can

overcome 'small group mentality' or not is a sign whether or not we are really proletarian revolutionaries or not." We must study this in order to realise the great alliance in our university.

Down with "small group mentality"!

Strengthen Party spirit in our university!

Long live the PLA!

Long live our great leader, great teacher, great supreme commander, great helmsman, Chairman Mao!'

Ching (Rebellious Committee)

'Throughout the whole country, the people are eliminating "small group mentality" in order to achieve the all-round victory of the Great Proletarian Cultural Revolution in our country.

The New Year's Day editorial says, whether you can overcome "small group mentality" or not, shows whether or not you are a true revolutionary. Members of the Rebellious Committee have a lot of "small group mentality." We hope the PLA here and the Red Flag Commune will give us help and criticise us . . .

People's Daily says, "In such a great mass movement, the Red Guards and other revolutionaries make mistakes — this is quite natural." We should recognise the main political orientation. As for me, I hardly ever admitted this of the Red Flag Commune. I sometimes reversed the main current. I seldom affirmed their correct orientation. Sometimes the Red Flag and "August 31st" did nothing right, so I said we should never learn from them. Their rebellious spirit is stronger than ours, we should learn from this. When Premier Chou said the Red Flag and the "August 31st" were revolutionary red Rebels, I did not agree. However, the contributions you have made to the Cultural Revolution in the university and the province show us facts. When the Red Flag side criticised the mistakes of our Rebellious Committee, we considered them attacks and slanders . . .

Last January and February, the Red Flag made some errors when they took part in the seizing of power in the province. Their political orientation was correct but we did not see this point ; we did not take an enthusiastic attitude towards them. We thought that the contradictions between us were between us and the enemy, thus there must have been some bad elements in the Red Flag side.

When five members of the Red Flag side were asked to return secret documents or else be put in prison, they were given five days to comply. Our Rebellious Committee members were very pleased by this. The Red Flag side made some mistakes at that time but we did not help them to correct their mistakes. We were happy, and hoped that the Red Flag would be disbanded. We broadcast many articles condemning the Red Flag side, and held two meetings of Canton workers on March 5th. I apologise to members of the Red Flag (*clapping*).

As for the reversals of judgement (on various organisations that had been dissolved in March 1967, *J & EC*) I was willing to accept it. When the organisation of the workers here was dissolved as counter-revolutionary I was pleased. When Premier Chou said it should be reinstated, I was unwilling to agree. I apologise (*clapping*).

As for the "August 1st Workers' Group", we did not know whether or not it should be re-instated. We thought it would harm our side as it had many members. Eventually leaders of our Rebellious Committee said we should support its reinstatement.

. We also criticised the PLA and raised the slogan; "Pull out the handful of reactionary PLA leaders". At first we did not dare act aggressively towards the PLA – we thought, "It is the reliable pillar of the revolution. If the PLA were paralysed, who would defend our motherland?" but later, when *Red Flag* number twelve was published, we followed its lead. (This editorial called for the exposure of "those handful of people in authority taking the capitalist road in the army". It was later repudiated by the Centre, *J & EC*). Some members of the Rebellious Committee put up slogans and posters in the university and in the town.

In August 1967 there was coercion here in Canton and some of our members went to seize arms from the PLA. At first, I thought, as proletarian revolutionaries we should not do so, because the PLA needed their arms and ammunition. If we took arms to shoot at our class brothers it would be wrong. In August we left for the countryside. If we had managed to get some hand grenades we would have stayed here. So we had wanted to get arms. Some of our members went to seize some from the PLA. Some of our leaders opposed this, and said, "You are full of Conservative spirit."

On September 10th, workers and Red Guards of our East Wind side formed a new headquarters organisation, but the PLA did not send a representative to the meeting. On the 11th some of our members went to hold a sit-down protest outside the Canton PLA headquarters. This was wrong, because of the "September 5th" order of the Central Committee, State Council, Military Commission, and Wen-ge. (This order directed that no new groupings should be formed which might hinder alliances in work units – factories, schools, colleges, etc, *J & EC*). Many PLA commanders and fighters came out of their headquarters to try and persuade our members to go away, but the demonstrators stayed for many hours. At first some of our leaders opposed this action, but only because they thought it would not help our side. Some of our members withdrew from the demonstration, but later our leaders thought it better to support it, because at some later date they thought we might need the support of other groups who were involved in this action. This was an example of "small group mentality". . . .

Chairman Mao says, that holding study classes is a good thing, because by doing this we can solve many problems. As proletarian revolutionaries we must fight self-interest, expose our "small group mentality" to the public, and make public self-criticism.

I did not pay close attention to the study classes in Mao Tse-tung's thought. The PLA arranged two study courses here. Some of our leaders asked me to attend but I was unwilling. There are not many leading members of our Rebellious Committee. If I went to study, I thought. "Who would be in charge of my jobs? How could we deal with the Red Flag Commune, tactically and strategically?" I did not have faith in the masses. (*Laughter*). I did not understand or follow closely Chairman Mao's plans. As for fighting self-interest, I thought we did not have much to struggle against. . . .

When some of our members pushed me to say how we should form the great alliance, I did not know how to answer, because I did not think about this problem very much. On the question of the alliance in our university I have not been loyal to Chairman Mao, to his strategic plans. Out of "small group mentality", we wanted to gain more members. . . .

I hope the PLA in our university and members of the Red Flag side and the Rebellious Committee will criticise my "small group mentality". . . .'

A week later, our Provincial and Municipal Committees were set up. In preparation for this there had been many meetings of representatives of all the mass organisations of both sides. Meanwhile, in the university, there had been study groups formed for reviewing the situation and making self-criticism, but particularly on how to eliminate "small group mentality". Kang Hai ching described to us a course he had attended of language teachers: 'It lasted for two weeks, during which time we met together for eight hours a day or more. We started by discussing the world situation, the situation throughout the country, and the situation throughout the province, then we discussed the position here in terms of our mistakes and our achievements during the movement. Finally we made self-criticism.' These groups were held all over the campus, many in the open, with twelve to twenty people sitting in a circle on the grass.

On the 6th March we had a meeting for the whole university sponsored by the Municipal Committee, and chaired by a civilian from the city. Three people spoke, a girl student from the nearby art college from the Red Flag side, a boy student from the same college who belonged to the East Wind side, and a cadre from the city department of education. All three made self-criticisms and explained how they had reached unity through self-criticism.

Towards the end of the meeting, while the cadre was still talking, leaders of our Red Flag and Rebellious Committee went to the back of the stage where they held negotiations for forming their alliance. In the afternoon, agreement was reached that both sides should have thirteen members on the alliance committee. After this both sides called meetings of their whole membership. The Red Flag members rejected the agreement. In the evening the different sections of the Red Flag met separately. Later, the two sides came together again for negotiations. Finally, at 3 a.m., agreement was reached. The new committee was named 'The Great Revolutionary Alliance Committee of Zhongshan University'.

It met the demand for equal representation of the Rebellious Committee and the demand of the Red Flag side for representation of 'August 31st', which was allotted three of the thirteen Red Flag side places on the new committee, but many members of the Red Flag regarded the settlement as a sell out. As we were going to attend the inaugural meeting, we met several of our second-year students. We asked them where they were going, and they replied, 'To read posters'. It was clear they had no time for the new committee.

In the middle of March, we started teaching again after the Spring Festival break, and also formed a study group with Tung and Lo Tsu-min from the President's office. Our study group met about four times over the following six weeks. During our meetings we reviewed the course of the Cultural Revolution from June 1966, and discussed the meaning of various concepts that had arisen during the movement.

The fourth- and fifth-year students were involved in discussions about their graduation. In our department, as well as discussions held by all the graduating students, a committee was formed of ten people including two teachers, two cadres and six students. Five members were chosen from each side. Lo Tsu-min told us that in form this was the same as the practice before the Cultural Revolution, but in the past the final say had tended to rest with the cadres. We held the opinion that the sooner our graduates left the better, as they were obviously anxious to leave, and being very much concerned with this problem did not help the situation in the university. Further, as these students had been enrolled in 1961 and 1962 they had had the full 'bourgeois' treatment, referred to in Secretary Yang's self-criticism.

On the 13th March our Language department started a week's study course. A general meeting of the department was called on the 23rd to hear reports from the class groups and have free discussion on the alliance. Nearly all speakers spoke in more or less sectarian fashion. The groups had only met for two or three days, and had not succeeded in breaking through the initial obstacles, when other meetings were called which interrupted the 'course', such as meetings to hear workers and peasants talking about their experiences before Liberation. Following this came the call to focus on forming the departmental alliance. We felt the whole thing had been rushed, and the alliance meeting was certainly premature. Following this meeting the whole scheme fell through.

The last major effort we have recorded at this time towards strengthening unity took place on the 3rd of April. On that day Zui, the commander of the PLA group in the university, addressed a meeting in the Auditorium:

'In the latter half of 1967 when the Cultural Revolution had reached a critical stage. Chairman Mao inspected three areas and several provinces. He spent two months on this tour. . . . After investigation Chairman Mao gave us many important instructions concerning the Cultural Revolution – for example, how to handle cadres – the key to the solution of the Cultural Revolution. He also called on the revolutionary masses to form alliances. . . .

Revolutionary masses have run many study courses. Bourgeois and petit-bourgeois sectarianism have been greatly overcome and Party spirit has been strengthened. More and more revolutionary organisations have directed their spearhead against the capitalist roaders and have stopped fighting among themselves. Eighteen provinces have set up their revolutionary committees, and six more are about to be set up (with the addition of Taiwan, this makes up the total of Chinese provinces, *J & EC*).

The situation here in Zhongda is also better than ever before. The two sides and the three big organisations (*laughter*) have formed their alliance (*clapping*) . . . We consider this a great achievement. . . .

This first part of Commander Zui's speech was familiar to our interpreter and he was able to translate it fairly fully. However, Zui spoke with a broad northern dialect, and when he got on to the less general and less familiar part of his speech our interpreter had considerable difficulty in keeping up with him, and we missed a good deal. Translation was not made any easier by the laughter that followed Zui's frequent jokes. The remainder of the speech included the following points and proposals:

A special Provincial Committee meeting took place on March 22nd to review the situation in the province.

In Zhongda the new alliance committee had only met twice and had failed to come to agreement on the main problems facing the university. A third meeting had been called, but had failed to take place. The recent study courses that had been organised in the university had broken down because there had been a lack of unified leadership. . . .

Posters had been put up, speeches had been made, and meetings had been organised which were not conducive to strengthening unity. There was an alliance, but it was more or less only such in name, not in fact.

Some people said that the situation in the rest of China was good, but that in Kwangtung and in Zhongda it was not good – this was not true.

Commander Zui proposed that the alliance committee should meet and get down to the main problems. That it should arrange the holding of Mao Tse-tung's thought study-classes to sort out the question of the cadres, and deal with the question of the allocation of jobs to graduates, and other pressing problems.

He attributed the difficulties of consolidating the alliance to the leaders being too self-opinionated; the existence of still active reactionary elements, such as ex-landlords and ex-capitalists; the continued influence of capitalist roaders; the petit-bourgeois background of most of the students and teachers; and the interference from outside organisations.

At the start of the meeting the hall was packed and several hundred people sat or stood outside listening to the loudspeakers. By the end of Zui's speach most of those outside had left, and by the end of the meeting perhaps a third of the audience had already left. Even at the beginning, there was a certain amount of talking and inattentiveness, though most of the audience were listening carefully.

This meeting was the last manifestation of the movement to achieve unity that took place in Zhongda before the struggle between the two sides again flared up and, later in the summer, developed into violence, as had happened a year earlier. The turn from unity to disunity may be timed by the collapse of the organised week of group discussions that took place at the end of March. The main thrust came in Chairman Mao's assertion that the Cultural Revolution was the continuation of the class struggle against the Kuomintang, which he made in early April.

17 'The Working Class must Exercise Leadership in Everything'

Early in April a quarrel flared up in the physics' students dormitory about a Red Flag philosophy student who was alleged to have criticised Chairman Mao. On the 11th, I noted in my diary that there had been two university meetings for Red Flag members only. On the 13th, the situation seemed less tense when we went to a neighbouring state farm to plant rice and cut sugar cane, however, the two sides made their way to the farm separately. On the 22nd the Red Flag side held a mass meeting in the city to celebrate Chairman Mao's latest instruction to distinguish between bourgeois and proletarian factionalism, and his characterisation of the Cultural Revolution as the continuation of the struggle against the Kuomintang. Following this, the whole situation on the campus became very tense and antagonistic, with a new flush of aggressive posters and intense broadcasting on both sides. Our Red Flag 'pulled out' another university cadre, Pan, who enraged many Rebel students by saying in a self-criticism that his condemnation of the students who raided the Party offices for 'black material' in November 1966 was justified. The Red Flag students asserted that Pan was being defended by the Rebellious Committee.

Towards the end of May most of the Rebellious Committee students had left the university, but groups of them remained in several buildings, including the central library building. Just up the path, the Red Flag held the administrative building where we went for our post. From these two buildings some fighting developed, but nothing more serious than stone throwing. The quarrelling we heard about first arose on the question of broadcasting. Our Red Flag friends told us that the Rebellious Committee continued to broadcast late at night, when it had been agreed that there should be no broadcasting after ten so as to allow people to get to sleep. However, the event that seems to have raised most anger was a raid on some of our language students' dormitories by members of Chu-yi-bing. Following this, but probably not directly connected with it, was a serious battle for occupation of one of the science buildings.

On the 8th we were told that Comrade Huang from the office

wanted to see us. We guessed that it meant a move into town or even worse an early return to Britain. In fact, the former was the case, and within a couple of hours we had packed a ruck-sack and a basket and were on our way to town. We arrived at Shamien and were shown into the same hotel room I'd occupied on my first night in Canton!

While we were in the hotel, news kept coming in of the forma-tion of further revolutionary committees in various parts of China, but we heard little of what was happening in our pro-vince except that we were experiencing exceedingly serious flood conditions over large areas, the North River having risen to a record height. Something in the order of 200,000 PLA men were fighting the flood and so, too, were thousands of middle-school Red Guards.

We stayed at the hotel for about a month. During this time there were a few sporadic shots most nights, but we heard of no serious fights. It seemed that young people who had come back from the countryside in 1966 had occupied a number of buildings, and it was mainly they who were causing the disturb-ances at night. We gathered that after we left, there had not been any further serious fighting at the university.

At this time a workers' militia, without firearms, but armed with pick handles, was formed in the city, and some students' units of a similar kind were formed. Among the things they did were some general city cleaning work, and traffic control.

The main political activity we were told, was concerned with the movement to 'cleanse the class ranks'. This meant making investigations to identify ex-landlords, ex-capitalists and other rightists who had managed to hide their identity in various jobs. One day we saw a large demonstration passing over the new Pearl River Bridge, with columns of workers' militia and some-thing in the order of forty to fifty people, capped with dunces caps, forming a group in the middle. What lay behind this rather sudden break in the movement towards unity in the university?

With the development of the campaign for unity – the forma-tion of alliances among the mass organisations, and the encour-agement of leading cadres to return to activity leading to the setting up of revolutionary committees – grew the danger of a reaction due to the falling-off of revolutionary momentum; the danger of things relapsing into their old patterns. This danger was made the more critical because of the continued sectarianism of the leadership of the various groups and mass organisations. Thus, in a sense, both the movement towards unity, and the main obstacle to this movement combined to create conditions in which there was a danger of the achieve-ments of the Cultural Revolution being lost.

The initial reaction of the Centre to this situation was to call upon the people to identify the dangers as part of the struggle for unity. Later, when the various reactionary ten-dencies became more marked, the lead towards unity was for a time set aside with a call for renewed Rebel struggle.

The high tide of the unity campaign was summed up in the instruction: 'The two groupings should talk less about each other's shortcomings and faults, and let each talk about its own. They should make more self-criticism and seek common ground on major questions while reserving differences on minor ones.' There was emphasis on the campaign to 'support the army and cherish the people', for the PLA to 'support the left, but no special faction', and, perhaps most significant as a measure of the emphasis on unity, Chairman Mao's call for Party building.

In February, we heard that Chiang Ch'ing had made an important speech in which she had warned against a new rightist manoeuvre to exploit the general movement towards unity, in order to re-establish the authority of those who had taken the capitalist road. Early in March, meetings and discussion centred on the instruction to struggle against the 'Four Rights'. The first 'right' was described as 'right capitulationism', which was aimed at countering a tendency to feel that, with the formation of alliances, it was possible to relax and stop struggling against the old patterns of authority and organisation. A large proportion of our students and young teachers went back to their family villages for the Chinese New Year at the end of January, and when they returned during February they were anxious to get back to classes or, in the case of the fourth- and fifth-year students, to get away to jobs. With no clear ideas of what the future patterns of university education or administration should be and continued encouragement from the Centre to unite, capitulation was in the air. The second 'right' was opportunism, the tendency for some leaders of groups and organisations to compromise important aspects of the movement in order to establish themselves in new leading positions. At this stage, probably the most dangerous possibility was that Red Guard representatives would agree to joining new committees dominated by people who they knew were hostile to the movement. The third 'right' was 'right splittism', which meant disrupting alliances or revolutionary committees after they were set up by withdrawing or breaking away. This happened in our university alliance, as can be seen from Commander Zui's speech reported in the last chapter. Added to the injunction to continue the movement towards unity in terms of struggling against these rightist tendencies, was a warning against efforts to reverse decisions categorising individual leading cadres as 'those in authority in the Party taking the capitalist road'.

In April, a further general intensification of struggle was indicated by Chairman Mao's statement that, 'The Great Proletarian Cultural Revolution is, in essence, a great political revolution. . . .; it is a continuation of the prolonged struggle waged by the Chinese Communist Party and the masses of the revolutionary people under its leadership against the Kuomintang reactionaries, a continuation of the class struggle between the proletariat and the bourgeoisie.' This statement followed soon after the news from Peking of the 'pulling out' of three leading PLA commanders, including the commander of the Peking garrison, and also of Chi Pen-yu, editor of *Red Flag,* who had written the first public indictment of Liu Shao-chi, who was now himself identified as a leader of the ultra-left.

Finally, towards the end of April, the *People's Daily* carried a short editorial calling for a class analysis of factionalism, and quoting Chairman Mao's statement, 'Apart from uninhabited deserts, wherever there are groups of people they are invariably composed of the left, the middle and the right. . . .' The editorial went on to say, 'We oppose bourgeois factionalism precisely in order to safeguard and strengthen the factionalism of the proletarian revolutionaries, namely the Party spirit of the proletarian vanguard.'

In the summer of 1967, although the students had been fully involved in the fighting, the involvement of the workers and, to a lesser extent, the peasants had also been important because of the seriousness of economic dislocation and the fact that restored working-class unity was the necessary basis for the new organs of power – the revolutionary committees. In early 1968 the fighting resulting from the new shift to the right and the counteracting initiative from Chairman Mao was largely concentrated among the students. Certainly the trends were general. When we visited Shanghai at the end of July there was again a serious and violent struggle going on in the diesel factory, but the fact that most of the factories and other non-educational units had, by that time, formed their revolutionary committees, confirmed the reports we were given that all through the summer the movement towards unity had continued to develop in industry. In Canton, industry was not quite back to normal in the summer, but this appeared to be mainly due to a backlog of dislocation – ships had been held up, coal supplies ran out, electric power cuts created shortages and bottle-necks – and the effects of the summer flooding in the delta which was severe and cut important rail links. Where there was trouble caused by political actions, it was mainly young people causing transport difficulties.

I have put forward the view that the situation of struggle in 1967 was determined by the contradiction in the PLA – the need to maintain the capacity of the PLA to provide leadership, organisation and national defence, while at the same time carrying out the Cultural Revolution among the commanders and men – and that concerning the cadres – the need for the students, workers and peasants to assess them mainly in terms of their relationship to the Cultural Revolution, while at the same time gaining political experience and understanding by criticising them for the part they had played in developing the bourgeois line, particularly from 1960 to 1965. These contradictions still existed, if less acutely, in 1968. The struggle of the Red Flag Commune with the Rebellious Committee and the general struggle still involved arguments about particular cadres and particular initiatives of the PLA. However, in 1968 the struggle mainly concerned the young people themselves – the major contradiction in the situation concerned the educated youth. To some extent this contradiction paralleled that which concerned the PLA in 1967. On the one hand, the students who had rebelled again and again since May 1966 now needed to learn the standpoint of the workers and peasants, for only if they did this could they avoid becoming a generation of

214

'overlords'. They could only themselves acquire this standpoint by living and working with the workers and peasants and being prepared to learn humbly from them. On the other hand, politically the student Rebels constituted mobile detachments of the left and their initiative was necessary to balance Conservative rightist tendencies.

The solution of this contradiction was, in its simplest terms, initially to rouse the ardour and morale of the Rebels in order to assure their proper representation on the new revolutionary committees, and then follow this by a great movement for the educated youth to go into the countryside and factories, in the context of working-class and poor-peasant leadership, coupled with a campaign of social transformation.

Thus, the rapid setting up of new revolutionary committees which continued through the summer took place in a context of class struggle and renewed Rebel initiative. In Zhongda, and probably most colleges and schools throughout the country, this leftward swing resulted in renewed factionalism among the students.

In July a group of workers and poor peasants entered Tsinghua Engineering College in Peking where there was intense fighting between two groupings of students. They went in to help the students and teachers sort out their problems. At about the same time an article was published in *Red Flag* written by Yao Wen-yuan of Wen-ge, explaining the new initiative. The article was entitled, 'The Working Class must exercise leadership in everything', and was a development of the theme indicated in the following statement of Chairman Mao that Yao quoted in his article:

'In carrying out the proletarian revolution in education, it is essential to have working-class leadership ; it is essential for the masses of the workers to take part and, in co-operation with PLA fighters, bring about a "three-in-one" combination, together with the activists among the students, teachers and workers in the schools who are determined to carry the proletarian revolution in education through to the end. The workers' propaganda teams should stay permanently in the schools and take part in fulfilling all tasks in the schools of "struggle-criticism-transformation", and they will always lead the schools. In the countryside, the schools should be managed by the poor and lower-middle peasants as the most reliable ally of the working class.'

A month previously, in connection with the report of the Shanghai Machine Tool Plant, Chairman Mao had stated,

'It is still necessary to have universities ; here I refer mainly to colleges of science and engineering. However, it is essential to shorten the length of schooling, revolutionise education, put proletarian policies in command and take the road of the Shanghai Machine Tool Plant in training technicians from among the workers. Students should be selected from among the workers and peasants with practical experience, and they should return to production after a few years study.'

In the following weeks, millions of workers all over China went into the schools and colleges following the experience of the workers and peasants at Tsinghua. When we left Zhongda and Canton for home in early August a group of workers and peasants had already come in to join with the resident PLA group to help our students, teachers and workers in their discussions.

During our last weeks in China, we spent a lot of time discussing the meaning of the workers and peasants going into the schools and colleges, and the role they would play both immediately, in the context of the situation of the Cultural Revolution in mid-1968, and in the long term. It seemed clear that their immediate role was to create a socialist atmosphere in the schools and other units which would encourage the students and teachers to make self-criticism. This would allow them to establish alliances of the previously hostile groups, leading to the formation of revolutionary committees, while at the same time whole sections of students could leave to take up work in the countryside. In other words, the workers and peasants reinforced the role already being undertaken by the PLA men. In principle, this was not a new phenomenon because, throughout the movement and in the course of previous campaigns going back to before Liberation, workers and peasants had played such a role. What was new was the scale of the operation and the long-term political emphasis now put upon it.

To create this socialist atmosphere workers described the conditions of poverty and exploitation they had experienced before Liberation and contrasted these conditions with the conditions that existed in the present. Further, there were accounts of the conditions in some units due to the influence of the rightist line represented by Liu Shao-chi.

From our experience, another way in which unity could be encouraged was through describing how unity had been achieved in particular factories and other units. Perhaps the most important influence the workers would have on the students was merely by their presence, particularly in small group discussions. Just as with the PLA men at the small group discussions we attended, students discussing their own future, or the future of education, or the question of forming a new committee of leadership, would hesitate to put forward sectarian or élitist arguments in the presence of workers.

The long-term role of the workers and peasants in the schools and colleges is something which will develop over the years, but certain trends are already clear. Education at all levels will be more closely related to production, and to this end workers, technicians and industrial cadres will join students in their work in various roles – as fellow students, as teachers and as fellow workers. The students' lives will no longer be separated socially from the workers and peasants and, more directly, there will be workers and peasants taking part in the administration of educational units, and in the discussions concerning educational policy at various levels. Schools and colleges will be closely related to particular factories or other industrial units, and communes.

18 Some Patterns for the Future

By the summer of 1968, many of the patterns of social development and organisation which were going to characterise the
period of stabilisation following the Cultural Revolution were
already clearly visible. A number of them were being propagated
throughout the country by the papers and radio, and by visits
of groups of workers from one unit to another, and from one
part of the country to another. Many of the model units, which
featured in this campaign of propagating advanced experience,
were in Shanghai.

As we had been to a considerable extent isolated from the
Cultural Revolution in the weeks leading up to the time for our
departure from China, we were very anxious to find an opportunity to gain some direct information about the latest developments. Two weeks before our time ran out, it was arranged that
we could visit Hunan Province and Shanghai and, so that this
trip could be possible, our residence permits were extended for
a month. We were asked to make a list of the places we wanted
to visit in Shanghai. In the event, all our requests were met,
with several important additions that we had left out because of
lack of knowledge or due to the short period of time available.

In Shanghai, it had been arranged that we visit units where
specially advanced forms of organisation were being tried out
in industry, agriculture, education, public health and on the
Shanghai docks. We were also to visit a workers' housing area
to learn about study groups of housewives, young people and
retired workers, in which personal family attitudes came under
criticism.

We have not included a full report of each of these visits, but
have extracted out of some, material which illustrates new forms
of organisation, new policies and new attitudes of mind. They
should be seen primarily as models, illustrating the direction of
social change and the emphasis of the leadership in 1968, rather
than illustrations of the situation throughout the country.

Shanghai Machine Tool Plant

The main lesson of this was that it is not only possible, but economically efficient to train workers into technicians and engineers, and that this is a necessary part of the struggle to bring the educational and administrative superstructure into conformity with the socialist economic base of Chinese society. They have found that the young worker-technicians have the following advantages over the old specialists and the young university-trained experts: they are not overawed by advanced foreign technological achievements; they do not circumscribe their work with what has already been written down in textbooks; they are more economical in their designs, which tend to be simple and more in conformity with the needs of both production and those who will work the machines (whereas many machines designed by the 'experts' tend to be expensive, complicated and difficult to operate); they do not fear failure and the loss of face, but are prepared to carry on experimenting until final success, even after repeated failures; they work on their designs together with the workers on the shop floor, rather than behind office doors, thus in the process of designing they help to raise the technical level of their fellow workers.

The background to this is that with the Cultural Revolution it was realised that training specialists who were not workers was on the one hand, perpetuating the bourgeois concept of the expert and creating a new élite, strongly imbued with bourgeois attitudes which quickly spread from production to politics, and on the other hand, dulled the initiative of the workers, which also spread into the political sphere through increased concern for personal material gain, and a reduced interest in technical advance and political activity. In short, either the whole factory must participate in manual work, technical advance, and political and technical administration, or socialist integration would give place to bourgeois polarisation.

The second lesson of the plant was that problems are best solved by forming groups composed of workers, technicians and engineers, and leading cadres. These 'three-in-one' groups mean that those immediately concerned with the problem – usually the workers – those with first-hand practical experience of the problem – the workers and the technicians – those with special knowledge and understanding – in the main the technicians or engineers – and those with an overall view of the context of the problem and with most administrative authority best able to cut through red tape – the leading cadres – are all brought together and can form a well-balanced team able to work as an independent group. Each team has a leader who may be a worker, a technician or a cadre depending on the nature of the problem, but the team works together democratically, which facilitates the integration of the members technically, socially and politically.

This leads onto a third major aspect of the process of transformation in the Cultural Revolution. This is summed up in Chairman Mao's phrase, 'Better troops and simpler administration'. In the situation where administrative staff take part in technical and manual labour, and workers become members of leading committees, the struggle for simpler administration is considered vital. Here the Machine Tool Plant claims no lead,

218

and in fact they emphasised that they needed to learn from units where administrative work had been cut down and office staff reduced a great deal more than they had yet achieved. In all the units we visited, this question was being given great attention.

Number 5 Wharf of the Shanghai Docks

Two aspects of the current situation and orientation were particularly notable here. Firstly, during our walk round the docks we ran into three groups of managers and office staff doing manual dock labour loading ships, and we were told that all the members of the new committee spend as much time as possible working with the dockers, and only a small proportion of the leading cadres are employed on office work at any given time. Secondly, here they were in the thick of the process of 'purifying the class ranks'. After Liberation a number of ex-landlords, KMT officials and others, referred to as class enemics, managed to obscure their backgrounds and get employment on the docks at various levels – as dockers, office staff and in managerial positions. Most of these people had been identified early in the movement, but some had managed to avoid detection and, in the process of forming the alliance of the different groups and setting up the revolutionary committee, had managed to sow discord among the dockers, and hold up the process of achieving unity.

Tong Chi Architectural and Civil Engineering College

Tong Chi achieved its alliance of revolutionary organisations and set up its revolutionary committee of students, teachers and leading cadres early in 1967. In the autumn of 1967 it had launched out on the transformation of its system of education by forming a group of students and young students who went to a building site and joined the workers – working, eating and living with them. As well as taking part in all the manual operations of building, the students and teachers held classes on the site and invited veteran workers to give them lectures on various aspects of the work. Their work was completed in nine months. After studying their experience they have summed it up as follows:

> 'Before, we studied for six years and after graduation those who left our college could not undertake independent work for a further three years, so divorced from practice were our courses. Now, we believe that by integrating our courses with actual working experience on construction sites we will be able to shorten our courses to three years or so, and after completing work on three different building operations our graduates will be qualified to undertake independent assignments.'

What stood out was that they appeared convinced from their experience that by integrating architectural studies with practical building operations, not only will the future architects avoid becoming separated socially and politically from the workers, but standards will be raised and buildings more suited to the needs of the people will be built.

Hua Shan Hospital

Before Liberation this hospital had been a reserve of the rich, and most of the staff were closely associated with the KMT. After 1949 it was opened to the workers, and the out-patients department also treated peasants from the neighbouring country areas. However, after 1961 authority was largely turned over to the old professional staff of doctors and administrators, some of whom neglected their medical responsibilities, and adopted an authoritarian and aloof attitude to their patients, the young doctors, nurses and other staff. During the three years leading up to the Cultural Revolution, half the beds were taken up with cases of over-weight, and other ailments of the privileged self-indulgent. Three doctors were charged with neglecting diseases common among the workers and peasants in order to study endocrinology, which it was asserted, was virtually limiting themselves to the problems of the privileged. The point was put strongly like this, 'In our hospital before the Cultural Revolution, many doctors studied only rare diseases, yet in one mountainous district of our province (Anhwei) which has an area of 100 km square, there are only ten semi-trained medical workers.'

Hua Shan is now leading in the transformation of medical practice. The outpatients department has been reorganised so that peasants who have come in from the countryside can get prompt attention without formalities. Those who are in need of hospital beds get priority. A twenty-three member team of young doctors and nurses had gone out to the remote mountainous areas of the province to treat the peasants in their own villages. At the same time they joined the peasants in their work and took part with them in political study. While in the villages they initiated the training of more health workers amongst the peasants.

The staff of one of the wards, which includes doctors, nurses and workers, has formed a team which aims to break down the old professionalism. The doctors take part in manual work, such as cleaning and serving food, every member of the team is involved in the nursing work, and no one is barred from doing medical work because of lack of 'paper' qualifications, if they are capable. Thus, one of the nurses has carried out serious operations under supervision and has already earned a very high reputation for her work. The staff join the patients in criticising the shortcomings of the old system and the abuses of their power committed by some of the old authorities.

Pangpu Industrial Housing Estate of Shanghai

Pangpu is one of many housing estates that have been built for the workers of Shanghai to replace the old Shanghai shanty-town type slums.

We attended a study group composed of about a dozen residents, where we heard members of the group describe how they had criticised some of their individual selfish attitudes.

The following are typical of the self-criticisms made by members of this group:

Chu Ching Hua (a housewife of fifty)

'I have five children. I love them dearly. Before the Cultural Revolution I used to spoil them. I would not let them go out in the summer when it was too hot, or in the winter when it was cold, in case they got ill. My husband used to say, "We should cultivate our children to serve the proletariat – they should be tempered by life, yet you cosset and spoil them." I said, "You don't love our children as I do." I also said, "You have your social security through your factory – the children are my social security. When they grow up each will earn at least 50 *yuan* a month, and each will give me, say, 10 *yuan*. In this way I shall have 50 yuan a month to live on."

Since that time of quarrelling about the children we have formed our study group and I have come to realise that I was wrong. Now we are all of one mind, the children, my husband and I. We know that to serve China and to raise the living conditions of all us workers and peasants, our children must temper themselves in social struggle.'

Su Sen-jing (retired machinery worker)

'When I retired two years ago I said to myself, "Now I will sit back and enjoy myself". After forming our study group I realised this was wrong. We old workers have a heavy task to educate successors to the revolution. Before Liberation the capitalists said, "He is poor because that it his destiny". Under the guidance of Chairman Mao we learnt that we workers have the power. If our country is not to change its political colour, our sons must be revolutionary successors. I educate my sons about the old society. Before the Cultural Revolution we used to say, "Our sons will keep us prosperous". Now we say, "Our sons must prevent revisionism".'

Postscript

Chairman Mao teaches, 'Once (the) principle contradiction is grasped all problems can be readily solved'.

The principle contradiction in China today is the economic and cultural backwardness of the majority of the Chinese people (the peasants), in contrast to the level of modern, world technology and culture, and the relatively advanced level of the urban population of China. The future of Chinese socialism depends on maintaining a grasp of this contradiction until it is solved. This in turn requires, on the one hand, that the poor and lower-middle peasants practice self-sufficiency and maintain the initiative in solving their own problems, and on the other, that the urban population maintains the orientation of serving the countryside and recognising the positive contribution of the peasants, and learning from their lives of hard work and simple living.

Still today, as throughout the history of China, the over-riding physical problem is water control, in particular the harnessing of the Yangtse and Yellow Rivers. In the case of the latter water control involves a complex and co-ordinated process of re-afforestation, land terracing, creation of silt beds, population resettlement, and dam-building, involving the co-ordinated use of electrical power, all of which would require the participation of tens of millions of people (a task which in 1955 was considered by a leading American authority on Chinese geography to be such as to tax the total resources of the United States). Similarly, the over-riding social problem is, will this task go forward by the volition of the peasants or as a burden forced on them by the State? It is the decisive shift from coercion to volition which has characterised the forward movement of the Chinese revolution.

In principle, Chinese agriculture may take one of three roads: *the traditional way,* leaving the village to stagnate as largely isolated grain surplus-producing communities, from which corvée labour and soldiers are recruited as required ; *the capitalist way,* leaving economic polarisation in the villages to create large, economically viable farms, and an unemployed army of impoverished peasants to keep wages down in the towns, and provide what labour is needed for water control until such time as it is replaced by large capital equipment; or, *the socialist way*, maintaining and steadily extending the peasant collective, so that the corvée aspect of working on water control is increasingly reduced, and steadily raising and diversifying the village economy and culture, including a steady increase in mechanisation, in order to close the gap between town and country.

If the socialist road in relation to the countryside is to be adhered to, this requires that the assertion of the collective interest is maintained in all spheres of social activity – most particularly in the Party, and the living experience of the workers.

In the countryside itself during the Cultural Revolution, the struggle has been between the patterns of individual incentive that developed in the sixties, and the collective interest most clearly illustrated in the achievements of Ta-chai, the model commune production brigade in the Shansi mountains. A special feature of the Ta-chai experience through the sixties was the development of the concept of self-reliance. Ta-chai refused aid from the State to mitigate its material backwardness and won through by its own efforts. The self-reliance of China's 26,000 communes is the basis for defence through People's War, but it is much more than this. The principle of self-sufficiency in the communes means economic and cultural diversification, and progress throughout the whole of Chinese society, without the loss of initiative and self-respect. Ta-chai has proved to China and the world that even the most backward community can set an example to the most advanced – it is man and his ideas which, in the last resort, is decisive. The paradox is that as the concept of self-sufficient development is strengthened, so can material and cultural assistance from industry and the towns become greater and more beneficial to the countryside.

The Chinese countryside, in general, has had eleven years of good harvests, and twelve years of growing assistance from the cities. In the Cultural Revolution, the poor and lower-middle peasants' associations, which were re-established in 1964 and 1965, have emphasised class struggle and collective interest, and enhanced the initiative of the peasants. This initiative has gained encouragement by the national decision to shift educational authority from the government to the peasants' associations. Agricultural production was not seriously disrupted by the struggles in 1967 and 1968, and what harm was done to agriculture was probably more than compensated for by the vast assistance in water control, harvesting and planting that was rendered by the PLA soldiers, the Red Guards and other sections of the population (as in the Kwangtung floods of 1968). Not least important, Mao Tse-tung is seen in China as, in a special way, the champion of the poor and lower-middle peasants so his status is in some way also their status, his initiative is their initiative. The steady winding down of the Chairman Mao cult since 1968 should not necessarily weaken this, as it is, in China anyway, understood as mostly dramatisation, and the substance remains.

In industry, the major contribution to serving the countryside lies in maintaining a level of wages and salaries, which is not so much above that in the countryside as to create a breach in the unity of the workers and poor and lower-middle peasants (that is, maintaining a level far below that which could be achieved on the basis of the productivity of industry, particularly the modern sector).

The movement of increasing individual material incentives and transforming the trades unions into organisations for the assertion of the interests of particular sections of workers, coupled with the emphasis on managerial and professional status and privilege which characterised the 'Three Hard Years' in 1960–2, threatened to disrupt this relationship. The struggle against 'economism' and the increased participation of the workers in technical innovation and management is the alternative, which by its strengthening of the collectivist consciousness of the workers and cadres can maintain the relationship. The 'three-in-one' revolutionary committee is an expression of this political orientation. Apart from full workers' participation, the main factor in the consolidation of this policy is the remoulding of the cadres.

From September 1968 there have been established in China what are called 'May Seventh' cadres' schools. On this date in 1966, Mao Tse-tung made his assertion of the need to transform education in the spirit of all people becoming workers and peasants and soldiers with a high level of class-consciousness and culture. These schools are situated in the countryside, and those studying at them do manual labour while studying and applying Marxist theory and making criticism and self-criticism, so as to raise their level of social-consciousness and political understanding. Living and working conditions are those of the peasants, or harder, for sometimes the schools are established on waste land and farming has to be established from scratch – each school aims at self-sufficiency.

Factories, schools and offices have established their own 'May Seventh' cadre schools, and all their cadres have been going in rotation for periods ranging from a few months to a few years. Each cadre assesses his own degree of remoulding and by this decides himself when he should return to his normal work. (This probably does not apply to those who have been seriously criticised as rightists.) If the practice of hard work and simple living coupled with deep-going criticism is maintained, the 'May Seventh' schools may be expected to constitute a major factor towards consolidating the socialist unity of town and country. The 'May Seventh' cadre schools run by schools and colleges are an integral part of the transformation of education.

The effects of the Cultural Revolution in the schools and colleges is significant in two major respects. Firstly, there is the transformation of education, and secondly, there is the role in society of the millions of middle-school and college students who took part in the movement and who have now graduated.

Students who leave middle school now all go to work in industry or agriculture as workers and peasants, those who graduate in the country towns mostly going back to their own villages. There is an increase in the number of peasant pupils at middle school, and the curriculum is now more practical, more related to production and generally simplified. All these changes, together with the peasant associations' control of their own primary education, are calculated to bring the whole education system closer to the lives of the peasants. Those peasants who receive further courses in higher education will almost certainly return to the countryside and this, linked with a greater proportion of peasants receiving such education, will militate in the same direction. To the extent that the whole of Chinese society maintains its revolutionary orientation, the closer relationship between the educational system and the peasants, and the greater number of peasants receiving advanced education will serve the unity of town and country, but to the extent that the revolution faulters, the new impetus in peasant education could subserve polarisation, particularly as the old, rich, peasant families are likely to maintain their cultural advantage for some decades.

Most of our students at Zhongda left to spend a prolonged period in the countryside, as did their contemporaries all over China. Hundreds of thousands of those who took an active part in the Cultural Revolution will have left the towns to settle permanently in the villages, many in the remotest places where life is isolated, tough and simple. Because of their experience, and their high level of education and culture, they will play in relation to their numbers a disproportionately important role in the life of the villages where they settle. There will be those who through their own experiences and study will have gone dedicated to the revolutionary transformation of the countryside and qualified to serve this transformation technologically and socially; there will be others who will have gone reluctantly, with little understanding, and bitter feelings of disillusionment; most will have attitudes which lie between these extremes. Waves of Chinese youths have gone to the countryside from the towns and cities ever since 1919. They have all in various ways learnt from and, at the same time, taken education to the peasants, and fomented social change. This latest exodus will certainly be the most extensive, and most deeply penetrating. Its members will be at the centre of future developments in China's twenty-six thousand communes. It is idle to speculate on whether they will serve the revolution or serve a new class polarisation, for of necessity they may serve either, and to some degree, they will serve both, the balance will be determined not by them alone but by the total pattern of social development, in China and in the world.

China is still deeply under-developed. The vast areas of the interior are only beginning to build up their industry, commensurate to their enormous populations. The coming together of all the factors I have just discussed – the backwardness of the villages, the problem of the unity of workers and peasants; the remoulding of the cadres and their adherence to the revolutionary road; the transformation of education and culture in response to the establishment of a socialist economy, and the migration of large numbers of educated young people into the interior – can be seen in the pattern of Ta-Ching oil field. Old China, both the towns and cities, and the villages must move towards the integration of workers, peasants and cadres if China is to move forward to a communist society. But in human history, the transformation of old communities has always gone together with the building, from scratch, of new communities, in the new pattern. A necessary part of China's future is many thousands of Ta-Chings, where the three divisions between men – that between town and country, that between mental and manual work, that between those in authority and the masses – are rejected from the beginning.

During a visit to Canton in September 1972 Elsie saw some of our friends from Zhongda, and they told her of their experiences in a 'May Seventh' cadre school to which they had gone in November 1968 with a group of PLA men and some workers from a shipyard.

They went to a hill village in the north of the Province and stayed with the peasants until they had built themselves houses. They cleared land and cultivated it, and built a motor road for the peasants. They had political study groups with the workers and PLA men during which they studied works of Marx, Engels, Lenin and Mao Tse-tung, and they had study groups at which they discussed the problems of re-organising language teaching.

In August 1969, they moved to work in a tea-growing area of the Province where help was needed, and by the end of that year they had all returned to Zhongda.

The main Language department has now transferred to the Kwangtung Foreign Languages Institute, which was founded in 1965 and therefore has not the academic tradition of the university, and they are now all working on developing new language courses in which work in the countryside and in the factories are an integral part of the students' work.

Notes on Some Major Documents of the Cultural Revolution

The decisions of the Central Committee meeting issued on the 12th of August 1966 were outlined under sixteen headings. The directive came to be known as the 'Sixteen Points'. I summarise it here in relation to the following aspects: the immediate struggle within the leadership of the Party; the general aims of the movement; as a stage in socialist revolution; the particular tactics of the movement; and, finally, in relation to the general concept of social struggle as indicated in the works of Mao Tse-tung.

In the first point the focal aim of the movement is stated as, '. . . to overthrow those persons in authority who are taking the capitalist road . . .' In Point 5 this is made more specific in the phrase, 'those within the Party'. Here it is made clear that whatever else might arise in the movement – and it is stated in Point 2 that there would be twists and turns – the central issue was the inner-Party struggle, which was considered a matter of life and death for the socialist state. In Point 5, 'Firmly Apply the Class Line of the Party', both, 'ultra-reactionary bourgeois rightists and counter-revolutionary revisionists' are identified as the enemy. The former are such people as ex-capitalist factory managers, who still hate socialism, and old professors who arrogantly defended their scholarly privilege, boasted of their superior knowledge and culture and despised the new generation of worker and peasant students. The revisionists are leading cadres of the Communist Party who denied the dictatorship of the proletariat and were therefore engaged in the process of creating 'a Party of the whole people' and 'a State of the whole people', in which the still existing stratification of Chinese society was being strengthened and perpetuated, and within which context they, the revisionists, could find common ground with the rightists in stabilising a bureaucratic and hierarchic State after the pattern of the Soviet Union. Both rightists and revisionists are the enemy, but it is the revisionists in the topmost leadership of the Party, and their hold on the Party organisation through the Party Secretariat, which is the main target.

The general aims of the movement were summarised in three

tasks: the first is that stated in the previous paragraph; the second and third are to '. . . criticise and refute the reactionary bourgeois academic authorities and the ideology of the bourgeoisie and all other exploiting classes . . . transform education, literature and art and all other parts of the superstructure not in correspondence with the socialist economic base, so as to facilitate the consolidation and development of the socialist system.' The criticism was to be directed at professional élitism, bourgeois individualism and the ethics of private property and individual betterment. But, here again, the focus was to be on revisionism. When the process of criticism became methodically developed in mid-1967, it was done in terms of policies identified with particular leading members of the Party and, specifically Liu Shao-chi. The transformation was towards an education and culture fashioned to the needs and potentialities of the ordinary workers, peasants and soldiers, and involving them in its creation and management. In the case of education, some of the requirements were spelled out in Point 10, 'Educational Reform': 'The period of schooling to be shortened. Courses should be fewer and better. The teaching material should be thoroughly reformed, in some cases beginning with simplifying complicated material.' And, to weaken the academic tradition further, '. . . in addition to their studies they (the students) should also learn industrial work, farming and military affairs, and take part in the struggles of the cultural revolution to criticise the bourgeoisie . . .' The three aims were later referred to by the three Chinese characters and words, 'dou-pi-gai' meaning, 'struggle-criticism-transformation'. This was later given a further dimension when it became understood that in the three years starting in mid-1966, the first would emphasise struggle, the second criticism and the third -transformation. Whereas the bourgeois elements are attributed with still possessing ideological strength, it is within the Party leadership that the centre of this struggle for political power is seen to be.

Under the heading of, 'Cultural Revolutionary Groups, Committees and Congresses', it is recognised that there is a need for new democratic organisations which will act as a bridge between the Party and the masses. Later, the mass organisations of the Cultural Revolution became so polarised into the Rebel and Conservative sides all over the country and in all sections of the masses, that it became clear that they could not develop directly into a unifying national institution. Their role of bridge between Party and masses became expressed in the revolutionary committees, which evolved out of the struggle for power in early 1967.

During the stage of 'struggle' to overthrow the capitalist roaders, the emphasis was on the initiative of the students of the schools and colleges, and Point 7 states their right to struggle and criticise, without being interfered with, unless they commit crimes. The importance of the part to be played by youth is also emphasised in Point 2, however, here it also states that the main forces in the Cultural Revolution are, 'the workers, peasants, soldiers, revolutionary intellectuals and revolutionary cadres', thus indicating that the movement must eventually

228

involve the whole people, and inferring the traditional view of Mao Tse-tung that youth is normally the vanguard in revolutionary struggles, but can achieve nothing in the final analysis unless it merges its aims and struggles with those of the worker and peasant masses.

The central role of the students in the movement can be understood in different ways. Most importantly it was recognised that they constituted the future of the revolution, and thus if they did not rid their minds of revisionist ideas, and their lives of privileged and élitist habits and customs, they would later betray the revolution. Again, the students came from all sections of the people, they did not embody the vested interests of a particular section exclusively. The workers and peasants lacked the mobility of the students, or the soldiers, or if they had been so mobilised it would have crippled production. If the army had spearheaded the movement then the population would not have been involved in the endless meetings, quarrels and debates that were the very substance of the movement. Revisionist leaders might have been removed from their positions, but physical force would have inhibited the vital struggle, that which took place in the peoples' minds.

The following ideas which infuse the 'Sixteen Points' are fundamental to Mao Tse-tung's general concept of social struggle. The first of these is that all revolutionary struggle is a struggle for the liberation of the masses of the people, and only the people themselves can wage this struggle – they must liberate themselves. The second is that all mass movements must involve physical and cultural progress for the people, or they will not become fully involved, or they will quickly become disillusioned. (Even in the poverty-stricken areas of North-West China during the anti-Japanese war, the Party and Red Army constantly aimed to improve the conditions of livelihood of the peasants and, as was emphasised in the introductory chapters of this book, this concept was brought to bare anew with each campaign after Liberation.) The third, and most strongly emphasised idea, was that the first requirement of leadership in social revolution is faith in the masses and the courage to rouse them to struggle. In Point 6, 'Correctly Handle Contradictions Among the People', we find, 'In the course of debate, every revolutionary should be good at thinking things out for himself and should develop the communist spirit of daring to think, daring to speak and daring to act.' The final idea, I would emphasise, is introduced in Point 5 with the words, 'Who are our enemies? Who are our friends? This is a question of the first importance for the revolution . . .' with which Mao Tse-tung began his report in 1926, 'Analysis of the Classes in Chinese Society'. The conclusion is that if this question is correctly handled then ninety-five per cent of the people and ninety-five per cent of the cadres can be united with – the enemy reduced to 'a handful'. This idea is at the very heart of Mao Tse-tung's view of socialist society. Once the economic base of socialism is realised then all sections of the people can benefit as society develops. There will continually be new polarisations and class struggles, but as each of these new contradictions is resolved, the overwhelming majority of all sections of the people can be united for periods of relative stability and consolidation, in which there will be rapid economic and cultural development. It is partly for this reason that once the struggle for power is won, the subsequent campaign of criticism is focused on the smallest possible number of representative revisionists and rightists.

Finally, Point 16 states that Mao Tse-tung's thought is the overall guide to the movement. An essential aspect of the movemen was that, as it developed, conflicting views and sectional interests more and more came to be argued out and expressed in terms of the concepts and terminology of Mao Tse-tung's writings, and hence in terms of and related to the collective interest, revolutionary theory and social change, and the rejection of the concepts of bourgeois individualism and traditional Chinese dogma. Five works of Mao Tse-tung are recommended for special and repeated study by all Party committees:

On New Democracy (1940). This depicts pre-Liberation China and considers the Chinese revolution in the context of world revolution and, in particular, outlines the course of the Cultural Revolution in terms of the united front of the Chinese Communist Party with other sections of China's intellectuals, from the 'May 4th' movement of 1919 up to 1940.

On Correct Handling of Contradictions Among the People (1957), asserts that in a socialist society there are still class contradictions, which are of two fundamentally different kinds, those between the people and their enemies – which can only be resolved by struggle – and those among the people – which should be resolved through discussion, criticism and self-criticism. The point is emphasised that the latter, if not dealt with properly and in good time, may develop into antagonistic contradictions, whilst the former, if handled correctly, may be transformed into non-antagonistic contradictions.

Talks at the Yenan Forum on Literature and Art (1942), asserts the need for creative work to be subordinated to the revolution and the service of the workers, soldiers and peasants, and the need for the intellectuals to live and work among the people so as to develop the workers' class standpoint and rid themselves of their individualist élitist standpoint.

Speech at the Communist Party's National Conference on Propaganda Work (1957), emphasises the importance of the mass line and analyses its content and heralds the impending rectification movement which was aimed at the 'three evils' of bureaucracy, subjectivism and sectarianism.

Some Questions Concerning Methods of Leadership, discusses the need to combine the general with the particular. It indicates the method of solving general problems by first concentrating on limited particular problems, which by their solution will throw up a general solution. Closely related to this is the need for the formation of leading groups of Party members and other activists, drawn from amongst those who are intimately involved in the particular problems to be solved. Finally, this decision of the Party Central Committee asserts the importance of identifying the central problem in a given situation, and concentrating all available forces for its solution.

The 'Sixteen Points' is a Party directive and hence this reading list for Party committee members. However, it was also taken as a general guide by all those taking an active part in the movement, so these texts were read and studied by millions of rank-and-file Party members and non-Party activists. There were also two other groups of texts which were even more widely studied: the 'Three Old Articles', that is, *Serve the People, The Foolish Old Man who removed the Mountains* and *in Memory of Norman Bethune,* which were read, recited and quoted by the whole population down to young children; and the 'Five Must Read Articles', which consisted of the three just mentioned with the addition of, *On Correcting Mistaken Ideas in the Party* and *Combat Liberalism,* (included in this work as an appendix) and the *Little Red Book of Quotations* which most people came to carry about with them and quoted from at every meeting. Among other works of Mao Tse-tung which were widely studied during the movement are his two basic philosophical essays, *On Practice* and *On Contradiction,* and five short comments on literature and art made in the years 1944, 1951, 1954 and 1963, at which times the struggle in the cultural field was intense. The first of the five congratulates the Yenan Peking Opera Company for having created and performed a revolutionary work that is based on the idea that history is made by the people. The other four criticise leading Party intellectuals for failing to criticise the old culture and failing to assist in the creation of a new socialist culture.

The five longer articles are historical and theoretical groundwork for understanding and developing the Cultural Revolution. The 'Three Old Articles' convey the essence of the proletarian ethics required in a backward, yet revolutionary, society in the context of imperialism and world revolution.

Appendix I 'The Sixteen Points'

1 A new stage in the socialist revolution

The Great Proletarian Cultural Revolution now unfolding is a great revolution that touches people to their very souls and constitutes a new stage in the development of the socialist revolution in our country, a stage which is both broader and deeper.

At the Tenth Plenary Session of the Eighth Central Committee of the Party, Comrade Mao Tse-tung said: 'To overthrow a political power, it is always necessary first of all to create public opinion, to do work in the ideological sphere. This is true for the revolutionary class as well as for the counter-revolutionary class.' This thesis of Comrade Mao Tse-tung's has been proved entirely correct in practice.

Although the bourgeoisie has been overthrown, it is still trying to use the old ideas, culture, customs and habits of the exploiting classes to corrupt the masses, capture their minds and endeavour to stage a come-back. The proletariat must do the exact opposite: it must meet head-on every challenge of the bourgeoisie in the idealogical field and use the new ideas, culture, customs and habits of the proletariat to change the mental outlook of the whole of society. At present, our objective is to struggle against and overthrow those persons in authority who are taking the capitalist road, to criticise and repudiate the reactionary bourgeois academic 'authorities' and the ideology of the bourgeois and all other exploiting classes and to transform education, literature and art and all other parts of the superstructure not in correspondence with the socialist economic base, so as to facilitate the consolidation and development of the socialist system.

2 The main current and the twists and turns

The masses of the workers, peasants, soldiers, revolutionary intellectuals and revolutionary cadres from the main force in this great Cultural Revolution. Large numbers of revolutionary young people, previously unknown, have become courageous and daring pathbreakers. They are vigorous in action and intelligent. Through the media of big-character posters and great debates, they argue things out, expose and criticise thoroughly, and launch resolute attacks on the open and hidden representative of the bourgeoisie. In such a great revolutionary movement, it is hardly avoidable that they should show shortcomings of one kind or another; however, their general revolutionary orientation has been correct from the beginning. This is the main current in the Great Proletarian Cultural Revolution. It is the general direction along which this revolution continues to advance.

Since the Cultural Revolution is a revolution, it inevitably meets with resistance. This resistance comes chiefly from those in authority who have wormed their way into the Party and are taking the capitalist road. It also comes from the force of habits from the old society. At present, this resistance is still fairly strong and stubborn. But after all, the Great Proletarian Cultural Revolution is an irresistible general trend. There is abundant evidence that such resistance will be quickly broken down once the masses become fully aroused.

Because the resistance is fairly strong, there will be reversals in this. It tempers the proletariat and other working people, and especially the younger generation, teaches them lessons and gives them experience, and helps them to understand that the revolutionary road zigzags and does not run smoothly.

3 Put daring above everything else and boldly arouse the masses

The outcome of this great Cultural Revolution will be determined by whether or not the Party leadership dares boldly to arouse the masses.

Currently, there are four different situations with regards to the leadership being given to the movement of Cultural Revolution by Party organisations at various levels:

(1) There is the situation in which the persons in charge of Party organisations stand in the van of the movement and dare to arouse the masses boldly. They put daring above everything else, they are dauntless communist fighters and good pupils of Chairman Mao. They advocate the big-character posters and great debates. They encourage the masses to expose every kind of ghost and monster and also to criticise the shortcomings and errors in the work of the persons in charge. This correct kind of leadership is the result of putting proletarian politics in the forefront and Mao Tse-tung's thought in the lead.

(2) In many units, the persons in charge have a very poor understanding of the task of leadership in this great struggle, their leadership is far from being conscientious and effective, and they accordingly find themselves incompetent and in a weak position. They put fear above everything else, stick to outmoded ways and regulations, and are unwilling to break away from conventional practices and move ahead. They have been taken unawares by the new order of things, the revolutionary order of the masses, with the result that their leadership lags behind the situation, lags behind the masses.

(3) In some units, the persons in charge, who made mistakes

of one kind or another in the past, are even more prone to put fear above everything else, being afraid that the masses will catch them out. Actually, if they make serious self-criticism and accept the criticism of the masses, the Party and the masses will make allowances for their mistakes. But if the persons in charge don't, they will continue to make mistakes and become obstacles to the mass movement.

(4) Some units are controlled by those who have wormed their way into the Party and are taking the capitalist road. Such persons in authority are extremely afraid of being exposed by the masses and therefore seek every possible pretext to suppress the mass movement. They resort to such tactics as shifting the targets for attack and turning black into white in an attempt to lead the movement astray. When they find themselves very isolated and no longer able to carry on as before, they resort still more to intrigues, stabbing people in the back, spreading rumours, and blurring the distinction between revolution and counter-revolution as much as they can, all for the purpose of attacking the revolutionaries.

What the Central Committee of the Party demands of the Party committees at all levels is that they persevere in giving correct leadership, put daring above everything else, boldly arouse the masses, change the state of weakness and incompetence where it exists, encourage those comrades who have made mistakes but are willing to correct them to cast off their mental burdens and join in the struggle, and dismiss from their leading posts all those in authority who are taking the capitalist road and so make possible the recapture of the leadership for the proletarian revolutionaries.

4 Let the masses educate themselves in the movement

In the Great Proletarian Cultural Revolution, the only method is for the masses to liberate themselves, and any method of doing things in their stead must not be used.

Trust the masses, rely on them and respect their initiative. Cast out fear. Don't be afraid of disturbances. Chairman Mao has often told us that revolution cannot be so very refined, so gentle, so temperate, kind, courteous, restrained and magnanimous. Let the masses educate themselves in this great revolutionary movement and learn to distinguish between right and wrong and between correct and incorrect ways of doing things.

Make the fullest use of big-character posters and great debates to argue matters out, so that the masses can clarify the correct views, criticise the wrong views and expose all the ghosts and monsters. In this way the masses will be able to raise their political consciousness in the course of the struggle, enhance their abilities and talents, distinguish right from wrong and draw a clear line between ourselves and the enemy.

5 Firmly apply the class line of the Party

Who are our enemies? Who are our friends? This is a question of the first importance for the revolution and it is likewise a question of the first importance for the great Cultural Revolution.

Party leadership should be good at discovering the left and developing and strengthening the ranks of the left; it should firmly rely on the revolutionary left. During the movement this is the only way to isolate the most reactionary rightists thoroughly, win over the middle and unite with the great majority so that by the end of the movement we shall achieve the unity of more than ninety-five per cent of the cadres and more than ninety-five per cent of the masses.

Concentrate all forces to strike at the handful of ultra-reactionary bourgeois rightists and counter-revolutionary revisionists, and expose and criticise to the full their crimes against the Party, against socialism and against Mao Tse-tung's thought so as to isolate them to the maximum.

The main target of the present movement is those within the Party who are in authority and are taking the capitalist road.

The strictest care should be taken to distinguish between the anti-Party, anti-socialist rightist and those who support the Party and socialism but have said or done something wrong or have written some bad articles or other works.

The strictest care should be taken to distinguish between the reactionary bourgeois scholar despots and 'authorities' on the one hand and people who have the ordinary bourgeois academic ideas on the other.

6 Correctly handle contradictions among the people

A strict distinction must be made between the two different types of contradictions: those among the people and those between ourselves and the enemy. Contradictions among the people must not be made into contradictions between ourselves and the enemy; nor must contradictions between ourselves and the enemy be regarded as contradictions among the people.

It is normal for the masses to hold different views. Contention between different views is unavoidable, necessary and beneficial. In the course of normal and full debate, the masses will affirm what is right, correct what is wrong and gradually reach unanimity.

The method to be used in debates is to present the facts, reason things out, and persuade through reasoning. Any method of forcing a minority holding different views to submit is impermissible. The minority should be protected, because sometimes the truth is with the minority. Even if the minority is wrong, they should still be allowed to argue their case and reserve their views.

When there is a debate, it should be conducted by reasoning, not by coercion or force.

In the course of debate, every revolutionary should be good at thinking things out for himself and should develop the communist spirit of daring to think, daring to speak and daring to act. On the premise that they have the same general orientation, revolutionary comrades should, for the sake of strengthening unity, avoid endless debate over side issues.

7 Be on guard against those who brand the revolutionary masses as counter-revolutionaries

In certain schools, units, and work teams of the Cultural Revolution, some of the persons in charge have organised counter-attacks against the masses who put up big-character posters criticising them. These people have even advanced such slogans as: opposition to the leaders of a unit or a work team means opposition to the Central Committee of the Party, means opposition to the Party and socialism, means counter-revolution. In this way it is inevitable that their blows will fall on some really revolutionary activists. This is an error on matters of orientation, an error of line, and is absolutely impermissible.

A number of persons who suffer from serious ideological errors, and particularly some of the anti-Party and anti-socialist rightists, are taking advantage of certain shortcomings and mistakes in the mass movement to spread rumours and gossip, and engage in agitation, deliberately branding some of the masses as 'counter-revolutionaries'. It is necessary to beware of such 'pick-pockets' and expose their tricks in good time.

In the course of the movement, with the exception of cases of active counter-revolutionaries where there is clear evidence of crimes such as murder, arson, poisoning, sabotage or theft of state secrets, which should be handled in accordance with the law, no measures should be taken against students at universities, colleges, middle schools and primary schools because of problems that arise in the movement. To prevent the struggle from being diverted from its main target, it is not allowed, under whatever pretext, to incite the masses or the students to struggle against each other. Even proven rightists should be dealt with on the merits of each case at a later stage of the movement.

8 The question of cadres

The cadres fall roughly into the following four categories:
  (1) good;
  (2) comparatively good;
  (3) those who have made serious mistakes but have not become anti-Party, anti-socialist rightists;
  (4) the small number of anti-Party, anti-socialist rightists.

In ordinary situations, the first two categories (good and comparatively good) are the great majority.

The anti-Party, anti-socialist rightists must be fully exposed, refuted, overthrown and completely discredited and their influence eliminated. At the same time, they should be given a chance to turn over a new leaf.

9 Cultural revolutionary groups, committees and congresses

Many new things have begun to emerge in the Great Proletarian Cultural Revolution. The cultural revolutionary groups, committees and other organisational forms created by the masses in many schools and units are something new and of great historic importance.

236

These cultural revolutionary groups, committees and congresses are excellent new forms of organisation whereby the masses educate themselves under the leadership of the Communist Party. They are an excellent bridge to keep our Party in close contact with the masses. They are organs of power of the Proletarian Cultural Revolution.

The struggle of the proletariat against the old ideas, culture, customs and habits left over by all the exploiting classes over thousands of years will necessarily take a very, very long time. Therefore, the cultural revolutionary groups, committees and congresses should not be temporary organisations but permanent, standing mass organisations. They are suitable not only for colleges, schools and government and other organisations, but generally also for factories, mines, other enterprises, urban districts and villages.

It is necessary to institute a system of general elections, like that of the Paris Commune, for electing members to the cultural revolutionary groups and committees and delegates to the cultural revolutionary congresses. The lists of candidates should be put forward by the revolutionary masses after full discussion, and the elections should be held after the masses have discussed the lists over and over again.

The masses are entitled at any time to criticise members of the cultural revolutionary groups and committees and delegates elected to the cultural revolutionary congresses. If these members or delegates prove incompetent, they can be replaced through election or recalled by the masses after discussion.

The cultural revolutionary groups, committees and congresses in colleges and schools should consist mainly of representatives of the revolutionary students. At the same time, they should have a certain number of representatives of the revolutionary teaching and administrative staff and workers.

10 Educational reform

In the Great Proletarian Cultural Revolution a most important task is to transform the old educational system and the old principles and methods of teaching.

In this great Cultural Revolution, the phenomenon of our schools being dominated by bourgeois intellectuals must be completely changed.

In every kind of school we must apply thoroughly the policy advanced by Comrade Mao Tse-tung of education serving proletarian politics and education being combined with productive labour, so as to enable those receiving an education to develop morally, intellectually and physically and to become labourers with socialist consciousness and culture.

The period of schooling should be shortened. Courses should be fewer and better. The teaching material should be thoroughly transformed, in some cases beginning with simplifying complicated material. While their main task is to study, students should also learn other things. That is to say, in addition to their studies they should also learn industrial work, farming and military affairs, and take part in the struggles of the Cultural

Revolution to criticise the bourgeoisie as these struggles occur.

11 The question of criticising by name in the press

In the course of the mass movement of the Cultural Revolution, the criticism of bourgeois and feudal ideology should be well combined with the dissemination of the proletarian world outlook and of Marxism-Leninism, Mao Tse-tung's thought.

Criticism should be organised of typical bourgeois representatives who have wormed their way into the Party and typical reactionary bourgeois academic 'authorities', and this should include criticism of various kinds of reactionary views in philosophy, history, political economy and education, in works and theories of literature and art, in theories of natural science, and in other fields.

Criticism of anyone by name in the press should be decided after discussion by the Party committee at the same level, and in some cases submitted to the Party committee at a higher level for approval.

12 Policy towards scientists, technicians and ordinary members of working staffs

As regards scientists, technicians and ordinary members of working staffs, as long as they are patriotic, work energetically, are not against the Party and socialism, and maintain no illicit relations with any foreign country, we should in the present movement continue to apply the policy of 'unity-criticism-unity'. Special care should be taken of those scientists and scientific and technical personnel who have made contributions. Efforts should be made to help them gradually transform their world outlook and their style of work.

13 The question of arrangements for integration with the Socialist Education Movement in city and countryside

The cultural and educational units and leading organs of the Party and government in the large and medium cities are the points of concentration of the present Proletarian Cultural Revolution.

The great Cultural Revolution has enriched the Socialist Education Movement in both city and countryside and raised it to a higher level. Efforts should be made to conduct these two movements in close combination. Arrangements to this effect may be made by various regions and departments in the light of the specific conditions.

The Socialist Education Movement now going on in the countryside and in enterprises in the cities should not be upset where the original arrangements are appropriate and the movement is going well, but should continue in accordance with the original arrangements. However, the questions that are arising in the present Great Proletarian Cultural Revolution should be put to the masses for discussion at the proper time, so as to further foster vigorously proletarian ideology and eradicate bourgeois ideology.

In some places, the Great Proletarian Cultural Revolution is being used as the focus in order to add momentum to the Socialist Education Movement and clean things up in the fields of politics, ideology, organisation and economy. This may be done where the local Party Committee thinks it appropriate.

14 Take firm hold of the revolution and stimulate production

The aim of the Great Proletarian Cultural Revolution is to revolutionise people's ideology and as a consequence to achieve greater, faster, better and more economical results in all fields of work. If the masses are fully aroused and proper arrangements are made, it is possible to carry on both the Cultural Revolution and production without one hampering the other, while guaranteeing high quality in all our work.

The Great Proletarian Cultural Revolution is a powerful motive force for the development of the social productive forces in our country. Any ideas of counterposing the great Cultural Revolution to the development of production is incorrect.

15 The armed forces

In the armed forces, the Cultural Revolution and the Socialist Education Movement should be carried out in accordance with the instructions of the Military Commission of the Central Committee of the Party and the General Political Department of the People's Liberation Army.

16 Mao Tse-tung's thought is the guide to action in the Great Proletarian Cultural Revolution

In the Great Proletarian Cultural Revolution, it is imperative to hold aloft the great red banner of Mao Tse-tung's thought and put proletarian politics in command. The movement for the creative study and application of Chairman Mao Tse-tung's works should be carried forward among the masses of the workers, peasants and soldiers, the cadres and the intellectuals, and Mao Tse-tung's thought should be taken as the guide to action in the Cultural Revolution.

In this complex great Cultural Revolution, Party committees at all levels must study and apply Chairman Mao's works all the more conscientiously and in a creative way. In particular, they must study over and over again Chairman Mao's writings on the Cultural Revolution and on the Party's methods of leadership, such as *On New Democracy, Talks at the Yenan Forum on Literature and Art, On the Correct Handling of Contradictions Among the People, Speech at the Chinese Communist Party's National Conference on Propaganda Work, Some Questions Concerning Methods of Leadership* and *Methods of Work of Party Committees.*

Party committees at all levels must abide by the directions given by Chairman Mao over the years, namely that they should thoroughly apply the mass line of 'from the masses, to the masses' and that they should be pupils before they become teachers. They should try to avoid being one-sided or narrow. They should foster materialist dialectics and oppose metaphysics and scholasticism.

The Great Proletarian Cultural Revolution is bound to achieve brilliant victory under the leadership of the Central Committee of the Party headed by Comrade Mao Tse-tung.

Appendix II Five Articles by Chairman Mao Tse-tung

Serve the People
(September 8th, 1944)

Our Communist Party and the Eighth Route and New Fourth Armies led by our Party are battalions of the revolution. These battalions of ours are wholly dedicated to the liberation of the people and work entirely in the people's interests. Comrade Chang Szu-teh was in the ranks of these battalions.

All men must die, but death can vary in its significance. The ancient Chinese writer Szuma Chien said, 'Though death befalls all men alike, it may be weightier than Mount Tai or lighter than a feather.' To die for the people is weightier than Mount Tai, but to work for the fascists and die for the exploiters and oppressors is lighter than a feather. Comrade Chang Szu-teh died for the people, and his death is indeed weightier than Mount Tai.

If we have shortcomings, we are not afraid to have them pointed out and criticised, because we serve the people. Anyone, no matter who, may point out our shortcomings. If he is right, we will correct them. If what he proposes will benefit the people, we will act upon it. The idea of 'better troops and simpler administration' was put forward by Mr Li Ting-ming, who is not a communist. He made a good suggestion which is of benefit to the people, and we have adopted it. If, in the interests of the people, we persist in doing what is right and correct what is wrong, our ranks will surely thrive.

We hail from all corners of the country and have joined together for a common revolutionary objective. And we need the vast majority of the people with us on the road to this objective. Today, we already lead base areas with a population of 91 million, but this is not enough ; to liberate the whole nation more are needed. In times of difficulty we must not lose sight of our achievements, must see the bright future and must pluck up our courage. The Chinese people are suffering; it is our duty to save them and we must exert ourselves in struggle. Wherever there is struggle there is sacrifice, and death is a common occurrence. But we have the interests of the people and the sufferings of the great majority at heart, and when we die for the people it is a worthy death. Nevertheless, we should do our best to avoid unnecessary sacrifices. Our cadres must show concern for every soldier, and all people in the revolutionary ranks must care for each other, must love and help each other.

From now on, when anyone in our ranks who has done some useful work dies, be he soldier or cook, we should have a funeral ceremony and a memorial meeting in his honour. This should become the rule. And it should be introduced among the people as well. When someone dies in a village, let a memorial meeting be held. In this way we express our mourning for the dead and unite all the people.

In memory of Norman Bethune
(December 21st, 1939)

Comrade Norman Bethune, a member of the Communist Party of Canada, was around fifty when he was sent by the Communist Parties of Canada and the United States to China; he made light of travelling thousands of miles to help us in our War of Resistance against Japan. He arrived in Yenan in the spring of last year, went to work in the Wutai Mountains, and to our great sorrow died a martyr at his post. What kind of spirit is this that makes a foreigner selflessly adopt the cause of the Chinese people's liberation as his own? It is the spirit of internationalism, the spirit of communism, from which every Chinese communist must learn. Leninism teaches that the world revolution can only succeed if the proletariat of the capitalist countries supports the struggle for liberation of the colonial and semi-colonial peoples and if the proletariat of the colonies and semi-colonies supports that of the proletariat of the capitalist countries. Comrade Bethune put this Leninist line into practice. We Chinese communists must also follow this line in our practice. We must unite with the proletariat of all the capitalist countries, with the proletariat of Japan, Britain, the United States, Germany, Italy and all other capitalist countries, before it is possible to overthrow imperialism, to liberate our nation and people, and to liberate the other nations and peoples of the world. This is our internationalism, the internationalism with which we oppose both narrow nationalism and narrow patriotism.

242

Comrade Bethune's spirit, his utter devotion to others without any thought of self, was shown in his boundless sense of responsibility in his work and his boundless warmheartedness towards all comrades and the people. Every communist must learn from him. There are not a few people who are irresponsible in their work, preferring the light to the heavy, shoving the heavy loads on to others and choosing the easy ones for themselves. At every turn they think of themselves before others. When they make some small contribution, they swell with pride and brag about it for fear that others will not know. They feel no warmth towards comrades and the people but are cold, indifferent and apathetic. In fact such people are not communists, or at least cannot be counted as true communists. No one who returned from the front failed to express admiration for Bethune whenever his name was mentioned, and none remained unmoved by his spirit. In the Shansi-Chahar-Hopei border area, no soldier or civilian was unmoved who had been treated by Dr Bethune or had seen how he worked. Every communist must learn this true communist spirit from comrade Bethune.

Comrade Bethune was a doctor, the art of healing was his profession and he was constantly perfecting his skill, which stood very high in the Eighth Route Army's medical service. His example is an excellent lesson for those people who wish to change their work for the moment they see something different and for those who despise technical work as of no consequence or as promising no future.

Comrade Bethune and I met only once. Afterwards he wrote me many letters. But I was busy, and I wrote him only one letter and do not even know if he ever received it. I am deeply grieved over his death. Now we are all commemorating him, which shows how profoundly his spirit inspires everyone. We must all learn the spirit of absolute selflessness from him. With this spirit everyone can be very useful to the people. A man's ability may be great or small, but if he has this spirit, he is already noble-minded and pure, a man of moral integrity and above vulgar interests, a man who is of value to the people.

The Foolish Old Man who removed the Mountains
(June 11th, 1945)

We have had a very successful congress. We have done three things. First, we have decided on the line of our Party, which is boldly to mobilise the masses and expand the people's forces so that, under the leadership of our Party, they will defeat the Japanese aggressors, liberate the whole people and build a new-democratic China. Second, we have adopted the new Party constitution. Third, we have elected the leading body of the Party – the Central Committee. Henceforth our task is to lead the whole membership in carrying out the Party line. Ours has been a congress of victory, a congress of unity. The delegates have made excellent comments on the three reports. Many comrades have undertaken self-criticism ; with unity as the objective unity has been achieved through self-criticism. This congress is a model of unity, of self-criticism and of inner-Party democracy.

When the congress closes, many comrades will be leaving for their posts and the various war fronts. Comrades, wherever you go, you should propagate the line of the congress and, through the members of the Party, explain it to the broad masses.

Our aim in propagating the line of the congress is to build up the confidence of the whole Party and the entire people in the certain triumph of the revolution. We must first raise the political consciousness of the vanguard so that, resolute and unafraid of sacrifice, they will surmount every difficulty to win victory. But this is not enough ; we must also arouse the political consciousness of the entire people so that they may willingly and gladly fight together with us for victory. We should fire the whole people with the conviction that China belongs not to the reactionaries but to the Chinese people. There is an ancient Chinese fable called 'The Foolish Old Man who removed the Mountains'. It tells of an old man who lived in northern China long, long ago and was known as the 'Foolish Old Man of North Mountain'. His house faced south and beyond his doorway stood the two great peaks, Taihang and Wangwu, obstructing the way. With great determination, he led his sons in digging up these mountains hoe in hand. Another greybeard, known as the 'Wise Old Man', saw them and said derisively, 'How silly of you to do this! It is quite impossible for you few to dig up these two huge mountains.' The Foolish Old Man replied, 'When I die, my sons will carry on ; when they die, there will be my grandsons, and then their sons, and grandsons, and so on to infinity. High as they are, the mountains cannot grow any higher and with every bit we dig, they will be that much lower. Why can't we clear them away?' Having refuted the Wise Old Man's wrong view, he went on digging every day, unshaken in his conviction. God was moved by this, and he sent down two angels, who carried the mountains away on their backs. Today, two big mountains lie like a dead weight on the Chinese people. One is imperialism, the other is feudalism. The Chinese Communist Party has long made up its mind to dig them up. We must persevere and work unceasingly, and we, too, will touch God's heart. Our god is none other than the masses of the Chinese people. If they stand up and dig together with us, why can't these two mountains be cleared away?

Yesterday, in a talk with two Americans who were leaving for the United States, I said that thhe US Government was trying to undermine us and this would not be permitted. We oppose the US Government's policy of supporting Chiang Kai-shek against the communists. But we must draw a distinction, firstly, between the people of the United States and their government and, secondly, within the US Government between the policy-makers and their subordinates. I said to these two Americans, 'Tell the policy-makers in your government that we forbid you Americans to enter the Liberated Areas because your policy is to support Chiang Kai-shek against the communists, and we have to be on our guard. You can come to the Liberated Areas if your purpose is to fight Japan, but there must first be an agreement. We will not permit you to nose around everywhere. Since Patrick J. Hurley has publicly declared against co-operation with the Chinese Communist Party, why do you still want to come and prowl around in our Liberated Areas?'

The US Government's policy of supporting Chiang Kai-shek against the communists shows the brazenness of the US reactionaries. But all the scheming of the reactionaries, whether Chinese or foreign, to prevent the Chinese people from achieving victory is doomed to failure. The democratic forces are the main current in the world today, while reaction is only a counter-current. The reactionary counter-current is trying to swamp the main current of national-independence and people's democracy, but it can never become the main current. Today, there are still three major contradictions in the old world, as Stalin pointed out long ago: first, the contradiction between the proletariat and the bourgeoisie in the imperialist countries; second, the contradiction between the various imperialist powers; and third, the contradiction between the colonial and semi-colonial countries and the imperialist metropolitan countries. Not only do these three contradictions continue to exist but they are becoming more acute and widespread. Because of their existence and growth, the time will come when the reactionary anti-soviet, anti-communist and anti-democratic counter-current still in existence today will be swept away.

At this moment two congresses are being held in China, the Sixth National Congress of the Kuomintang and the Seventh National Congress of the Communist Party. They have completely different aims: the aim of one is to liquidate the Communist Party and all the other democratic forces in China and thus to plunge China into darkness; the aim of the other is to overthrow Japanese imperialism and its lackeys, the Chinese feudal forces, and build a new-democratic China and thus to lead China to light. These two lines are in conflict with each other. We firmly believe that, led by the Chinese Communist Party and guided by the line of its Seventh Congress, the Chinese people will achieve complete victory, while the Kuomintang's counter-revolutionary line will inevitably fail.

On Correcting Mistaken Ideas in the Party
(December 1929)

There are various non-proletarian ideas in the Communist Party organisation in the Fourth Red Army which greatly hinder the application of the Party's correct line. Unless these ideas are thoroughly corrected, the Fourth Army cannot possibly shoulder the tasks assigned to it in China's great revolutionary struggle. The source of such incorrect ideas in this Party organisation lies, of course, in the fact that its basic units are composed largely of peasants and other elements of petit-bourgeois origin; yet the inadequacy of the Party's leading bodies in waging a concerted and determined struggle against these incorrect ideas and in educating the members in the Party's correct line is also an important cause of their existence and growth. In accordance with the spirit of the September letter of the Central Committee, this congress hereby points out the manifestations of various non-proletarian ideas in the Party organisation in the Fourth Army, their sources, and the methods of correcting them, and calls upon all comrades to eliminate them thoroughly.

On the purely military viewpoint

The purely military viewpoint is very highly developed among a number of comrades in the Red Army. It manifests itself as follows:

(1) These comrades regard military affairs and politics as opposed to each other and refuse to recognise that military affairs are only one means of accomplishing political tasks. Some even say, 'If you are good militarily, naturally you are good politically; if you are not good militarily, you cannot be any good politically' – this is to go a step further and give military affairs a leading position over politics.

(2) They think that the task of the Red Army, like that of the White Army, is merely to fight. They do not understand that the Chinese Red Army is an armed body for carrying out the political tasks of the revolution. Especially at present, the Red Army should certainly not confine itself to fighting; besides fighting to destroy the enemy's military strength, it should shoulder such important tasks as doing propaganda among the masses, organising the masses, arming them, helping them to establish revolutionary political power and setting up Party organisations. The Red Army fights not merely for the sake of fighting but in order to conduct propaganda among the masses,

organise them, arm them, and help them to establish revolutionary political power. Without these objectives fighting loses its meaning and the Red Army loses the reason for its existence.

(3) Hence, organisationally, these comrades subordinate the departments of the Red Army doing political work to those doing military work, and put forward the slogan, 'Let Army Headquarters handle outside matters'. If allowed to develop this idea would involve the danger of estrangement from the masses, control of the government by the army and departure from proletarian leadership – it would be to take the path of warlordism like the Kuomintang army.

(4) At the same time, in propaganda work they overlook the importance of propaganda teams. On the question of mass organisation, they neglect the organising of soldiers' committees in the army and the organising of the local workers and peasants. As a result, both propaganda and organisational work are abandoned.

(5) They become conceited when a battle is won and dispirited when a battle is lost.

(6) Selfish departmentalism – they think only of the Fourth Army and do not realise that it is an important task of the Red Army to arm the local masses. This is the 'small group mentality' in a magnified form.

(7) Unable to see beyond their limited environment in the Fourth Army, a few comrades believe that no other revolutionary forces exist. Hence their extreme addiction to the idea of conserving strength and avoiding action. This is a remnant of opportunism.

(8) Some comrades, disregarding the subjective and objective conditions, suffer from the malady of revolutionary impetuosity; they will not take pains to do minute and detailed work among the masses, but, riddled with illusions, want only to do big things. This is a remnant of putschism.

The sources of the purely military viewpoint are:

(1) A low political level. From this flows the failure to recognise the role of political leadership in the army and to recognise that the Red Army and the White Army are fundamentally different.

(2) The mentality of mercenaries. Many prisoners captured in past battles have joined the Red Army, and such elements bring with them a markedly mercenary outlook, thereby providing a basis in the lower ranks for the purely military viewpoint.

(3) From the two preceding causes there arises a third, overconfidence in military strength and absence of confidence in the strength of the masses of the people.

(4) The Party's failure actively to attend to and discuss military work is also a reason for the emergence of the purely military viewpoint among a number of comrades.

The methods of correction are as follows:

(1) Raise the political level in the Party by means of education, destroy the theoretical roots of the purely military viewpoint, and be clear on the fundamental difference between the Red Army and the White Army. At the same time, eliminate the

remnants of opportunism and putschism and break down the selfish departmentalism of the Fourth Army.

(2) Intensify the political training of officers and men and especially the education of ex-prisoners. At the same time, as far as possible let the local governments select workers and peasants experienced in struggle to join the Red Army, thus organisationally weakening or even eradicating the purely military viewpoint.

(3) Arouse the local Party organisations to criticise the Party organisations in the Red Army and the organs of mass political power to criticise the Red Army itself, in order to influence the Party organisations and the officers and men of the Red Army.

(4) The Party must actively attend to and discuss military work. All the work must be discussed and decided upon by the Party before being carried out by the rank and file.

(5) Draw up Red Army rules and regulations which clearly define its tasks, the relationship between its military and its political apparatus, the relationship between the Red Army and the masses of the people, and the powers and functions of the soldiers' committees and their relationship with the military and political organisations.

On ultra-democracy

Since the Fourth Army of the Red Army accepted the directives of the Central Committee, there has been a great decrease in the manifestations of ultra-democracy. For example, Party decisions are now carried out fairly well; and no longer does anyone bring up such erroneous demands as that the Red Army should apply 'democratic centralism from the bottom to the top' or should 'let the lower levels discuss all problems first, and then let the higher levels decide'. Actually, however, this decrease is only temporary and superficial and does not mean that ultra-democratic ideas have already been eliminated. In other words, ultra-democracy is still deep-rooted in the minds of many comrades. Witness the various expressions of reluctance to carry out Party decisions.

The methods of correction are as follows:

(1) In the sphere of theory, destroy the roots of ultra-democracy. First, it should be pointed out that the danger of ultra-democracy lies in the fact that it damages or even completely wrecks the Party organisation and weakens or even completely undermines the Party's fighting capacity, rendering the Party incapable of fulfilling its fighting tasks and thereby causing the defeat of the revolution. Next, it should be pointed out that the source of ultra-democracy consists in the petit-bourgeoisie's individualistic aversion to discipline. When this characteristic is brought into the Party, it develops into ultra-democratic ideas politically and organisationally. These ideas are utterly incompatible with the fighting tasks of the proletariat.

(2) In the sphere of organisation, ensure democracy under centralised guidance. It should be done on the following lines:

1. The leading bodies of the Party must give a correct line

of guidance and find solutions when problems arise, in order to establish themselves as centres of leadership.

2. The higher bodies must be familiar with the situation in the lower bodies and with the life of the masses so as to have an objective basis for correct guidance.

3. No Party organisation at any level should make casual decisions in solving problems. Once a decision is reached, it must be firmly carried out.

4. All decisions of any importance made by the Party's higher bodies must be promptly transmitted to the lower bodies and the Party rank and file. The method is to call meetings of activists or general membership meetings of the Party branches or even of the columns (when circumstances permit) and to assign people to make reports at such meetings.

5. The lower bodies of the Party and the Party rank and file must discuss the higher bodies' directives in detail in order to understand their meaning thoroughly and decide on the methods of carrying them out.

On the disregard of organisational discipline

Disregard of organisational discipline in the Party organisation in the Fourth Army manifests itself as follows:

A. Failure of the minority to submit to the majority. For example, when a minority finds its motion voted down, it does not sincerely carry out the Party decisions.

The methods of correction are as follows:

(1) At meetings, all participants should be encouraged to voice their opinions as fully as possible. The rights and wrongs in any controversy should be clarified without compromise or glossing over. In order to reach a clear-cut conclusion, what cannot be settled at one meeting should be discussed at another, provided there is no interference with the work.

(2) One requirement of Party discipline is that the minority should submit to the majority. If the view of the minority has been rejected, it must support the decision passed by the majority. If necessary, it can bring up the matter for reconsideration at the next meeting, but apart from that it must not act against the decision in any way.

B. Criticism made without regard to organisational discipline:

(1) Inner-Party criticism is a weapon for strengthening the Party organisation and increasing its fighting capacity. In the Party organisation of the Red Army, however, criticism is not always of this character, and sometimes turns into personal attack. As a result, it damages the Party organisation as well as individuals. This is a manifestation of petit-bourgeois individualism. The method of correction is to help Party members understand that the purpose of criticism is to increase the Party's fighting capacity in order to achieve victory in the class struggle and that it should not be used as a means of personal attack.

(2) Many Party members make their criticisms not inside, but outside, the Party. The reason is that the general member-

ship has not yet grasped the importance of the Party organisation (its meetings and so forth), and sees no difference between criticism inside and outside the organisation. The method of correction is to educate Party members so that they understand the importance of Party organisation and make their criticisms of Party committees or comrades at Party meetings.

On absolute equalitarianism

Absolute equalitarianism became quite serious in the Red Army at one time. Here are some examples. On the matter of allowances to wounded soldiers, there were objections to differentiating between light and serious cases, and the demand was raised for equal allowances for all. When officers rode on horseback, it was regarded not as something necessary for performing their duties but as a sign of inequality. Absolutely equal distribution of supplies was demanded, and there was objection to somewhat larger allotments in special cases. In the hauling of rice, the demand was made that all should carry the same load on their backs, irrespective of age or physical conditions. Equality was demanded in the allotments of billets, and the Headquarters would be abused for occupying larger rooms. Equality was demanded in the assignment of fatigue duties, and there was unwillingness to do a little more than the next man. It even went so far that when there were two wounded men but only one stretcher, neither could be carried away because each refused to yield priority to the other. Absolute equalitarianism, as shown in these examples, is still very serious among officers and soldiers of the Red Army.

Absolute equalitarianism, like ultra-democracy in political matters, is the product of a handicraft and small peasant economy – the only difference being that one manifests itself in material affairs, while the other manifests itself in political affairs.

The method of correction: We should point out that, before the abolition of capitalism, absolute equalitarianism is a mere illusion of peasants as small proprietors, and that even under socialism there can be no absolute equality, for material things will then be distributed on the principle of 'from each according to his ability, to each according to his work' as well as on that of meeting the needs of the work. The distribution of material things in the Red Army must be more or less equal, as in the case of equal pay for officers and men, because this is required by the present circumstances of the struggle. But absolute equalitarianism beyond reason must be opposed because it is not required by the struggle; on the contrary, it hinders the struggle.

On subjectivism

Subjectivism exists to a serious degree among some Party members, causing great harm to the analysis of the political situation and the guidance of the work. The reason is that subjective analysis of a political situation and subjective guidance of work inevitably result either in opportunism or in putschism. As for subjective criticism, loose and groundless talk or suspiciousness, such practices inside the Party often breed unprincipled disputes and undermine the Party organisation.

Another point that should be mentioned in connection with inner-Party criticism is that some comrades ignore the major issues and confine their attention to minor points when they make their criticism. They do not understand that the main task of criticism is to point out political and organisational mistakes. As to personal shortcomings, unless they are related to political and organisational mistakes, there is no need to be over-critical or the comrades concerned will be at a loss as to what to do. Moreover, once such criticism develops there is the great danger that within the Party attention will be concentrated exclusively on minor faults, and everyone will become timid and over-cautious and forget the Party's political tasks.

The main method of correction is to educate Party members so that a political and scientific spirit pervades their thinking and their Party life. To this end we must: (1) teach Party members to apply the Marxist-Leninist method in analysing a political situation and appraising the class forces, instead of making a subjective analysis and appraisal; (2) direct the attention of Party members to social and economic investigation and study, so as to determine the tactics of struggle and methods of work, and help comrades to understand that without investigation of actual conditions they will fall into the pit of fantasy and putschism; and (3) in inner-Party criticism, guard against subjectivism, arbitrariness and the vulgarisation of criticism; statements should be based on facts and criticism should stress the political side.

On individualism

The tendency towards individualism in the Red Army Party organisation manifests itself as follows:

1. *Retaliation.* Some comrades, after being criticised inside the Party by a soldier comrade, look for opportunities to retaliate outside the Party, and one way is to beat or abuse the comrade in question. They also seek to retaliate within the Party. 'You have criticised me at this meeting, so I'll find some way to pay you back at the next.' Such retaliation arises from purely personal considerations, to the neglect of the interests of the class and of the Party as a whole. Its target is not the enemy class, but individuals in our own ranks. It is a corrosive which weakens the organisation and its fighting capacity.

2. *The 'small group mentality'.* Some comrades consider only the interests of their own small group and ignore the general interest. Although on the surface this does not seem to be the pursuit of personal interests, in reality it exemplifies the narrowest individualism and has a strong corrosive and centrifugal effect. The 'small group mentality' used to be rife in the Red Army, and although there has been some improvement as a result of criticism, there are still survivals and further effort is needed to overcome it.

(3) *The 'employee mentality'.* Some comrades do not understand that the Party and the Red Army, of which they are mem-

bers, are both instruments for carrying out the tasks of the revolution. They do not realise that they themselves are makers of the revolution, but think that their responsibility is merely to their individual superiors and not to the revolution. This passive mentality of an 'employee' of the revolution is also a manifestation of individualism. It explains why there are not very many activists who work unconditionally for the revolution. Unless it is eliminated, the number of activists will not grow and the heavy burden of the revolution will remain on the shoulders of a small number of people, much to the detriment of the struggle.

(4) *Pleasure-seeking.* In the Red Army there are also quite a few people whose individualism finds expression in pleasure-seeking. They always hope that their unit will march into big cities. They want to go there not to work but to enjoy themselves. The last thing they want is to work in the Red areas where life is hard.

(5) *Passivity.* Some comrades become passive and stop working whenever anything goes against their wishes. This is mainly due to lack of education, though sometimes it is also due to the leadership's improper conduct of affairs, assignment of work or enforcement of discipline.

(6) *The desire to leave the army.* The number of people who ask for transfers from the Red Army to local work is on the increase. The reason for this does not lie entirely with the individuals but also with: (1) the material hardships of life in the Red Army, (2) exhaustion after long struggle, and (3) the leadership's improper conduct of affairs, assignment of of work or enforcement of discipline.

The method of correction is primarily to strengthen education so as to rectify individualism ideologically. Next, it is to conduct affairs, make assignments and enforce discipline in a proper way. In addition, ways must be found to improve the material life of the Red Army, and every available opportunity must be utilised for rest and rehabilitation in order to improve material conditions. In our educational work we must explain that in its social origin individualism is a reflection within the Party of petit-bourgeois and bourgeois ideas.

On the ideology of roving rebel bands

The political ideology of roving rebel bands has emerged in the Red Army because the proportion of vagabond elements is large and because there are great masses of vagabonds in China, especially in the southern provinces. This ideology manifests itself as follows: (1) Some people want to increase our political influence only by means of roving guerrilla actions, but are unwilling to increase it by undertaking the arduous task of building up base areas and establishing the people's political power. (2) In expanding the Red Army, some people follow the line of 'hiring men and buying horses' and 'recruiting deserters and accepting mutineers', rather than the line of expanding the local Red Guards and the local troops and thus developing the main forces of the Red Army. (3) Some people lack the patience to carry on arduous struggles together with the masses, and only want to go to the big cities to eat and drink to their hearts' content. All these manifestations of the ideology of roving rebels seriously hamper the Red Army in performing its proper tasks; consequently its eradication is an important objective in the ideological struggle within the Red Army Party organisation. It must be understood that the ways of roving rebels of the Huang Chao or Li Chuang type are not permissible under present-day conditions.

The methods of correction are as follows:

(1) Intensify education, criticise incorrect ideas, and eradicate the ideology of roving rebel bands.

(2) Intensify education among the basic sections of the Red Army and among recently recruited captives to counter the vagabond outlook.

(3) Draw active workers and peasants experienced in struggle into the ranks of the Red Army so as to change its composition.

(4) Create new units of the Red Army from among the masses of militant workers and peasants.

On the remnants of putschism

The Party organisation in the Red Army has already waged struggles against putschism, but not yet to a sufficient extent. Therefore, remnants of this ideology still exist in the Red Army. Their manifestations are: (1) blind action regardless of subjective and objective conditions; (2) inadequate and irresolute application of the Party's policies for the cities; (3) slack military discipline, especially in moments of defeat; (4) acts of house-burning by some units; and (5) the practices of shooting deserters and of inflicting corporal punishment, both of which smack of putschism. In its social origins, putschism is a combination of *lumpen*-proletarian and petit-bourgeois ideology.

The methods of correction are as follows:

(1) Eradicate putschism ideologically.

(2) Correct putschist behaviour through rules, regulations and policies.

Combat Liberalism
(September 7th, 1937)

We stand for active ideological struggle because it is the weapon for ensuring unity within the Party and the revolutionary organisations in the interest of our fight. Every communist and revolutionary should take up this weapon.

But liberalism rejects ideological struggle and stands for unprincipled peace, thus giving rise to a decadent, philistine attitude and bringing about political degeneration in certain units and individuals in the Party and the revolutionary organisations.

Liberalism manifests itself in various ways.

To let things slide for the sake of peace and friendship when a person has clearly gone wrong, and refrain from principled argument because he is an old acquaintance, a fellow townsman, a schoolmate, a close friend, a loved one, an old colleague or old subordinate. Or to touch on the matter lightly instead of going into it thoroughly, so as to keep on good terms. The result is that both the organisation and the individual are harmed. This is one type of liberalism.

To indulge in irresponsible criticism in private instead of actively putting forward one's suggestions to the organisation. To say nothing to people to their faces but to gossip behind their backs, or to say nothing at a meeting but to gossip afterwards. To show no regard at all for the principles of collective life but to follow one's own inclination. This is a second type.

To let things drift if they do not affect one personally; to say as little as possible while knowing perfectly well what is wrong, to be worldly wise and play safe and seek only to avoid blame. This is a third type.

Not to obey orders but to give pride of place to one's own opinions. To demand special consideration from the organisation but to reject its discipline. This is a fourth type.

To indulge in personal attacks, pick quarrels, vent personal spite or seek revenge instead of entering into an argument and struggling against incorrect views for the sake of unity or progress or getting the work done properly. This is a fifth type.

To hear incorrect views without rebutting them and even to hear counter-revolutionary remarks without reporting them, but instead to take them calmly as if nothing had happened. This is a sixth type.

To be among the masses and fail to conduct propaganda and agitation or speak at meetings or conduct investigations and inquiries among them, and instead to be indifferent to them and show no concern for their well-being, forgetting that one is a communist and behaving as if one were an ordinary non-communist. This is a seventh type.

To see someone harming the interests of the masses and yet not feel indignant, or dissuade or stop him or reason with him, but to allow him to continue. This is an eighth type.

To work half-heartedly without a definite plan or direction; to work perfunctorily and muddle along — 'So long as one remains a monk, one goes on tolling the bell.' This is a ninth type.

To regard oneself as having rendered great service to the revolution, to pride oneself on being a veteran, to disdain minor assignments while being quite unequal to major tasks, to be slipshod in work and slack in study. This is a tenth type.

To be aware of one's own mistakes and yet make no attempt to correct them, taking a liberal attitude towards oneself. This is an eleventh type.

We could name more. But these eleven are the principle types.

254

They are all manifestations of liberalism. Liberalism is extremely harmful in a revolutionary collective. It is a corrosive which eats away unity, undermines cohesion, causes apathy and creates dissension. It robs the revolutionary ranks of compact organisation and strict discipline, prevents policies from being carried through and alienates the Party organisations from the masses which the Party leads. It is an extremely bad tendency.

Liberalism stems from petit-bourgeois selfishness, it places personal interests first and the interests of the revolution second, and this gives rise to ideological, political and organisational liberalism.

People who are liberals look upon the principles of Marxism as abstract dogma. They approve of Marxism, but are not prepared to practise it or to practise it in full; they are not prepared to replace their liberalism by Marxism. These people have their Marxism, but they have their liberalism as well – they talk Marxism but practise liberalism; they apply Marxism to others but liberalism to themselves. They keep both kinds of goods in stock and find a use for each. This is how the minds of certain people work.

Liberalism is a manifestation of opportunism and conflicts fundamentally with Marxism. It is negative and objectively has the effect of helping the enemy; that is why the enemy welcomes its preservation in our midst. Such being its nature, there should be no place for it in the ranks of the revolution.

We must use Marxism, which is positive in spirit, to overcome liberalism, which is negative. A communist should have largeness of mind and he should be staunch and active, looking upon the interests of the revolution as his very life and subordinating his personal interests to those of the revolution; always and everywhere he should adhere to principle and wage a tireless struggle against all incorrect ideas and actions, so as to consolidate the collective life of the Party and strengthen the ties between the Party and the masses; he should be more concerned about the Party and the masses than about any individual, and more concerned about others than about himself. Only thus can he be considered a communist.

All loyal, honest, active and upright communists must unite to oppose the liberal tendencies shown by certain people among us, and set them on the right path. This is one of the tasks on our ideological front.

Appendix III The Liberation of the Foreign Workers in China

Early in February 1967, our situation in relation to the Cultural Revolution underwent a radical change after the issuing of a directive from the Bureau of Foreign Experts in Peking. The main content of the directive was that, henceforth, foreign workers in China should be enabled to join in the Cultural Revolution in their own places of work. The background to this event went back to September 1966, when four Americans working in Peking put up a poster in the Friendship Guest House denouncing the existing treatment of foreign workers and calling for a new policy. The poster came to the attention of Chairman Mao, who strongly approved of it and wrote a comment. Apparently, no further action was taken until December when a new policy towards foreign workers was in fact adopted. In January, Foreign Minister Chen Yi assembled together the foreign people working in Peking and outlined to them the new policy. The directive from the Bureau arrived at Zhongda in late January, but, with the Red Flag taking over the administration, the cadres in the President's Office did not know what to do. At the beginning of February the language teachers held a meeting and from this arose Kang and Wu's visit to us with the directive, and the text of the Americans' poster. The text of the poster, Chairman Mao's comments and the Chinese Foreign Office directive were given to us as follows:

The Americans' poster

Five No's (of the existing policy towards foreign workers)

1   No physical labour
2   No ideological remoulding
3   No chance to come into contact with Chinese workers and peasants
4   No participation in class struggle
5   No struggle to increase production

Two Yeses (of the existing policy towards foreign workers)

1   High pay and especially good living conditions

2 Enjoyment of all kinds of privileges

The guiding thought in this attitude is that of Kruschev, not Mao Tse-tung.

Eight Point Request (of the 4 foreign workers)

1 We should be treated as class brothers, not bourgeois specialists
2 We should be allowed to take part in physical labour
3 We should be helped to remould our ideology
4 We should be enabled to form close ties with the Chinese workers and peasants
5 We should be allowed to take part in the three revolutionary movements of class struggle, the struggle for higher production, and scientific experiment
6 Our children should be treated the same as Chinese children are treated
7 Our living standards should be the same as our Chinese colleagues
8 All privileges should be abolished

Mao Tse-tung's comment (3rd September 1966)

I agree with this *dazibao*. Revolutionary foreign experts and their children should be treated in exactly the same way as Chinese. There should not be any difference. Please discuss this point. All foreign experts *who are willing* should be treated in this way. Please consider how to go about this.

Foreign Office directive

1 Propagate Mao Tse-tung's thought among foreign experts, and help them to study Chairman Mao's works
2 Expound to foreign experts the significance and policies of the Cultural Revolution. Foreign experts should be enabled to read posters put up in their place of work. They should also be enabled to write posters and take part in mass meetings organised to overthrow those who have taken the bourgeois road, or to repudiate and criticise those academic authorities who are taking the reactionary road. Foreign experts may form their own organisations and make contact with Chinese revolutionary Rebel organisations
3 Bring the initiative of foreign experts into full play and consider them as class brothers. Let them join in discussion on the Cultural Revolution with their colleagues to exchange views, criticism and self-criticism
4 Foreign experts – if willing – are to be encouraged to take part in physical labour with students and colleagues and to live, eat and labour with their Chinese colleagues
5 Foreign experts may have their pay reduced if they wish. It should be made clear that if this should make difficulties, then old levels of pay will be restored. No effort

should be made to persuade those who do not want to have their pay reduced

6 Try in every possible way to allow foreign experts to live in the same way as their Chinese friends – emphasising that sanitary conditions should meet their needs

7 Children should be treated in the same way as Chinese children – to take part in work, join Red Guards, visit other areas etc. This to be approved by Red Guard groups in their area. We rely on revolutionary people to do this among foreign experts

An English friend of ours in Peking had written to us about the meeting with Chen Yi in January, and since receiving the letter we had increased our agitation to be enabled to attend meetings, have posters read to us and work in a factory. Now the way seemed wide open for our participation. We were all very excited. We started working at the Electric Motor Factory on the 22nd of February. However, things still moved slowly towards our participation in university activities so we composed a letter addressed to the whole English department, asking to take part in their discussions and to have posters read to us methodically. Gan Su-wan suggested having our letter translated into Chinese and put up at the Language department office. There was some days' delay about this, so eventually we took the letter over to the students' dormitory. We met an English student who was coming out as we went into the dormitory building. When we had explained our purpose, he became very enthusiastic, took our letter and promised to get it translated and put up on the hoarding outside the dormitory and at the department office. A couple of days later the letter duly appeared in the form of two posters on the wall of the department – one in English, the other in Chinese. We received a number of favourable comments and soon after this did, in fact, have a number of important posters read to us. From this time, and for the following year, we also attended all the meetings we wanted with someone to interpret for us and, when we wished, we ourselves also spoke at meetings.

Appendix IV   Working in the Electric Motor Factory

The wall of the university campus runs along the main road into town for about a mile and a half. The west gate, nearest town, looks across the road to a diesel factory, which became the local headquarters of Di-cong, the largest Conservative workers' organisation of Canton. During the periods when our campus was dominated by the Red Flag side, the relative positions of the university and this factory turned the road into a front line, along which unarmed young soldiers of the PLA worked with great patience and courage to persuade the contestants to solve their differences through argument and discussion rather than by resorting to violence. Between the west gate and the main gate, a mile to the east, lay a row of shops, some small residential areas, and a large middle school – deserted during most of the two years we were there. Further along, past the main gate, occupying perhaps a square half mile was the Canton Electric Motor Plant. This plant, which was really seven small factories joined into one, produced electric motors and fans. Like most Chinese engineering factories it had its own foundry and machine shops where they made some of their machine tools.

We had been agitating for some months to be enabled to work in a factory, but on the morning of February 22nd, 1967, when we set out for our first morning's work, we had no idea where we were going, and our first surprise was to find that we were to work more or less on our own doorstep.

Comrade Lin, one of the young English teachers who interpreted for us, came to work with us. We were greeted warmly at the entrance gate by a group of four men, but with the minimum of fuss. A number of children from the nearby flats gathered around us. The site also included nursery schools and clinics, as well as housing for some of the people who worked there.

We went straight to a small office. Having all found seats between desks covered with papers, we were given a very brief outline of the history of the factory which, like so many others we had visited, was formed out of repair workshops in 1958. With some words of polite appreciation of our stated desire to

259

help production, while at the same time getting a wider view of Chinese life to help us in our work as teachers, we set off again. We were taken to a large open-plan factory building, which contained two main sections – the assembly of electric motors and a machine shop. Down two parallel spaces, which ran the length of the building, overhead cranes shifted heavy parts of sub-assemblies and finished electric motors.

Comrade Jong, our foreman, and the shop manager showed us quickly round, and then took us to the section where we were to work. Twenty to thirty people were assembling large electric motors, measuring about two foot high and weighing perhaps a quarter of a ton. Most of the workers were young or middle-aged women, but there were several young men, one worker who looked to be in his fifties, and half a dozen middle-school Red Guards. After friendly informal greetings, Comrade Jong started demonstrating how to do a soldering operation on one of the motors. Ten minutes of this and we were asked if we would like to start. We started. Jong came back after several minutes to see how we were coping, did a little more demonstrating, and again left us to it.

The score or so coils of wire that were fitted into the stationary case of the motors had to have the insulating varnish scraped off their ends, which were then twisted round copper hoops, soldered and finally bound with tape.

The quarter-ton castings came to us carried by the overhead crane. This was usually worked by a young woman, who travelled ceaselessly up and down the shop in her little cabin high up above the workers and machines. She communicated in sign language with a man on the shop floor who hooked and unhooked the crane to its various loads. We were told by our fellow workers that the young woman had been chosen for her job because of her care and sense of responsibility.

When we broke for dinner there was quite a fuss. Comrade Jong decided that the bowls we had brought were too small and insisted on searching out three aluminium canisters for us. When we got across to the dining hall, we had a great argument about whether we should queue or not. The compromise reached was that since it was our first day and we could not easily be told what was to be had, we were to go into the kitchen to take a look before we selected our meal, but that after this we should queue like everyone else.

Public catering in China seems to be universally based on a 12 *yuan*-a-month minimum food bill. This works out at about 8p a day. Rice, vegetable and a little fish or meat cost us about 4p. Many of the workers took their food back to their sections to eat. Others ate in the open, outside the canteen. Only in the coldest weather were there more than a handful eating inside the canteen.

After the meal, most people drank tea, and those who smoked lit up. More than half the section was sitting round their work benches. For our first two weeks, before we went over to afternoon working only, we joined our colleagues in the section, where we chatted and held singsongs.

Some women went home to feed their children, and some of

the young mothers went to the crèche to feed their babies. One day a new baby was brought into the section by his proud mother to be admired, and off and on children came in. The day the baby was brought in most of the section was away visiting another factory in Fushan. Two little children came in with their mother, and played about the section with a small trolley all the morning.

All the jobs in our section were done at various times by every member of the section, and everyone moved about from one job to another. They had all been together with the same foreman, our friend Comrade Jong, since 1958 when the factory was set up, except for one woman who had joined the team in 1962, and one or two of the younger ones. The foreman's wife was in the team, so were a mother and daughter. Jong was conspicuous as a hard worker and general handiman, and was also involved in design work. The wire strippers we used, he made from old hacksaw blades, with the aid of a small forge that he brought to the section. When we had a couple of days without motors to assemble, we turned to making bamboo tools which were used for inserting the coils into the cases. The bamboo came in two-inch diameter poles. We sawed the poles up, sliced the pieces, then with knives and sandpaper shaped the different tools for various jobs. All the solder that was dropped on the floor was swept up, and we had a melting pot from which we cast new rods. On several days, we were engaged in assembling the rotating part of the motor.

There was no clocking on or off. Every section worked a six day week. At first we had Monday off, later it was Sunday. Sunday is both the main day off from work, and the main shopping day in China, when people also come into town from the countryside.

If the section was slack, as it usually was for a day or two at the end of the month, extra days would be taken off and made up later. If an individual wanted to take a day off, they could also arrange to make it up later. Overtime was usually dealt with in the same way. If one man worked very late he would often come in late the next day, or perhaps not at all. Nursing mothers had extra time off. Tea breaks were flexible. There was tea (or, in the summer, often marrow soup) on tap most of the day, but there was also a regular tea break. But although the whole section stopped at the same time for tea, people got started again when they felt like it.

In China today, a very important idea is of people achieving efficiency through understanding the situation, rather than achieving efficiency by making and observing rules and regulations. Our section kept good time because we wanted to fulfil or over-fulfil the monthly target, and because it meant good team work. When the monthly figures came through, and we knew that production was up we were all very pleased. The general level of time-keeping and work was high. This does not mean everyone was equally diligent, far from it. Our friend Jong worked like a beaver, and obviously put in a lot of overtime. Most of the team worked well, at an easy rhythm, but one or two were rather lazy. One young technician, who was our tester, only spent about a couple of hours a day testing the motors. The rest of the day he would sit himself down beside someone who was working and chat to them by the hour.

To ensure that advanced techniques become generally adopted, workers and technicians make periodic visits to similar plants elsewhere. While we were at the factory, our whole section went to visit a plant in Fushan, about thirty miles away. Also, while we were there, a party of electrical workers came from Nanking, a day's journey away by train.

A young technician, Chen Li-yang – in Britain he would probably be called a design engineer – who spoke a little English, came to the section to speak to us quite often. The first day he explained to me the circuitry of the motors. Chen was excited about a new, rotary, voltage regulator that they were developing. The basic design was Hungarian and he lent me the paper on its principle, which was a translation into English from the Hungarian.

One day, when there was not much work to do in our section, we were given a tour of the factory. The three other sections were the electric fan shop, the main machine shop and the foundry. The foundry was very primitive, and to bring it more up to date they were constructing a new building. In addition to the engineering side, they were building a whole new machine shop. We also visited the crèche and kindergarten.

While we were working at the factory there was a minor epidemic of meningitis. We had been issued with clinical face masks at our own clinic on the campus, but when we turned up at the section without them, our comrades insisted on getting us more masks from their clinic. Both at the gate of the campus and at the factory entrance gate, medical workers were on duty, and as we went out we were given a throat spray and nose drops of peroxide (both doctors and nurses took turns on the gate). Spring being the cholera season, we also had injections. A team came to the factory shop complete with kit of swabs, cleaning spirit, serum and hypodermics, and was in action within minutes. We all queued up and, amidst much hilarity, feigned pain and teasing, were jagged one by one. This informal process certainly saved much time, trouble and anxiety.

The Cultural Revolution had deeply affected the factory, as it had the university. Every wall, and any other flat surface, was plastered with *dazibaos* (big character posters) hand-written on multicoloured paper, or sheets from newspapers. In every shop, loudspeakers were on all day long. For most of the period of our stay, news-sheets were brought round the section several times a day—bringing work to a stop while everyone scanned quickly through the contents in search of new information or controversial assertions, and then broke into argument. Every day there were meetings, including at least ten mass meetings of the whole factory during our stay, which worked out at about once a week.

In mid-March a small group of PLA men took up residence in the factory. They took part in meetings for studying Mao Tse-tung's thought. They helped in negotiating the formation

262

of a new factory management committee by the various revolutionary groups, and came round the shops, stopping to work with us and talk. The commander of the group worked with us one afternoon, wiring up motors.

The first factory meeting we attended was called to emphasise the need to 'carry out revolution and promote production', and to report on a five-day provincial production conference. The next meeting was to launch a new fourteen-man revolutionary factory committee that was to take over the authority of the old management committee, and the last two meetings we attended were called to struggle against the old manager of the factory.

The procedure at the factory meetings was for each section to line up at their own shop, and march to the canteen where the meeting was held. However, this plan was poorly adhered to, either in the spirit or in the letter. Certainly we lined up. One of the workers (not a foreman) stood in front and shouted some orders. There was a certain amount of shuffling about to form a reasonably straight line, and we more or less started off simultaneously, but although we only had about fifty yards to go, by the time we were nearing the canteen, everyone had split up into pairs or little groups and were strolling along chatting, just as they did when they left work.

As at nearly all meetings we attended, except the most serious and intense, there was a great deal of chatter. About half the women of our section knitted throughout the meeting and, in the main, the knitters talked while they plied their needles. The talk was partly argument concerning the subject of the meeting, but much of it was just friendly chat. The meeting to meet the new committee, who all sat on the platform, was begun by a tremendous beating of drums and setting-off of fire-crackers. This gave the meeting an exciting send-off, but here too was room for the light-hearted touch – several of the younger men throwing fire-crackers in among the young women workers, who responded with shrieks and laughter.

Periodically, groups from the factory took off for the city with banners and drums. In April, when the struggles in Hong Kong started with the strike at the artificial flower factory, we arrived for work one morning to find that the whole section was going to march into Canton for a protest meeting. We asked some of our fellow workers what they were doing and they told us adding, as if to reassure us, 'The Hong Kong police are very bad – you are good'.

In early June we stopped working in the factory so as to be free to attend university meetings in the afternoons, as well as the mornings and evenings. From time to time, groups of friends from our group in the assembly shop visited our house, and we occasionally went back to visit them at the factory.

Index